THE
EXORCISM OF
ANNELIESE
MICHEL

THE EXORCISM OF ANNELIESE MICHEL

FELICITAS D. GOODMAN

Resource *Publications*

An imprint of *Wipf and Stock Publishers*
199 West 8th Avenue • Eugene OR 97401

Resource Publications
A division of Wipf and Stock Publishers
199 W 8th Ave, Suite 3
Eugene, OR 97401

The Exorcism of Anneliese Michel
By Goodman, Felicitas D.
Copyright©1981 by Goodman, Felicitas D.
ISBN: 1-59752-432-8
Publication date 11/1/2005
Previously published by Doubleday & Company, Inc., 1981

TO BUCKING BULL
in gratitude for his advice and
encouragement

CONTENTS

INTRODUCTION

In a rural community in Bavaria called Klingenberg, in a modern, two-storied house on Mittlerer Weg, a young student by the name of Anneliese Michel died in the summer of 1976 of what appeared to be severe battery and starvation. She had contusions on her face, hands, arms, and legs and was frightfully emaciated. The physician whom her father asked for a death certificate refused to issue it because he could not be sure that she had died of natural causes. A priest who had called the district attorney's office in Aschaffenburg the same day spoke of demonic possession and exorcism. Other details soon became public. Her physicians, it was said, had suspected that she was suffering from epileptic fits. Her parents, however, believed that she was possessed by demons. In response to their request, and with the official permission of the bishop of Würzburg, Dr. Josef Stangl, two priests carried out a ritual of exorcism. It was done in total secrecy and lasted for months, up to the time of Anneliese's death. Despite her obvious physical deterioration, none of the persons in on the secret, it was alleged, sought medical help for her, help that supposedly could have saved her life.

The German wire services promptly picked up the story. The American film *The Exorcist* had been seen in Germany. The public was also perturbed over a debate that had followed some theses published by a well-known Tübingen theology professor, Herbert Haag: Was the devil only a symbolic representation of the concept of evil or did demonic forces have an objective existence? There had been strident comments, much publicized, on both sides. Here, now, was an actual case where the two opposing views met head on. The Catholic Church, apparently, had flown in the face of modern science and had upheld the idea of the objective existence of horned devils and the rest of the hellish horde. Magic rites had been carried out in back rooms, secreted behind the silk curtains of the Mother Church, resulting in the death of an innocent young girl. There was no end to sensationalism.

Nor did public interest wane with the passage of time. In August—nearly two months after Anneliese's death—the Bavarian Radio Service reported that the case continued to fire the public imagination. Not many people knew what exorcism was, the commentator said, since permission for it had been granted only rarely in the twentieth century. Not many, that is, until the Anneliese Michel case came along. "At her bedside, it seems, there were not only prayers against evil. What the priests attempted was rather a kind of magical expulsion of demons in the style of religious fanatics of the early Middle Ages," the speaker opined. Priests, however, were not magicians. The German Catholic Church would do well to follow the lead of the bishop of Essen and make a clear distinction between magic and religion. When asked about exorcism, this bishop had stated that he had never granted any permission for exorcism and would not do so in the future, for "Christian faith is too sacred a property and must be protected against all manner of superstition."

Just a week before this broadcast, and apparently unbeknown to the Bavarian Radio Service, the "superstition" had proved its power once more in a striking way. A citizen of the community of Bretzingen, which is not too far from Klingenberg, called the authorities in Aschaffenburg. He would not give his name, but reported that the Catholic priest of the village, Pastor Hermann Heim, was playing some tapes over the loudspeaker of the "Zum

Ross," a local tavern. He assumed that these tapes had been made during exorcism sessions with Anneliese Michel. The screams and throaty obscenities of the demons were causing a near panic in Bretzingen, he said. The district attorney ordered them confiscated as probable material evidence in the Anneliese Michel case. He also ordered the priest frisked—an unheard-of action against a man of the cloth—and his living quarters and belongings searched. Stunned by the vindictive reaction of the legal authorities and the witch-hunt mood of the public, the bishop of Würzburg now denied any support to what the radio commentator had called "elements of primitive culture." But it was too late. Laymen from around the country filed suit against him, from Munich, Nuremberg, Ludwigshafen, Remscheid, Karlstadt, and other places, among them a number of lawyers.

After a prolonged and very thorough investigation, Anneliese's parents and the two priests who had carried out the exorcism were accused of negligent homicide. The case came up for trial in the spring of 1978 in the District Court of Aschaffenburg. The media had another field day. Bavaria was characterized in the headlines as "the land where the demons howl." "Such nonsense must be rooted out," was the demand. The parents and the priests must be punished to the fullest extent of the law. Bishop Stangl carried part of the blame for the girl's death. Eventually the Court in Aschaffenburg dismissed the suits against the bishop. But the attacks had done their work. He laid down his office and soon after suffered a stroke, brought on, his friends said, by the grief the case caused him. He lost his power of speech and died on April 8, 1979, without ever regaining it.

The severity of the sentences meted out to the four accused, going well beyond what the prosecution had asked for, surprised even the most vocal exponents of public outrage against "back-country demon frenzy." Partly for this reason and partly because some very fundamental religious issues were at stake, the debate about the case has not subsided to this day—a year or more after the trial. A number of books have been published, principally dealing with the reality of demons. These works quote extensively from a statement of Pope Paul VI, given at the general audience on November 15, 1972, where he said, among other things, "Sin,

on its part, affords a dark, aggressive evil-doer, the Devil, an opportunity to act in us and in our world . . . Anyone who disputes
the existence of this reality places himself outside biblical and
Church teachings." As late as January 1979, a Catholic reporter,
Leo Waltermann, broadcast a program over the radio station of
the Westdeutscher Rundfunk, in which he highlighted the dilemma
of the Catholic Church. It was caught, he felt, between what he
termed nonsensical beliefs in the devil and traditional teachings
about him.

Clearly, in this debate the gentle principal of the drama, the
young girl who lost her life, was more or less forgotten. The psychiatrists had dismissed her by labeling her mentally ill. The court
had avenged her death. What more was there to say?

A great deal more, I felt, when I first read about her case in
Newsweek (August 23, 1976). Entitled "The Exorcist," the brief
report said that a twenty-three-year-old epileptic named Anneliese
Michel died in Germany while being exorcized. There were tapes
containing "incoherent screams mixed with furious profanity"
supposedly uttered by her demons, who included such infamous
characters as Lucifer, Judas, Nero, and Hitler. Her parents and
the two priests involved had accepted the diagnosis of demonic
possession, "but," *Newsweek* continued, "more liberal Catholics
challenged it. 'Possession is a question of belief, not an empirical
fact,' said theologian Ernst Veth, Michel's tutor at the University
of Würzburg. 'They should have called a doctor.' "

Three elements in particular aroused my avid interest in this
news story. One was the association between epilepsy and what
was obviously a religious experience. Western observers, as I
knew very well from early anthropological literature, often reported the fact that "entire tribes" had "epileptic fits" during religious observances. Supposedly it was possible for an entire population to go into epileptic convulsions on command and then carry
out, while in a grand mal seizure, complex ritual dramas. The conjecture was obviously absurd. Had such a misconception prevailed
in this case?

The second matter was the alleged "possession" by evil spirits.
Contrary to what Ernst Veth had been quoted as saying, "possession" was very much an "empirical fact," that is, an experience

reported about uncounted millions around the world. In my fieldwork in Apostolic churches in this country, in Mexico City, and
among Mayan peasants in Yucatán, I had seen many people who,
within their own religious context, experienced a sense of being invaded by an entity from the realm of the supernatural, from the
region that Carlos Castaneda calls the "separate reality." Some
had, in their experience, been filled by the Holy Spirit, others by
Satan. Catholic charismatics in this country had what they called
"deliverance services" designed to expel "evil spirits." And a fellow faculty member had told me of exorcism sessions in the
Lutheran Fellowship, located in a midwestern town, that he
belonged to. "You should hear how the demons plead because
they do not want to leave their victims," he said, obviously
shaken, "and what obscenities they come up with."

Third, there were those tapes, a record of the exorcism sessions.
I had done extensive research on the speech patterns of subjects
reporting the experience of being possessed; this research was
based not only on my own collection of sound tapes of English,
Spanish, and Mayan speakers but also on material from Brazil,
Malaysia, Borneo, and Africa. I had discovered that irrespective
of their native tongue, these speakers all shared a few highly characteristic features. Would these diagnostic traits also be detectable
on the German tapes? I dearly wanted to find out, but other proj-
ects had to be taken care of first, and I more or less forgot about
the matter.

In the spring of 1978 a news item broadcast over a national television network unexpectedly dredged up the Anneliese Michel
case once more. There had apparently been a criminal investigation in the matter, and it had led to a trial. The four defendants,
Anneliese's parents and the two priests who had carried out the
exorcism, had been convicted of negligent homicide and sentenced
to suspended jail terms and court costs. This was a most curious
conclusion. Was there actually evidence that they had caused her
death? None of the people that I had seen or read about who had
experienced "possession" had ever died. What had been different
in this case?

I wrote to my niece in Germany, herself a young lawyer, and
asked her for additional information. The articles she sent me

from German newspapers about the trial further convinced me that the case was worth examining more closely. It was clear from these articles that the parents had simply done what their daughter had wanted. Anneliese said she was plagued by demons and, as believing Catholics, the parents had called in the priests. The priests, in turn, had tried to help her, with the knowledge and express permission of their bishop. Yet all four of them had not only been convicted by the courts but had also been put down, ridiculed, and condemned by public opinion because of their belief in possession. Perhaps by chance the law court had not called in any psychiatrist who might have known something about this type of human behavior. There was, for instance, Professor Wolfgang Pfeiffer of the Medical School of the University of Münster. In his book on cross-cultural psychiatry [*Transkulturelle Psychiatrie* (Stuttgart, 1971)] he speaks of "possession" as one of the basic human religious experiences. Instead, the Court called on experts not in *trans-cultural* but in *clinical* psychiatry. They were clearly unaware—a regrettable result of professional specialization—that around the world millions of people regularly became "possessed" in the context of the most varied rituals. The mere belief, possibly, and the experience most certainly, that an alien entity might take over the body of a subject and speak through his mouth was taken as proof of insanity by these experts. So overawed was the law court, apparently, by the pronouncements of the experts it had marshaled, pronouncements couched in the most convoluted technical language, that it never even thought of comparing them with each other. Had the members of the court bothered to do so, they would no doubt have discovered that their experts had, in a number of instances, obviously contradicted each other.

Early in the summer of 1978 I had an opportunity to call Professor Pfeiffer. He had also followed the case but was so overburdened with teaching duties that he had no time to concern himself with the matter any further. Yet I felt that something had to be done to help the persons involved. Not only had they been judged on the basis of clinical opinions not, to my mind, relevant to the case, but under the barrage of public opinion even the Catholic Church had buckled under and had deserted them. I felt deeply sorry for them.

Upon my request, my niece procured the address of Frau Marianne Thora, one of the defense lawyers. After checking out my scientific credentials, Frau Thora decided to cooperate with me. She kindly placed at my disposal her entire dossier of documents, totaling close to eight hundred pages of reports, letters, statements by witnesses, and depositions by Anneliese's physicians and by the psychiatrists consulted by the court. In short, due to the thorough criminal investigation by the court, I was put in the enviable position of receiving the results of what amounted to extensive fieldwork covering most of the relevant aspects of the case.

In order to be able to gauge the personal involvement of the various participants, I started a correspondence with both exorcists, who kindly answered the many questions I directed to them. Father Renz, who had carried the greatest share of the exorcism sessions, lent me some of his exorcism tapes. On the basis of this material, I wrote a forty-odd-page German "minority opinion," so to speak. The ideas expressed there form the basis of the theoretical section of the present book. This opinion was widely circulated among friends and supporters of the parties to the case. Frau Thora wrote that had the Court been able to read it before sentence was passed, the defendants would not have been convicted. Her optimism has not been put to the test. She encouraged all four defendants to appeal their case on the basis of the new arguments, but as of this writing they have refused to do so. They have been hurt so badly that it is understandable that they do not want to expose themselves to another round of publicity and attacks no matter how the appeals court would eventually rule.

The case is so many-sided, so well documented, that I think it would be a true loss if the wider public did not come to know of it in an age where there is an avid interest in such occurrences but also so much uninformed speculation. I therefore asked the defendants if they would consent to a treatment of the case in book form. Anneliese's parents, contacted by Father Alt, were leery of opening up wounds that had just barely begun to heal. They did not, however, object to my quoting them from the documents in my possession. The two priests were most cooperative. Father Renz sent me relevant publications, additional material from Anneliese's diaries, and some answers to questions from the parents.

He let me have photographs and a sound track of a television show on the "Fall Klingenberg"—the Klingenberg case, as it is now referred to in Germany. His most important contribution, however, was a complete copy of all forty-two cassettes he made during the exorcism sessions. They are carefully numbered and dated and were recorded on high-quality equipment. Without these Anneliese's story would be just another scary tale. With them I was able to do what amounts to extensive fieldwork. They are probably even better than if I had been there recording the events. For in a way any outside observer "contaminates" the scene. Here only insiders were present.

From Father Alt came letters written to him by Anneliese, some more publications, a taped account of the trial, and other comments, among them a description of a visit to the shrine at San Damiano, in northern Italy, where Anneliese had gone several times. Both Fathers patiently answered my many questions in a lengthy correspondence. In addition, Anneliese's boyfriend, Peter, and her youngest sister, Roswitha, provided me with personal reminiscences. Friends in Germany and Austria sent me newspaper articles. I was also hoping to hear from those psychiatrists who had been principally involved with treating Anneliese, namely, Dr. Lüthy and Dr. Schleip, but telephone calls were turned aside and my letters went unanswered.

To complete the picture, I went to Germany in November 1979 and had an opportunity to speak to all the principal participants, to visit the churches that Anneliese had frequented, and to see her grave. I am most grateful for all the cooperation and gracious hospitality that was extended to me.

From this extensive material I have been able to assemble what I think is a reliable picture of Anneliese's life and the story of the exorcism. I painstakingly sifted, evaluated, and fitted together countless bits and fragments, composing a picture more complete than any one participant could have had at the time when all this happened. On occasion I had to flesh out the account a bit, which I was able to do because I know Germany and attended the University of Heidelberg, which is not too far away from the region where it all took place. But nothing in the presentation was invented. The events are described as they emerged from the documents in my files, occasionally amplified from taped narrations or from interviews. In other words, they are all substantiated. So are all statements, contradictions, and equivocations attributed to individual actors in the drama. To refer to the source in each instance would have made tedious reading, but the documentation is often mentioned, or it is at least clear from the context.

The point of view of the narrative is, as much as possible, that of the participants, who shared a set of often unspoken assumptions about the world. What contributed to the tragedy was the fact that these were not shared by others—more powerful than they—in the same society. And the compromises they tried to arrive at proved disastrous.

In the last two chapters I have attempted to present an analysis of what transpired. To do this, two different aspects had to be considered: the medical and the anthropological. With respect to the former, I assumed the role of an investigative reporter. I am not entirely a stranger to the field. As a multilingual scientific translator, I worked for many years with medical material, especially in hematology and in biochemistry. In graduate school I took courses in neurophysiology and in psychiatry. I checked my suppositions against the relevant literature, spoke at length with counselors at the Epilepsy Association, and discussed the salient points of the case with a physician friend. As to the anthropological side of the matter, I speak as a trained researcher with twelve years' experience in the area of religious trances. With all of this, I am, in the end, offering a different hypothesis of what happened to Anneliese Michel than the one that served as a basis for the judgment by the Court, an alternate hypothesis that takes into account the general validity, the reality, of the possession experience.

AUTHOR'S NOTE

The dating of the various events in Anneliese's life is of crucial importance. Not all participants in the events agreed on what happened or when, but it was usually possible to clear up discrepancies from the context and from the many dated letters included in the Court's files. Conversations among the participants are all based on file material, although I occasionally had to rely on allusions or asides, especially for the early part of Anneliese's life. These conversations are conjectural. For the latter part of her life, many witnesses supplied paraphrases or recalled statements verbatim, which I was then able to use to present a good reconstruction of what was said. Before publication, the German translation of the manuscript, prepared by me, was checked for accuracy by Father Alt, Father Renz, and Frau Marianne Thora. Their suggestions were incorporated, where feasible, into both the English and the German version. Luckily, the file on Anneliese was so complete, and the material collected during the interviews in Germany in November 1979 so satisfactory, that only minor changes had to be made.

PROLOGUE

The first item in the collection of documents of Frau Marianne Thora, the defense lawyer of Father Alt, is an entry in the office records of the district attorney of Aschaffenburg, seat of the administration of the district by the same name.

Today, at half past one, I had a telephone call from a Father Alt. He did not give his address. He described a case of exorcism (driving out of devils) to me, which he said that he had carried out on a young girl, Anneliese Michel of Klingenberg. He described previous treatments that the girl had undergone, all without success, by psychiatrists and neurologists in Aschaffenburg, specifically Dr. Siegfried Lüthy, and in Würzburg. He described the symptoms that she had been suffering from and the successes and failures of the exorcism. He mentioned that during periods of arousal she was at times unable to eat or drink, and that this had also happened recently. Everyone had hoped, however, that she would soon start taking nourishment again. Finally he mentioned that the girl had died this morning. '
When I called the courthouse in Klingenberg at about

three, the clerk told me that Josef Michel, the dead girl's father, had come to the office there at about one o'clock and had applied for a death certificate for his daughter. He said that she had suddenly developed a very high fever and had quite unexpectedly died this morning. When he was informed that only a physician could issue such a certificate after properly having viewed the body, he said that there was a physician at his house right now. The clerk called his home and spoke to a Dr. Roth. Whether this person was indeed a physician is not known. Dr. Roth said that he did not have the requisite forms. He did not carry out any postmortem examination.

Burial is to be Saturday morning.

Upon calling the general practitioner in Klingenberg, Dr. Martin Kehler, I was informed that the latter had found at his postmortem that the corpse was totally emaciated and still warm. It exhibited a number of skin abrasions. He did not issue the death certificate because he could not attest to a natural cause of death. He suggested that an autopsy be carried out.

He also told me that he had last seen the girl in a good nutritional state in October 1975. Two months ago her father had called him and asked him to come and make a house call. A little later, however, he canceled it.

I have asked the Institute of Forensic Medicine at the University of Würzburg to make preparations for the autopsy.

Signed at Aschaffenburg, July 1, 1976
Stenger
District Attorney

The end of the path. Even through the factual reporting of the district attorney, we can feel the agony of Father Alt as he talks about something so odd and out-of-the-way for a district attorney, who needs to ask: "What, exactly, is exorcism? Oh, I see, the driving out of devils . . ." Then, almost as an afterthought, Father Alt adds that the girl has just died. The end of the path.

THE
EXORCISM OF
ANNELIESE
MICHEL

CHAPTER ONE

THE CHILDHOOD YEARS

Anneliese Michel was not quite twenty-four years old when she died. She was a child of the stable, frugal, industrious, slow-moving German middle class, more peasant than urban, law-abiding, and in Bavaria, where she was born, solidly Catholic. The Michels had been village artisans for centuries, mainly builders and bricklayers. Her father's father owned a sawmill in Klingenberg. So did her mother's father, grandfather Fürg, in Leiblfing, a small community in Lower Bavaria. Anneliese was born there on September 21, 1952, the second child of her mother. A first daughter, Martha, died at the age of eight of a kidney ailment. "Everyone loved little Martha," the family is wont to tell. "She liked to pray and was a gay and gentle child. 'I prayed three rosaries today,' she'd tell everyone when she came in from playing with the three little lambs that Papa had given her.'" The image of the pious child recalls altar paintings from the Bavarian baroque.

When Anneliese was little, she often visited with her grandparents in Leiblfing; throughout her life she retained some of the special lilt of the dialect of the village of her mother. The latter, Anna Fürg, had attended three years of a secondary school and then went on to commercial training, the usual choice of the girls of her class. Only the brightest went on to become nuns or enrolled in a college of education for training as schoolteachers. It is a persistent pattern. Two of Anna's daughters chose the same course in the next generation. Before her marriage to Josef Michel, Anna worked in the office of her father's sawmill; as a matter of course she had lived at home.

Anneliese's father, Josef Michel, was sent to secondary school in Miltenberg when he was ten; this was done according to his mother's wishes, who wanted him to become a priest. Dedicating some of one's children to an ecclesiastical career was a family tradition of long standing: three of her own sisters were teaching nuns. The boy received good grades in everything but Latin, the one subject most important at the time for a future priest. Reluctantly his mother finally agreed that he change over to a trade school, an outcome presumably not too distressing to his father. He had always wanted his "Sepp" to take over the family business. So he learned carpentry from a master carpenter in his father's establishment. After passing his journeyman's examination three years later, he worked in that trade. At twenty-two he was drafted at the outbreak of the Second World War. He fought first on the western front, in Belgium and France, and was then sent to Russia. Concerning this experience, there is a touching little entry, dated October 29, 1975, in Anneliese's diary.

> Saint Joseph told me that he was the one who saw to it that Papa found those boots in Russia. Papa often told about this, that in Russia his feet nearly froze off. Then suddenly, in the snow, he found a pair of wonderful Russian boots.

Toward the end of the war Josef Michel became a prisoner of the Americans. He was released in June 1945 and went to Munich to attend a school for construction work in 1946. In the summer of 1948 he passed his master's examination. He took over the family business in Klingenberg and married two years later.

Upon returning from the war, Josef Michel found his parents' home and his community nearly untouched by the ravages of the air attacks that had destroyed the larger cities. In earlier centuries it was considered dangerous to live in a small community in time of war. It was much more likely to be looted and its inhabitants murdered by armies passing through because its fortifications were so much weaker than those of the larger cities. In the period of modern warfare, being a small community proved to be an advantage. And Klingenberg is very small. It houses not quite three thousand souls. Located in the district of Obernburg in Bavaria, one of the lands of western Germany, it looks out on the narrows of the Main River. This is where the latter breaks through between the rolling, forested hills separating the Odenwald and the Spessart. Anneliese loved her hometown, and a print of its peaked roofs nestling into the valley hung over the sofa bed in which she died.

On the hillsides vineyards climb the slopes in frayed rectangles. The peasants whose home Klingenberg remains to this day have known how to make red wine for over two millenia, for the art of wine making was introduced to them by the Romans. Here and there a stone from the ancient Roman settlement that once stood here turns up in the walls of the terraces on which the grapes are grown. Tourists come to taste the wine in the taverns of Klingenberg, and in the church the priest's blessing turns it into the blood of the Lord.

A castle guards the break through the narrows between the folding hills. In its time it housed some petty nobles, robber barons who took their toll of the boats floating toward the Rhine with their cargoes of grain and wine. Today schoolchildren come in on the train that connects Klingenberg with the larger town of Miltenberg and with Aschaffenburg, the district capital where Anneliese attended high school. The children climb over the tumbled walls of the castle, layed low by the powder charge of some long-forgotten French soldier. The brick battlements had blocked the path of the armies of Louis XIV, which came through here in the late 1680s to assert the claim of their Sun King to the wine-rich Palatinate. They left behind dead peasants, felled fruit trees, and scorched vineyards. It had been the second time in a century that this had occurred, for two generations earlier the plundering mercenaries of the Thirty Years War had left similar scars. So did the peasant uprisings a century earlier, when some of the restless young of Klingenberg attacked the nobles in the castle, only to be tortured and beheaded after their defeat. But in time there were other sons, new vineyards were planted, and the cultivators carried on as before. There is great persistence in these village towns.

Where fifty years ago passive cows glanced with one eye through tiny first-story or cellar windows and warmed the upper floor for the people with their massive body heat, the large homes of the winegrowers today form the core of a popular recreation area. New streets with modern houses reach out among the hills and along the Main River. That is where the owners and the workers of the clay pits live. The latter are located in the hills near Klingenberg, as is the small plant where pressure gauges are assembled. Anneliese's family also has a house like that. It is surrounded by trees and ornamental shrubs, and the vineyards rise at the back fence. The windows on the left side look out over the cemetery where Anneliese lies buried.

Some of the workers in Klingenberg's industry and commercial enterprises are newcomers, flotsam carried along by the whirling waters of the Great War. But most, like Anneliese's parents, are from families founded by the younger children of the winegrowers, for whom there were no terraces or fields left to subdivide. Modern industry created new ways of living for them in their ancient town.

Even with new areas of employment, though, these descendants remain tied to the culture that is as much a part of the land as is the forest fragrance of the Spessart and the Odenwald or the mist over the Main. This is a culture common to all cultivators, no matter where they break their furrows or what they call their gods. There is a godhead from whom grace rains down to undeserving sinners, so high, so exalted that it can hardly be approached. But life is onerous and the cultivator needs the help of the powers on the "other side." So there are kind intermediaries who will listen, protect, and intercede. Highest among them, in Klingenberg and elsewhere in the Catholic world, is the Virgin Mary, closest to God, God's mother. "Holy Mary, have mercy on us," Father

Renz's voice proclaims on the first of the tapes he made of Anneliese's exorcism sessions, after invoking the personages of the Trinity. But then the prayer of the group around her rises to the other intermediaries. "St. Michael, pray for us. St. Gabriel, pray for us. All the sacred angels and archangels, pray for us. Saintly souls, pray for us. John the Baptist, the Patriarchs, St. Peter, St. Paul, St. Andrew, St. Jacob, St. John, St. Thomas . . . pray for us, pray for us." There are so many of them. Occasionally some are expelled from the calendar of saints. Others have not yet gone through the lengthy trial for admittance. In Klingenberg people hope for the awarding of the "blessed" title to Barbara Weigand. Anneliese had great affection for this peasant woman, dead before her time, from a village in the Spessart. She spent most of the ninety-seven years of her life in untiring work, in prayer and in ecstasy, and laid the foundation for the spacious church in Rück-Schippach, Father Renz's parish.

Anneliese's parents and sisters pray, while from her mouth demons rave and curse. The demons are fallen angels who hate God and are locked in eternal combat with those of the heavenly host that remained faithful. Humans also have their role in the drama, some aiding on one side, some on the other. Good always wins, and those fighting the good fight go to their glory. A terrible fate awaits the others. "Hell must be monstrously horrible," Anneliese sighs in the only extensive conversation Father Renz recorded with her. In school the Klingenberg children learn about Doctor Faustus, a brilliant swindler, according to early versions of his tale, who passed through Würzburg where Anneliese attended college, many times. They learn how he made a pact with the devil, who in the end murdered him, tearing him limb from limb and spattering his brains against the walls. They also talk of women in Klingenberg, women who have evil powers. During the dark days of witchcraft trials, there were so many of them that the Pankratius gate of the town could not house them all. They are no longer called witches these days, but there are those who are envious, who can utter a curse and imbue it with life. Long after they are dead it may sicken an innocent person or rob him of his mind, and no doctor has any cure for it. There were those in Klingenberg who thought that Anneliese was the victim of such a curse.

And then there is Hitler. In Bavaria, where he started on his road to power, the obscene terror of his presence hovers in the treetops like dark-winged bats.

The Trinity and the Virgin, the intermediaries and Lucifer, sin and redemption—all this is, of course, Catholic dogma. It persists. But details change over time, and changes decreed from Rome often do not sit well with the people in the village churches. When a pope ordered celibacy for the priests many centuries ago, Bavarian women stayed on with their priest-husbands for a generation or more. There was much opposition to Rome down through the centuries in Bavaria. The Gymnasium (secondary school) that Anneliese attended in Aschaffenburg was named for Reichsfreiherr Karl Theodor von Dalberg, bishop of Konstanz, prince of Aschaffenburg, and later in life archbishop of Regensburg. In his sermons and writings he fought for the independence of the German bishops from papal power. And later in the nineteenth century, when the popes compromised with liberal political views, the people in Bavaria did not want their priests to go along with this decision. It is only logical that in Bavaria the reforms agreed upon in the Second Ecumenical Council were not too popular. In a backhanded way, some of Anneliese's demons were archliberals, lauding the reforms that Anneliese loathed.

It was in Klingenberg, so firmly embedded in the past, that Josef Michel started settling into the tasks of the house father. The role suited him well. It was not hard to learn; he had seen it played out by the men of his father's generation. There was no break in tradition in Klingenberg. Anna properly left all decisions to him, whether large or small. He was the head of the house, just as he was the head of the family business. He provided for all their needs and demanded obedience, but he was also fiercely protective, the shield of his family toward the world. Although often curt and blustering, the girls sensed his passionate love for them. Anneliese's voice becomes caressing when she tells Father Renz, in that recorded conversation, how "Paba" scolds if she does not eat. "You are not exactly fat, you know," he says.

After Anneliese, Anna gave birth to three more girls, Gertrud Maria (1954), Barbara (1956), and Roswitha Christine, her last (1957). The three younger sisters were quite robust, but Anneliese had little resistance to childhood diseases. She caught the measles when she was quite small and had the mumps and scarlet fever when she was only four or five. Seeing the delicate child, the grade-school teacher thought her too small for her age and counseled the parents to keep her at home a year longer. She attended kindergarten for a while, but it was not a happy time; the more aggressive children kept pushing her around.

Anna often felt defensive about Anneliese's being sick so much. There is a shadow of shame attached when an adult is often sick. Perhaps he or she wants to get out of work. But when a child is sickly, well, that is a misfortune, and who knows why some people have bad luck that way? "I was still weak when I carried her," she would say to the neighborhood women as she waited for the pound of sugar and the flour to be weighed out—and sauerkraut in this pot, please—in the grocery store around the corner. "You know how it was, we were all so hungry. Even after the war, all that hunger. It is bound to make a woman weak, and the second child after the war, *net*? There just wasn't much she could get from me." The women knew. It hadn't been as bad in Klingenberg as in the big cities, but they had all been hungry. Some remembered going into the Spessart for berries, and how clean the people had picked the forest floor for twigs for the kitchen fire, for mushrooms, and for beechnuts. But still, there was sometimes a reason why a woman had a sick child. Maybe there was envy somewhere.

At first communion Anneliese was still slighter than the others, wearing her fine white lace dress, a veil on her head, the small bride of Christ, carrying that tall candle. But she seemed to be outgrowing her health problems, and by the time she entered the Dalberg-Gymnasium in Aschaffenburg in 1965, she had caught up with her fellow classmates. It was fun taking the train every morning, squeezing into the narrow compartment with the other children attending school there, and watching the landscape go by through the train window. Besides, now "Oma" (grandmother Fürg) had to help watch her lively little sisters, and that was also a welcome change. "She was just like the rest of us," her friend and fellow classmate in the Gymnasium, Maria Burdich, told the court investigator. "She was a jolly girl, participating in the usual schoolgirl pranks and jokes." Josef Michel, in a letter to me, remembered her the same way.

When Anneliese and her sisters became bigger, we often took the car and went on outings on Sundays, and the girls sang to their hearts' content. They all had a good ear for music, played various instruments, and loved to harmonize when they sang. That was always very lovely, a very happy time. Especially Anneliese had a way of just glowing with joy.

Anneliese played the accordion and, as was expected of girls from well-off families, she took piano lessons. She also studied hard. "I will not have you bring home any poor grades," her mother said with her usual nervous severity. "You are good at learning, and your father and I want to see that in your report card." That was how all parents talked, and Anneliese put forward a great deal of effort. It was hard going in the new school for a while, but eventually she caught on, even in Latin, which she especially liked. "She would take watch in hand and recite Latin vocabulary assignments with breathtaking speed," Anna recalled in some notes written for me.

Anna often talked about Anneliese's good grades. "She is so good, she will very likely become a schoolteacher someday," she might say to the butcher's wife, who had come up to the office on the second floor of the Michel house to pay for some planks her husband had bought. "It's in the family," the butcher's wife would answer. "Look at yourself, doing all that difficult bookkeeping." And perhaps a *Bäuerin,* the wife of a winegrower from a nearby village, who was waiting for her bill for new trellises, might be listening to the talk a bit wistfully. A person could have three cows in the stable, a number of productive vineyards, big barrels of red wine in an orchard, and even a field or two, but to have a child that was going to be a schoolteacher was still something special. Her Hans had not made it into high school. And even in the trade school, where he was now, the teacher was always down on him. "You're only good in religion, but in arithmetic you flunk," the teacher would say, and the other boys would laugh. If Anneliese

Michel were really to become a schoolteacher and would come to call, her Hans would feel honored. He would get up from the kitchen chair and pull up the chair with the cushion for her to sit on, and her opinion would carry more weight with him than that of his parents. She sighed a little to herself as Anna Michel typed out the bill. It was not hard to see that Frau Michel had ambitions. Everyone in Klingenberg knew that she had bought new rugs for the house. She had seen on the way up how even the glass doors inside the house had curtains on them, thin ones and flowery, heavy ones on top of that. There was a maid working in the kitchen, and her girls had their own rooms on the second floor. It wasn't like with many people, where the daughters slept on a couch in the living room until they left to get married. It was easy for such a family to have a girl become a schoolteacher.

Josef Michel also talked about Anneliese's grades while sitting around the *Stammtisch,* "his" table at the tavern, the "Winterstübchen" in the Bergwerkstrasse, where he drank an evening "Klingenberger red one" with his friends, men of substance like the other sawmill owner, maybe the master butcher, the master shoemaker, and one or the other mechanic from the gauge factory. "She's so good, I'll let her become a schoolteacher," he would say. They obviously approved. It was useful to have an educated person in the family, even if only a girl. Girls who had an education married a better type of husband. Besides, the Michels were already in that class. There was their cousin in Mömbris, where Anneliese occasionally went during summer vacation. Josef Michel talked about him often. *He* was a schoolteacher. "I hope you know, Sepp, how expensive it is to send your child to the Pädagogische Hochschule, the teachers' college," someone would observe. "All the way to Würzburg, and then the expensive dormitory . . ." "Expenses are no matter," Josef Michel would counter. The men nodded. It was profitable to have a sawmill and a store with it, even though Sepp did not talk about his income, only about how he and his family always worked hard, every day, from morning till night.

"Still," one of the *Stammtisch* members ventured, "it isn't without danger to let one's daughters go to the big city." Josef Michel knew that, too, and sometimes he worried about it, although all of

this was still in the distant future, with Anneliese only fourteen
and Roswitha, the youngest, in grade school. "My girls will be
good girls," he blustered, "very good girls!" He brought his fist
down on the table, jostling the wineglasses on their blue-and-white
paper napkins. "And if they are used to being good girls at home,
they will also be good in the city." He went on with the topic for a
while, and his friends let him, knowing him as a man more given
to talking than to listening. Besides, there was really nothing to
say. The way Sepp was raising his girls, they were not going to
grow up spreading their legs for anyone, like some big-city girls
nowadays. He was strict, sure. But, then, how else could he protect them? Besides, no one heard his girls complaining about how
they were treated at home. They went to church with their parents
on Sundays and sometimes even on weekday evenings. At home
they all said the rosary together. But they also had some decent
fun, going to sports classes at the local club. There was nothing
wrong with the Michel girls.

Anna was not all that happy about her girls going to the sports
club. And the fact that they were taking ballroom-dancing classes
with boys was even less desirable. One never knew what might
happen when boys and girls were together. She had heard the ad-
monition many times when she was a girl: A girl's honor is like a
white sheet; every spot shows. She wanted her girls to be pure
when they went to their marriage bed, virgins like the Virgin
Mary. The priests always asked about these things in confession.
You had to listen to your priest, for he was the guardian of your
soul. She had managed to keep Anneliese away from boys and
from dancing by arguing, "You are too delicate, you must not
exert yourself. If you are not careful, you'll get sick again." But
Anneliese was her oldest. With all the work in the office now, she
had less time for the younger ones, less strength to stand up
against their insistent argument, "But everybody else has dancing
lessons." Besides, Anneliese always took their part.

There were occasions when her sisters would find Anneliese
crying in her room about yet another time that she had been forbidden to go dancing. "All girls my age are allowed to," she
would sob. "After all, I am nearly fifteen." "Don't cry," Gertrud
would console her. "Look, Mama will not even allow us three to

go and visit girl friends." "I know why," Barbara suggested. "It's because Mama thinks that we would get to read some of those sinful books there that she always warns us about. I bet Anneliese has one of those, too." Then they would all fall on her, laughing. "Come on, Anneliese, hand it over." But she would just shrug and threaten to chase them out of her room. Roswitha had another idea, seeing that Anneliese was starting to cry again. "Mama won't let any of us, not even Anneliese most of the time, go visit girl friends, because girl friends have brothers." "Hey," all of them laughed again, and they nudged Anneliese, for they knew that their big sister had a boyfriend. "You're in love," Roswitha teased. "Confess, we know it anyway. How about it? Does he have a good job? Do his parents have any money?" That would make even Anneliese laugh, for Roswitha had a knack for mimicking their mother's scolding voice. She pulled her little sister's hair playfully and blushed. Years later she told her psychotherapist about this boy, and about how happy she had been with him, but we do not know his name.

CHAPTER TWO

ENTER THE GHASTLY FACES

After the long and lazy days of summer, it was great fun to go back to school in September, Anneliese thought as she boarded the train for Aschaffenburg for the first school day of the 1968–69 academic year. And it *was* fun. All the old friends were there, especially Maria Burdich, with whom she spent the "long" intermission, the one at ten o'clock, walking in the school yard. Usually they talked about going to the "PH," the Pädagogische Hochschule in Würzburg, and what the professors would be like there, and the boys. "And then I'll teach in some nice little village, and all my kids will be well behaved, and you'll come and visit me," Anneliese would say.

Then, about the time of her sixteenth birthday at the end of that month, it happened. It came up suddenly, like a thunderhead boiling up over the horizon, pregnant with lightning. The day before she had been sitting in class, at her place next to Maria. Without warning she had blacked out. Maria had pressed her arm.

"Mensch," she had whispered to her, "Anneliese, what's the matter with you? Are you asleep or something?" "I suppose so," Anneliese shrugged, still dazed. "Maybe I studied too much." They both giggled a little and then forgot about it.

That night, shortly after midnight, she woke up and could not move. A giant force was pinning her down. It pressed on her abdomen and she could feel her warm urine spilling out. Her breathing became labored. In utter panic, she wanted to call to her sisters, but no sound came out. Her tongue was as if paralyzed. "Holy Mother of God," she thought, "I must be dying." By the time the tower clock of the church sounded the quarter hour, it was over. All pressure ceased as if blown away. Only her tongue felt sore.

Whimpering with terror, so exhausted she could hardly move, she got up and changed the linen on her bed. Next day she told her mother that she was too tired to go to school. "Mama," she said, "I must have been awfully sick last night. My bed was all soaked through." So Anna let her stay home and made her tell what had happened. A sick worry swept through her. What could this have been? But when it did not happen again, she put it out of her mind. Anneliese continued in school as before, got good grades, played the piano. She started learning to play tennis. Christmas came and went, there were the final examinations, and then the summer vacation. All was well.

Then, nearly a year later, during the night of August 24, 1969, whatever it was struck again, exactly as before. There was the brief blacking out during the day, where she just sat and did not know what it was she was about to do. And in the middle of the night that frightening paralysis, with her arms completely stiff, the inability to breathe, the desperate attempt to call out, to scream for help, and the total futility of it all, for there was that force that would not let her.

"This is the second time," her mother said when Anneliese told her about it the next morning. "What, in the name of all the saints, is the matter with you?" She put a comb to her neatly waved hair and rushed down the street to the office of Dr. Vogt, the family physician. An hour later she and Anneliese had boarded the train to Aschaffenburg to consult Dr. Siegfried Lüthy, the neurologist to whom Dr. Vogt had referred them.

"Oh, my God, my God, what is going on with you?" her mother kept sighing over and over again. "Dr. Vogt said it may be something with your brain. Let's not talk about this to anyone outside the family, *net*? You know how people talk. They are so uneducated. 'Michel's Anneliese is crazy,' they will say. 'Did you hear about it? She had to go to a nerve doctor.' Unthinkable." Anneliese, too spent to care much, watched her mother's hand trembling as she pulled her embroidered handkerchief from her handbag. It was hot in the train, and little beads of perspiration had formed on Mama's forehead. With jerky little movements she daubed them off, shaking her head all the while. "If this gets around, you might not even be admitted to the Pädagogische Hochschule."

Anneliese felt her heart contract. And then what about her dream of teaching in some quiet village, of a little school, of children smelling of hay and freshly threshed wheat?

Dr. Lüthy, tall and imposing, asked many questions and ran a number of tests to check her various reflexes. As he told the criminal investigator who came to his office to interrogate him on February 9, 1977, he could find nothing wrong with her. "Neurologically and psychologically all findings were negative." He asked them to come back on August 27 for some electroencephalographic recordings. Again he came up empty-handed, as we read in the record of this interrogation: "The EEG recorded on August 27, 1969, showed a normal, physiological alpha-type brain activity." Yet he had to account for the convulsions his young patient had reported, and so he continued, "I judged from the description I was given that this was *probably* a case of cerebral seizures of the nocturnal type, with the symptoms of a grand mal epilepsy." One detects a note of anxiety, for a bit further on during the same interrogation he repeated once more, "Judging from the description, this was *probably* a cerebral disease of the convulsive kind" (emphasis added). There are two versions of what followed next. The first version is contained in a letter he had written to the state investigator on July 16, 1976. It is missing from the files, but Dr. Lüthy refers to it at his interrogation. In this letter he had apparently maintained that at this first consultation in 1969 he already prescribed Zentropil to Anneliese, an anticonvulsant drug known in the United States as Dilantin (phenytoin sodium). The second version was given during the interrogation: "Let it be emphasized at this point that I did not treat Miss Michel with Zentropil . . . as early as August 25, 1969, as stated in my letter of July 16, 1976." Rather, he maintains, "since only two attacks occurred within an interval of a year, I suggested no anticonvulsant therapy and advised further observation."

Be this as it may. When school started after this visit to Dr. Lüthy, Anneliese was not well. Roswitha, who was eleven at the time, remembers how much her sister complained about a sore throat. Finally her tonsils had to be removed. Soon after she contracted pleurisy and pneumonia, complicated by a tuberculous infection, and had to drop out of school. She was confined to bed at home. No midnight mass on Christmas Eve for her, so beautiful with all the flickering candles. And no getting up for Roswitha's twelfth birthday on the first day of Christmas either. With still no improvement in her condition in January, she was transferred to the hospital in Aschaffenburg in February, and from there, on the twenty-eighth of the month, to a clinic in the mountainous southern region of Bavaria. This was a sanatorium in Mittelberg, in the Allgäu, specializing in bronchial and lung disease of children and juveniles.

Day after day Anneliese looked out of the window at the towering peaks of the Allgäu, close and threatening, not gently undulating like the hills of home but abruptly rising in rocky clefts, their peaks capped with snow and brooding clouds. In the large dormitory where she lay there were some girls from the Oberpfalz, the Upper Palatinate. They all seemed to know each other and gossiped noisily about the nurses, the doctors, about the food, their boyfriends, and about when they would be discharged. Their dialect was just different enough that Anneliese could not catch the key phrase that made them laugh, and it locked her out. They used to laugh together that way at home, she and her sisters. Now she was alone, very alone. The letters she was getting did not help much. It made the loneliness even more cruel, like a pain in her chest, a dark pain with ragged, red edges. All had written her,

Gertrud, Barbara, and even little Roswitha, who always sounded like she had copied a sermon from a devotional book at home. "I hope you can bear the cross intended for you with love and uncomplainingly . . ." Uncomplainingly? She was not complaining. She was willing to suffer as Christ had taught people by his example. But was it a sin to ask for it to end sometime? Was it wrong to pray for a speedy discharge, as she was doing every evening? She hoped not, for her homesickness often seemed to smother her with its crushing weight until she just had to cry for help. Perhaps Papa should make a pilgrimage to the church of Padre Pio da Pietralcina of San Giovanni Rotondo (who died in 1968), that saintly Capuchin friar who had borne Christ's wounds visibly on his limbs and body. Papa had been there before and knew the way. If he prayed for her recovery there, that might help. Everyone knew that such prayers were very efficacious. In the meantime, she kept up her own supplications to the Virgin, and every morning she waited for the nurse to tell her that she was doing better. Was her temperature down? Were her tests negative? Did the doctor say anything that was hopeful?

Spring came. One of the girls from the Oberpfalz was allowed to go home, and another, even more boisterous, had taken her place. Anneliese was permitted to go on short walks in the park of the sanatorium, but she longed to see the Odenwald, not these rocky faces where melted snow was oozing from monstrous scars. At home the linden trees would be blooming. There were none here. But perhaps she would soon be let go. It would be the right time, June was coming, and school would let out. Was that possible? "Why not, *Schäfle,* silly little girl," one of the nurses had said.

It did not happen. Her parents were told that there were some heart and circulatory problems, and she could not yet be discharged safely. Anneliese was numb with disappointment. Maybe she should just walk out into the mountains, up to one of those sheer cliffs. No one would even notice. And she would jump off, and the pain would lift, and she would be light as a butterfly and rise and rise into God's heaven.

It was then that she was struck again, on a Wednesday night, June 3, 1970. There had been the stiffness in the arms, the crushing sensation, the struggle for breath, the warm urine. Desperately she tried to free herself. Finally the scream tore loose and everyone—the night nurse, the young doctor on duty—came running. Even the girls from the Oberpfalz jumped out of bed. But by that time it was all over. Limply she allowed herself to be changed and moved to a fresh bed. Then she fell asleep.

The girls left her alone the next morning. Even they could sense that she was too spent to talk. But the following day they descended on her like a swarm of chattering magpies. "What, you don't know what's wrong with you? It's in your head, don't you see? Maybe you have water on the brain. It got in there, you know, before you were born," one of them suggested. "I had an aunt . . ."

"No, no," another interrupted. "Maybe you fell on your head. My cousin did once, and he was never right since. His mother dropped him on the kitchen floor after she gave him his bath. He hit the back of his head smack on the tiles."

"I did fall once," Anneliese admitted.

They all started talking at once. How? When? Where?

"I stumbled and hit my forehead. I was about eleven."

"Did you vomit afterwards? My cousin did."

"No, I didn't. The doctor said it wasn't a concussion. You only vomit after a concussion."

"So that can't be it." The girls ran out of conjectures. "Besides, you are pretty together," one of the girls said, and they started on something else.

But Anneliese kept remembering the suggestions as she tried to figure out just what was the matter with her. She talked about the "water on the brain" theory to her friend Mechthild Scheuering at the PH. The fall on the forehead came up in a conversation with Father Alt, and she also mentioned it to Dr. Irmgard Schleip, her neurologist at the clinic in Würzburg. But at the autopsy there was no sign of either "water" on or injury to the brain.

A few days after the seizure, Anneliese was sitting on the chair beside her bed. Dusk was welling up outside and made the objects of the large dormitory indistinct. The nurses took their time about turning on the lights. Anneliese started praying the rosary. Dusk. It was a good time of day. The girls usually went down to the lounge or roamed the corridors before supper, and she could think

of home. They said the rosary in the kitchen about this time of the
day, all of them together, even Papa. It made you feel good,
warm, and sheltered. As she fingered bead after smooth bead, she
tried to call up that special mood. Blessed are you among women,
and blessed is the fruit of your womb, Jesus. On and on. The
mood came, as if on tiptoes. Ave Maria, full of grace. The mood
grew stronger, more powerful than she had ever felt it at home.
There was a gentle prickling in her cheeks and her lips trembled.
Ave Maria . . . Ave Maria. The end of the prayer. She let her
hands drop in her lap, still holding the rosary. Something was so
different this evening. A sweetness she had never known before
made her ring. I am a bell, she thought, I ring the praise of the
Mother of God . . . a bell . . . a bell . . .

She looked out the window, as if trying to discover if that
unearthly sweetness had perhaps entered from there. Those mountains? How strange. She had not previously noticed that those for-
bidding mountains out there were so beautiful. The peaks glowed
in altar gold and pink, and silver streamers tumbled toward blue-
black depths.

"Wos is'n mit dere los?"—what's wrong with her there, she
heard, startled. She had not noticed that some of the girls had
come back, nor that the light was now turned on. "What were you
doing, anyway?" Their voices were awfully loud, even louder than
usual.

"Praying, of course."

"We can see that, dummy. But what's with your hands?"

"My hands?"

"Yea, your hands. We were watching you. Like you had a
cramp or something. Like when my cat stretches her claws."

Anneliese looked down at her hands in her lap. There was still
the rosary, and it, too, was transformed in beauty. But she could
see nothing different about her hands. "Like you had paws or
something."

"You're all daffy, you know that? Nothing wrong with my
hands."

"And your eyes," another girl persisted. "I thought they were
blue. Now they are all black."

"Don't be silly," Anneliese could not help laughing. There was still that sweetness wafting about her like the fragrance of violets. No amount of teasing was going to spoil it for her. But she did get up and walk to the mirror over the washbasin. Her eyes really appeared darker than usual. Like looking into the well at Oma Fürg's house. But what struck her more was her face. She was all rosy, real, real well. "Too bad the doctor can't see me tonight," she thought. "He would discharge me this minute." But to the girls she just said, "Leave me alone, will you? You're just imagining things."

A feeling of well-being lingered on into the next day. "It must be the Virgin helping me," she thought gratefully. That prayer last night had been so special. As if the Virgin had been there with her, lighting up the world with her presence and making everything glow with her glory. She longed to speak to someone about it, but that would have to wait till she was out of here and back in school. Maria Burdich would listen and not laugh about her.

On Tuesday morning (June 16) the nurse came in as Anneliese was brushing her teeth.

"Get dressed, young lady, you're going to Kempten today."

"I am? Why?"

"They're going to try and find out what's going on in your head."

Anneliese blushed. She hated being surprised by what they were going to do to her. It was like being a rag doll; anybody was allowed to throw you back and forth. They could take blood from you, poke you, stick needles in you, put electrodes on your head with that awful paste that was so hard to wash out of your hair. You never had a say about anything. I wish I could close my eyes, she thought, and be in my room, and Mittelberg would just disappear. But it's no use. I am a prisoner, and they will never, never let me go.

The report of Dr. von Haller, the Kempten neurologist, is not among the documents on the Anneliese Michel case. We know that he recorded an EEG of her that showed an irregular alpha pattern with some scattered theta and delta waves—nothing pathological. Stimulation—of what nature we are not told—triggered no access firing of any particular group of cells, any "locus" in the brain, and she did not respond with any seizure. Still, in view of

the fact that she had had seizures before, he recommended anticonvulsant medication, according to the summary of Anneliese's
medical history submitted during the trial by Dr. Sattes, the court-
appointed expert. According to the Drs. Kehler, the husband-and-
wife team who were the Michels' family physicians since April
1973, "EEGs were recorded and the epilepsy was treated with"
followed by the name of a drug. Unfortunately, it is smudged and
illegible in their letter to the district attorney.

In the days following that special prayer she had often tried to
call up the same experience once more. A few times it almost happened again. You can't blame the Mother of God for not coming
every time you asked her, she consoled herself. She must be very
busy, with so many people calling to her for help every hour of
the day and night. But one evening, about a week after the trip to
Kempten, she felt sure she was going to succeed. It was one of
those still days, no wind coming through the window, the foot of
the mountains shimmering in the heat. She sat with her rosary en-
twined around her hands. "I would want to touch the seam of your
mantle," she thought. Suddenly, like sheet lightning on the distant
horizon, she saw a huge, cruelly grimacing face. It was gone almost as soon as she had seen it, but it left her with a chill of
nameless fear. In a letter to her parents earlier that day she had
written, "God I place first in my life." Now, after seeing that face,
she felt she could not pray. She put the rosary away into her
nightstand drawer.

Anneliese, growing more and more despondent, was kept in the
sanatorium for another six weeks after the consultation in Dr. von
Haller's office in Kempten. Sometimes she was afraid to say the
rosary in the evenings, something that had meant so much, calling
up home and the Virgin, comfort in both her worlds. For who
could know if instead of the sweet perfume of the presence of the
Mother of God that ghastly, grimacing horror would not intrude,
dreaded, uninvited? It had already done so a few times, and when
it did it made her swirl, as if she were being hurled into a dark pit.
The last time it had happened a terrifying thought had hit her afterwards: What if that monstrous shape were really in her, not

outside, where she seemed to see it? It's in me, in me, in me . . . the fear of it kept echoing through her mind.

On August 11 Dr. von Haller checked her EEG once more, and again he found no irregularities. "How are you feeling, young lady?" he asked her. "Sometimes I am dizzy," she said. To tell more seemed impossible. It was her private panic, and she was not ready yet to surrender it to the scrutiny of a stranger's eye. "Any more seizures?" She shook her head. On August 29 she was allowed to go home.

Her sisters found her changed. "You're so moody," Roswitha complained. "What's the matter with you? Aren't you glad you're home? Don't you love us anymore?"

"You're *depp,* crazy. Of course I do. I love you all very much. I know that I do. I am just too exhausted to feel it. I don't seem to be able to feel anything at all."

"Leave her alone," said Josef. "Of course she is tired. She should go upstairs and go to sleep early. We want to go to the first mass tomorrow morning."

So Anneliese went upstairs right after praying the rosary with her family. Her room was unchanged and smelled pleasantly of sun-dried bed linen. She sat down at her small desk in the corner, between the wide wardrobe and the window. The trees nodded darkly under a pale sky, with just a spangle of the first stars. She had done so many pleasant things at this desk, scribbling gossip about boys into her diary, writing letters to cousins, pressing a little bunch of violets into her prayer book. I wish I could be that carefree again, she sighed. She idly turned on her desk lamp. The light of its round, milky globe reflected off the slanting ceiling and made the flowers of the wallpaper stand out in bas-relief. She turned it off and walked across the room to the small table with a framed picture of Jesus on it. Mama had put a freshly ironed embroidered cloth on the table. Or was it perhaps Roswitha? She would have to thank her tomorrow.

Slowly she drew the heavy, flowery curtains over the glass door leading into the corridor and put her wristwatch on the nightstand. Wearily she undressed. She shivered a little as she pulled the cool sheet and the flowery quilt over herself. How many times had she imagined just this moment in the sanatorium. Now the glow of its happiness was eluding her. "Oh, Lord," she thought, slipping into the idiom of her prayer book, "oh, Lord, I am willing to take up my cross. But please, please don't let it be *that*." She could not bring herself to name it, and it took awhile before she fell into a troubled sleep.

CHAPTER THREE

PHYSICIANS AND PRIESTS

"I thought I was going to be happy going back to school again," Anneliese sighed. "Now I am worried."

"What about?" asked Gertrud, who was sitting beside her in the train on this September morning in 1970. She had graduated from the Mittelschule (high school) in Erlenbach and was starting further training in the Euroschule in Aschaffenburg.

"To begin with, those girls are going to be two years younger than I. Mere babies."

"Two years?"

"Of course two years. I started a year late, and now I missed another year."

"Maria Burdich will be there."

"True. But she is now in a class above me. And in the eleventh grade, where I am going, I won't know a soul."

As it turned out, there was one girl in the class that she did know. This was Ursula Kuzay. They had played together when

Anneliese had visited her second cousin, Walter Hein, in
Mömbris, where he was then a grade-school teacher. It was the
only familiar face in the class, though, as she looked around, and
she longed for true intimacy. She wanted to talk with someone,
some trusted friend, like Maria Burdich, for instance, about that
strange, unearthly sweetness that she so longed to experience
again. And perhaps . . . maybe . . . possibly . . . Maria could
also be trusted with that other secret, the secret that made her
tremble with dread.

Maria did greet her affectionately during the long intermission.
She asked about the sanatorium and how she was feeling now. But
then the conversation drifted to summer fun, to boys, and to what
Herr Völkl, the homeroom teacher, had said in his first class.
Anneliese's heart sank. She had tried to bring Maria around to the
topic of topics, but at that point the conversation lagged and
Anneliese stopped insisting. It was no use. Maybe it would be better not to wait for her again at the school yard door. Maria was
no less disappointed. "After her illness," she told the court investigator, "Anneliese was changed. She was quiet and withdrew
from her friends. I also noted that she kept wanting to carry on
mostly religious conversations."

Anneliese's new classmates agreed with Maria. "She was quiet
and serious," Karin Gora stated, "a loner if not an outsider, in-
troverted and dreamy, who participated in silliness or pranks only
if we drew her in." Some of the girls talked behind her back.
"Let's do something nice for her," one said. "Let her try some
hashish." "*Haschen* with us?" The other one laughed until she
nearly choked. "Most likely she would tell you that *haschen* was a
sin, and that to save us somebody would have to do penance for
us." "What a religious nut. I bet you she'd much rather go to
church than to the movies." "Don't let Ursula Kuzay hear you,"
another warned them. "She thinks Anneliese is all right." At her
interrogation this erstwhile Mömbris playmate was to state, "I recognized that she was deeply religious and also lived accordingly."

Dejected and alone, Anneliese earned only average grades. She
was not feeling very well, either. The sanatorium had instructed
her parents to take her for a checkup a month after her discharge.
Always worried about her health, and anxious to do everything

that the physicians thought necessary, on October 6, 1970, her mother took her to a specialist for lung diseases in Miltenberg, a city close to Klingenberg, which is too small to support any specialists. This was a Dr. Reichelt. When, during the consultation, he quizzed her mother about the seizures that were noted in her daughter's file, Anna told him that Anneliese had had another one "recently." In other words, this new seizure must have coincided, more or less, with the start of the new school year.

Anneliese's lungs checked out fine, but Dr. Reichelt found some circulatory problems and wrote a referral to an internist also practicing in Miltenberg, a Dr. Packhäuser. "All I ever do is sit around in doctors' offices," Anneliese complained. "You drag me to one, then you drag me to another, then I have to go to a third. I wish I could be rid of the lot of them and just live like other girls." Anna felt sorry for her. It was hard for her, too, taking time off from all that work in the office of the family sawmill, and spending days in Miltenberg, waiting for the doctors to examine Anneliese, for all the good they were doing her. You would think that after such a long time in the sanatorium she would finally be healthy. But if this Dr. Reichelt thought that Anneliese also needed an internist to look at her, then they would have to do it. Better was better.

There is no record of what Dr. Packhäuser, the internist, suggested should be done about Anneliese's circulatory problem. But he was also interested in the seizures and wrote a note concerning them to the Michels' family physician, Dr. Vogt. Since Anneliese had had numerous seizures that year, he said, something ought to be done about them. Her mother seemed to think that they had to do with the girl's circulation, but of course he could not concur with that. The family should take her to a neurologist. Dr. Packhäuser may have been in a hurry to do other things that day. Not only had he exaggerated the number of seizures—there had only been two in 1970, one in June in the sanatorium, the other at the start of the school year—but he also labeled them "apoplectic." Now, whatever was ailing Anneliese, it most certainly had not been a stroke.

Dr. Vogt apparently did not think that a consultation with a neurologist was necessary at this time. According to Anna, however, he did prescribe some sort of anticonvulsant. There is nothing to indicate that Anneliese took it very long, but she was generally not well. She was plagued by a succession of brief absences, accompanied by depression. It became hard for her to concentrate on her increasingly difficult homework.

"In the last two years of the Gymnasium [i.e., 1971–72 and 1972–73], I just didn't care beans about anything anymore," she told Dr. Lenner, a young internist at the Institute for Psychotherapy and Medical Psychology of the University of Würzburg, where she went for a consultation in the fall of 1973. "Things got worse and worse that way. I became completely apathetic in those years, with no interest in anything that was going on." With remarkable introspection she later elaborated on the same point at a different interview. "I was able to perceive but not to experience." Her mother, however, looked forward to Anneliese's graduating from the Gymnasium with joyous anticipation. "Just think, I will have a daughter who is going to earn her *Abitur*," she would say. And Anneliese kept plugging away to please her, although her grades were no longer as good as they were before her stay in the sanatorium in Mittelberg.

Toward the end of her twelfth school year, in June 1972, there was another very severe seizure. Anneliese was totally spent for days afterwards and dreaded the next one. However, the seizures stopped as abruptly as they had started. Like aftershocks following an earthquake, there were a few minor ones, and then the problem disappeared altogether. Her mother often quizzed her. Was she all right? Wasn't she playing too much tennis? Was she getting enough rest? "They say that the last year of the Gymnasium is the hardest, and then the *Abitur* examinations, I hear they have made them much tougher recently. So please take care of yourself."

As September approached, Anna's anxiety became increasingly intense. "I'm all right," Anneliese would assure her. "You know it isn't so," her mother replied. "How about all those times when all of a sudden you become stiff, or when you no longer know where you are?" To which Anneliese rejoined, "That doesn't happen very often."

Still, Anna fretted. "You no sooner start school and you have another seizure. Let's go to Dr. Lüthy now, before school starts, just to be sure, all right? Maybe he can give you a pill or something to get you through the school year and the *Abitur.*"

"Mama will make herself sick with worrying," Anneliese told her sisters. "I had better let her take me to Dr. Lüthy again."

So on September 5, 1972, mother and daughter once more made the trip to Aschaffenburg, to Dr. Lüthy's office in the Bismarckallee. There is a brief report extant from Dr. Lüthy about this visit. He told the court investigator during that frequently mentioned interrogation in his office on February 9, 1977, that Anneliese admitted that there had still been some seizures. "I now prescribed the anticonvulsant *Zentropil,* one tablet in the morning, two at night. No pathological EEG could be elicited."

Dr. Lüthy asked her to come back for regular checkups, and obediently she saw him on January 18, March 27, and June 4 and 6, 1973. Despite a heavy burden of studying and considerable anxiety about the approaching *Abitur* examinations, there were no new seizures except for one on November 8, 1972, according to Dr. Lüthy's case history. Since Anneliese did not mention this seizure in the interviews with the neurologists in Würzburg, we may assume that it was a minor one, an "aftershock," as were the ones during the summer of that year. Concerning the results of the examinations in the first half of 1973, according to Dr. Lüthy, "Also during these examinations no pathological findings could be elicited. During the entire time Miss Michel was free of seizures." The EEG he recorded on June 4 was normal.

It is an indication of the rather distant relationship that must have existed between Anneliese and Dr. Lüthy that he apparently had no inkling at all of what her reaction may have been to the daily Dilantin doses. Perhaps he never asked her, being only interested in the suppression of the seizures. She obviously did not tell him that just a few weeks after taking this medication, in October 1972, absences and "turning stiff" became much more frequent— something she did mention to Dr. Lenner in Würzburg a year and a half later. Nor did she tell Dr. Lüthy what we also know from Dr. Lenner's report, namely, that she started smelling a horrid stench not perceived by others. What a psychological burden it must have been for her to hold back on all of this, especially since those hellish faces also occasionally came back to haunt her! Why didn't she trust him? The reason may have been nothing more than conflicting personalities. But it *could* have been more. Dr. Lüthy was born in Bernau, near Berlin, while Anneliese was a child of Bavaria. Cultural differences cut deep between northern and southern Germany, daily honed by stereotypes about the punctilious north and the easygoing south, by striking deviations in dialect, and by a mutual lack of understanding of Bavarian religiosity and northern Protestant worldliness. Nothing need be said. A barely perceptible shrug, a fleeting, deprecating smile, and the message has been received, the separation made visible. In the exchange between Anneliese and Dr. Lüthy, the young girl was the patient, the disadvantaged partner, Dr. Lüthy the power figure, invested with all the aura that a man of science bears in Germany. Without knowing it, he must have set up the kind of relationship that expressed this superior-inferior role. We can assume this because Anneliese perceived the need to defend herself against him. She did it by means of the one effective weapon she had: silence.

In the early spring of 1973, new, disturbing things began happening. "There is this knocking in my room," Anneliese would tell her mother. "You must have dreamed it," Anna countered. "I heard nothing at all." Anneliese kept insisting. Exasperated, Anna finally sent her to Dr. Vogt. "If you did not dream it, maybe there is something wrong with your ears." But Dr. Vogt could find nothing out of the ordinary and referred her to a specialist.

"The ear doctor could find nothing wrong with Anneliese's hearing," Anna told her husband that evening.

"Didn't I tell you he wouldn't? Dr. Lüthy thinks she has epilepsy. By the way, I hope you didn't tell her that, did you?" Anna shook her head. "Well, it may have something to do with that. *Sie spinnt halt,* she's a bit off her rocker, that's all."

"No, Sepp, no. It wasn't just Anneliese. She was the first one to hear it, but then the others did too. Like rapping, or a chair falling over, or someone thumping inside the wardrobe, then underneath the floor and above the ceiling."

Sepp did not look at her and continued unbuttoning his shirt. "So?"

"What I mean, Sepp," Anna dropped her voice to a hoarse whisper, "what I mean is that this might be something supernatural." She kept nervously smoothing out the pillows.

Josef's temper began to rise. "I'll tell you what I think, if you want to hear it. Anneliese is sick. And as to her sisters, well, young girls are sometimes hysterical. Everybody knows that. So maybe that's why they heard those things. But, you, a grown woman—I must say."

"But Sepp, listen. There is more. Anneliese has been telling me recently that no matter what she might be doing—making her bed, playing the piano, or just looking out the window—she sees those ghastly distorted faces, those *Fratzen*. It isn't just occasionally, like before."

Josef sighed. "Yes, she told me that too. God only knows what that is about."

"Well, if she told you that, did she also tell you that those faces are like devils? With horns? And she thinks that they are after her, and she hears those voices that tell her that she is damned and will go to hell forever. . . ." She trailed off into a dry sob.

"Who put that stupidity in her head?" Josef had been unlacing a shoe and he now let it drop with a thud. "Damned? That pure, innocent child?" His voice rose, flaring with anger. "That is silly. That is bullshit."

"But Sepp, listen," Anna kept her voice low. "They could be devils, don't you think? The priests talk about Satan and how he is everywhere trying to tempt us."

His anger left him as quickly as it had arisen. He sat down beside his wife on the edge of the bed and patted her hand. "Calm down, Anna. The girl is an epileptic. Someday she'll be well again. All of this will blow over, you'll see."

She would not be comforted. "No, Sepp, no. Believe me, something terrible, something supernatural is going on. You know that statue of the Virgin on the mantel in the living room downstairs? Well, the other day I happened to walk through there and saw Anneliese looking at the Mother of God. Only it wasn't with respect or with adoration. Her face was like a terrible mask, full of hatred. Her eyes turned black, jet black. And her slender hands— you know how delicate her hands are—well, they twitched, and

seemed to turn into thick paws with claws. I tell you, it was awful.
I was so scared, I rushed up to the office and tried to calm myself
by writing out some bills. Only I couldn't. My hands shook so, I
couldn't hold the pen. And I could not see the letters on the type-
writer."

Josef was silent for quite a while. "We'll have to ask for guidance in prayer," he finally said.

Prayer had always been a rallying point for the family. But the
evening rosaries and the masses and services of penance did very
little for Anneliese. Instead, she now suffered a new kind of
hellish torment, one that grew worse as the examinations drew
nearer. She talked about it in that conversation that Father Renz
recorded with her on February 1, 1976.

It was especially gruesome at the time of the *Abitur*. Oh,
Herr Pater, you cannot imagine that most awful dread
[*Grausen*]. It is a terror that goes through all my limbs
and settles there. It is a dread that makes you think that you
are right there, in the middle of hell. You are totally, utterly
deserted. You can call all you want to for help, to the
Mother of God maybe, but they are all deaf. I think that's
how it must have been for the Savior on the Mount of Olives,
where they say he was beset by the shudders of death. Although I think for him it must have been even worse, for,
after all, he had taken all the sins of the people on himself,
the sins of all the world. . . .

Later that spring Anneliese caught the German measles. Because this childhood disease came so late, her parents consulted
the family physicians. "Just leave me alone," Anneliese pleaded.
"I'll get over it." But one of the Kehlers who had taken over the
practice of Dr. Vogt just a few weeks previously (on April 1) was
asked to make a house call anyway. Despite the loss of several
weeks of school because of this illness, Anneliese did pass the
difficult *Abitur* examinations and graduated. It was also gradua-
tion year for the other Michel girls. Gertrud completed her
courses at the Euroschule. For Barbara classes finished at the
Kraus Handelsschule (commercial school). And the youngest,

Roswitha, left the high school in Obernburg am Main with a tenth-grade certificate. It should have been a time for celebration. For Anneliese it was not. "I feel like I am in a deep hole," she kept complaining. To Dr. Lenner she later confessed that she had recurring ideas of suicide but had been too much of a coward to go through with it.

The summer brought no relief either. "Those pills of Dr. Lüthy's don't help me," she insisted. "All they do is make me tired and apathetic." Finally her father came up with a suggestion. "Why don't I take you to San Damiano? It'll be a change, a pleasant bus ride through northern Italy, the pretty Po valley and all that. And Frau Hein, who is organizing the trips, is a nice woman. You'll like her."

Anneliese perked up. Her father had been to the shrine earlier that summer. He had brought back a small book about it entitled *The Mother of God in San Damiano?* It was a bit effusive, but she had occasionally thought how pleasant it might be to pray the rosary there. It was a nice story about how the shrine came into existence. There was this humble peasant woman, Rosa Quattrini or Mamma Rosa, who had trouble giving birth, so she had to have her baby delivered by Cesarian section. After her third child she had such a serious infection that the incision would not heal. She was finally sent home, too sick to work. All she could do was just lie in bed. Then a woman came to her house, dressed in the local costume, with a sky-blue kerchief on her head, who was really the Virgin Mary. She made her get out of bed, closed her wound, and told her that she should go and visit Father Pio far to the south, where Papa had also been. Father Pio ordered her to go for two years and care for the sick. Papa said that Father Pio was famous throughout Italy for being a holy man and for always making people do difficult things that were good for their souls. Finally Mamma Rosa got back home. But miracles did not end there. For Mamma Rosa had been home for only a little while when, in October 1964, the Virgin appeared to her again. This time, a pear tree that the Virgin had brushed against started blooming out of season. Papa said that today there was also a picture of Christ at the shrine that changed colors according to how the affairs of the world went, whether there was good or bad news, but that he had

not seen that happen. Holy water came from a well dug according
to the instructions of the Mother of God, and although he didn't
think that it tasted any different from other water, the entire place
was still pretty holy. Too bad, Papa said, that the church would
not recognize San Damiano as a shrine and for years now had forbidden Mamma Rosa to tell any of the new messages she received
from the Virgin, because she said many good things, like that
families should say the rosary together, and that people should
love one another. Who knows, perhaps she could feel the presence
of the Mother of God there as she had in Mittelberg.

In a narration taped for me in July 1979, Father Alt described
San Damiano and the shrine, which he had visited in 1975, and
related what happened to Anneliese there. The village, located
south of Piacenza, is surrounded by spacious vineyards. The Quattrini homestead is a bit outside the community and has a garden
with a statue of the Madonna, the renowned pear tree, and the miraculous well. Around the garden there is an open space where
pilgrims come to kneel and pray. He then continued:

Now: Anneliese told me—and Frau Hein confirmed this—
that she was unable to enter the shrine. She approached it
with the greatest hesitation, then said that the soil burned like
fire and she simply could not stand it. She then walked
around the shrine in a wide arc and tried to approach it from
the back. She looked at the people who were kneeling in the
area surrounding the little garden, and it seemed to her that
while praying they were gnashing their teeth. She got as far
as the edge of the little garden, then she had to turn back.
Coming from the front again, she had to avert her glance
from the picture of Christ [in the chapel of the house]. She
made it several times to the garden, but could not get past it.
She also noted that she could no longer look at medals or
pictures of saints; they sparkled so intensely that she could
not stand it.

The pilgrims were usually a mixed crowd: a few members of a
prayer group from Miltenberg perhaps; a pinched-face housewife
wearing a hat fashionable several seasons back but too good to

throw away; a postal official from Ebersbach with his wife; a retired schoolteacher with binoculars and a camera around his neck.
They were strangers to each other, but still everyone watched to
see if everyone else behaved properly. *"Toll*—crazy," the postal
official said to his wife as they were walking toward the covered
part of the yard, "did you see that she refused to drink of the miraculous well water? As if it were bad or something." "Thea Hein
says she said that it burned." A girl from the prayer group walking
beside them shook her head. "She sure acts strange. Her father
bought her a medal but she wouldn't wear it. He kept coaxing, but
she said it pressed on her chest so she couldn't breathe. I heard
her say that." "Did she ever get as far as the chapel?" the teacher
wanted to know as he snapped a picture of the Quattrini house
from the back. "I don't think so," the housewife interjected. "I
saw her going around the shrine on the outside several times."
"Not so loud; they might hear you." There were sideways glances
in the direction where Anneliese was standing with her father, toward the back of the enclosures. He had his arm around her
shoulder as if to comfort her. "Did you hear Thea Hein say that
there was something sinister going on?" a young man asked his
companion. But the girl had not heard it and knelt down to pray.

Anneliese could not, of course, help noticing that people talked
about her. But neither was she able to change the way she was
behaving. "My will is not my own," she would say over and over
again later. "Someone else is manipulating me." It was that way in
the bus on the return trip. Father Alt tells what happened.

On the way home Anneliese behaved in a most unseemly
way toward Frau Hein. She spoke with a voice like a man's,
made fun, so to speak, of Frau Hein, was uncertain of herself; she simply was not Anneliese anymore. She tore off a
medal that Frau Hein was wearing. And she exuded a stench
like Frau Hein had never smelled before, like fecal matter or
something burning. Everyone in the bus could smell it. As
Frau Hein told me, the other passengers in the bus were
quite angry that a young girl would behave in that manner,
talking very loudly and all that. It was something completely
unbecoming under the circumstances. Her father then sat

down beside her, and apparently people began to understand
that something special was going on with Anneliese.

After her visit to San Damiano, Anneliese was feeling quite
well, but that lasted only for two or three weeks, and things re-
verted to the way they had been before. Her mother was pressuring her. "You'll have to get ready to register with the PH," she
kept reminding her. "I'm in no condition to go to college this
fall," Anneliese demurred. "I couldn't possibly study, as depressed
as I am and as plagued by those horrible faces." "Then let's do
something about it." "What?" "Let's go back to Dr. Lüthy.
Maybe these faces are simply part of those seizures you used to
have. Perhaps he has some medicine that will take care of all of
that and you can go to the PH. After all, why did you bother to
get the *Abitur* if now you don't want to go to college?" "All right,
do as you wish."

So Anna made an appointment for September 3, and dutifully,
although with reluctance, Anneliese trooped along. According to
Dr. Lüthy, as he recalled the conversation during the interrogation
on February 9, 1977—four years after it took place—she told him,
"I often see *Fratzen,* ghastly, distorted faces; the devil is in me, I
am all empty inside." Two years later, under oath during the trial,
he recalled a few more details. "She said that she often saw *Fratzen,* and that the devil was in her. She further asserted that a judgment of fire would be visited on everyone. She could not get her
mind off these things. She had no power of decision, and everything was empty in her." In response to his question as to what
those *Fratzen* looked like, she purportedly answered, *"Es sind halt
Fratzen*—well, just ghastly faces." She would give no further description. When he subsequently asked her how she recognized
that this was the devil, she remained silent.

On July 2, 1976, the day after Anneliese died, Anna Michel
was asked to make a statement to the police. At that time—before
she could possibly know what furor this simple statement would
create—she said the following: "We told Dr. Lüthy about these
things, and he advised us to consult a Jesuit."

Dr. Lüthy hotly denied this charge when confronted with it during the February 9, 1977, interrogation. "When I have a patient

whom I cannot handle either as far as diagnosis is concerned or as an outpatient, I always refer that patient to a clinic and not to a priest. The expression 'demonic possession' is not medical terminology, and I never used it." And then he repeated his assertion once more. "I should like to emphasize again that I never referred Miss Michel either to a Jesuit father or to the respective church authorities, nor did I use the term 'demonic possession.'" He also rejected the allegation of having said that medical help for Anneliese was no longer possible.

So here we have a confrontation. First, let us set the record straight. Neither Anneliese nor Anna ever stated that Dr. Lüthy used the term "demonic possession." In fact, as late as the end of 1973 Anneliese still felt that she was being "molested," not possessed by satanic beings. The two women only maintained to the various priests they contacted that he said that for the particular problem, namely, seeing those *"Fratzen,"* she might want to consult a Jesuit, not that she should stop seeking medical advice altogether. Due to circumstance, Anna could no longer call on corroboration from her daughter during the trial in the spring of 1978, and under oath Dr. Lüthy repeated his defense. In the words of the Opinion of the Court, "The expert witness, Dr. Lüthy, has not confirmed but rather emphatically denied the statement ascribed to him, namely, that useful medical help was no longer possible and that a Jesuit should be consulted." And then comes a curious statement from a court of law. "Because of the personal impression which he made on the Court, the chamber believes him." In other words, the Court had a good impression of him, a bad one of Anna Michel, and therefore preferred to believe him and not her.

The Opinion of the Court continued: "The expert witness, Dr. Lüthy, did not know that Anneliese Michel was a Catholic." Now *that* is hard to credit. Even with all the internal migration after the Second World War, the region around Aschaffenburg as still close to 90 percent Catholic. If Anneliese had been a Protestant, she would have been the exception, part of a small minority. Her entire psychological profile would have shifted. As a specialist doing psychiatric counseling, Dr. Lüthy would surely have been aware of that. Besides, as soon as the conversation turned to the devil, his culturally informed intuition should have told him that he was speaking to a Catholic girl. German Protestants rarely talk of Satan as a personal entity.

"Since he himself adheres to no organized religion [*konfessionslos*]," the Court continued in Dr. Lüthy's defense, "such counsel [namely, that Anneliese should consult a Jesuit] would have been alien to him." Well, perhaps. There is, of course, no evidence that he wrote out a formal referral to someone connected with the Catholic Church. The files of the case contain no piece of paper bearing his signature and saying, "To the Nearest Available Jesuit: Anneliese Michel, aged twenty, patient in my care, is seeing devils. Request exploration." On the other hand, there is still that testimony by Anna and Anneliese. So what happened? He may, in fact, have made a little joke. Here is this young girl sitting in his office, very polite, very well mannered, but to his eyes still lower middle class, the daughter of a tradesman. Her mother sits beside her, extremely protective, and obviously has few doubts about the ridiculous stuff the girl is talking about. The devil appearing is, of course, a folktale at best. In fact, it sounds rather funny in that dialect. So he allows himself a little joke. "Well, then, Fräulein Michel, if you see devils, how about asking some Jesuit about it?" And having said it, he promptly forgot about it. This is a conjecture, of course. But, in fact, he considered what she said of so little import that in his 1977 statement he remarked, "It could not be stated with certainty at that time that there was the beginning of a psychotic symptomatology." And, he added, "I merely noted that there was no experiential content behind what she was saying." Case closed. She did not really experience what she said she was experiencing. On the other hand, she was obviously not well. For this reason "I added Aolept drops to the anticonvulsant medication, a drug I customarily prescribe in cases of neurotic developmental disturbances in children and young people."

Pharmacologically, this is a drug of medium intensity (the active ingredient is periciazine) that depresses the readiness of the brain to go into convulsions. It dulls it, in other words, just like the Dilantin that Anneliese was already taking.

Anneliese never went back to Dr. Lüthy. She may have felt too humiliated, too much put down. On November 20, without giving Anneliese a new checkup, he wrote out another prescription for Dilantin for her following a telephone request, presumably by her parents. From then on she went to specialists in Würzburg. After this visit to Dr. Lüthy, Anneliese never again mentioned to any member of the medical profession the gruesome countenances or the devils bothering her, or even the prediction about the judgment of fire to be visited on the whole world. There is not a word about any of this in either Dr. Lenner's or Dr. Schleip's reports, both of whom she sought help from in Würzburg, or in the recollections of Dr. Martin Kehler, who had a long conversation with her later on. Instead, she consulted them only for what she felt they were competent to treat: her depression, her headaches, the stench that was plaguing her. So intent was she on shielding her sacred world from the other one, that we read in Dr. Lenner's interview with her, "Somebody recommended Professor Strick to her, who promptly sent her here." That "somebody" was Father Alt. And it is hard not to see traits of her physicians in the demons she tried to rid herself of: "We will torment that snotnose, we will torment her," they shriek from her mouth.

The first half of September 1973 was a busy time in the Michel household. Roswitha had taken charge of some of the office chores and Oma Fürg helped in the household. But there was still a lot to do getting Gertrud ready for her job in Bad Schwalbach, where she would begin working for the Medical Missionary Service on September 15. Only Anneliese was sitting around listlessly, not participating much in anything.

"You had better start getting your things ready for Würzburg," her mother kept reminding her.

"I don't know whether I want to go."

"What do you mean you don't want to go? Father Wenzel gave you a special recommendation in July already so that you could live in the Ferdinandeum [the dormitory]. On the first of this month we went to Würzburg specifically to sign the contract. All you have to do now is register."

Anneliese remained silent.

"Your whole life," her mother went on, "you wanted to become a schoolteacher. Now it's before your nose and you are just sitting there. Another girl would jump at the chance."

"I simply don't feel well. Dr. Lüthy's pills and drops are not helping me at all. They just make me depressed and tired. Besides, didn't you hear him say that I shouldn't start yet this fall? He is right. I don't think I could sit through lectures and pay attention. And those *Fratzen* . . ."

"If Dr. Lüthy's medicine is all that useless, maybe we could talk to a priest about those."

"He said a Jesuit."

"Well, we don't know any Jesuits. But Frau Hein thinks that Father Habiger, the pastor of the Mother of God parish in Aschaffenburg, might be interested."

"Does she know him?"

"No, but Father Herrmann, that retired priest in the parish who sometimes travels with her pilgrim groups to San Damiano, she knows him. So she also knows Father Habiger indirectly, so to speak. Maybe Papa would go along too," Anna added coaxingly.

What had happened, apparently, was that Thea Hein had been talking busily to various members of the staff of the Mother of God parish about what had by now become one of her favorite topics. Father Roth, one of the young priests of the parish, had heard of the case weeks before the Michels came to call and had talked to his friend, Father Alt, even before he saw the girl. The Michels wrote several letters to Father Habiger prior to their visit. However, there is little of these preliminaries in Father Habiger's statement, which he made to the criminal investigator in October 1976. As he recalled it,

> One day in the summer of 1973—I am no longer sure of the date—the Michels came to the parish house from Klingenberg with their daughter Anneliese to ask for my advice. I think they were sent to me by a Frau Hein of Ebersbach. . . .
>
> In the course of a brief conversation at which a young priest associated with my parish, Father Roth, was also present, the Michels told me that for some time now their daughter Anneliese had problems that might indicate that she

was possessed. They mentioned, for instance, that on a pilgrimage to San Damiano she had torn a rosary. During the same visit I also talked with Fräulein Michel and had the impression that she was an entirely normal young girl, somewhat reticent and shy in conversation. There was nothing that I could see that would indicate possession.

At the conclusion of the conversation I advised the Michels to take their daughter to a physician and have her examined.

"I am not going that route again," Anneliese declared on the way home. "Dr. Lüthy's medication did not chase away the devilish beings. Why would some other specialist's?"

"Some other specialist may know of a better medicine," her mother countered. But Anneliese remained adamant.

Then Thea Hein came up with a new suggestion. Having heard from the Michels of Dr. Lüthy's allusion to Jesuit counsel, she had, on her own, sought out Father Adolf Rodewyk in Frankfurt. Father Rodewyk *was* a Jesuit and, what's more, he was a recognized authority on possession, having written a number of books on the topic. One of these, published in English (Doubleday, 1975) under the title *Possessed by Satan* (originally published in German, 1963 [Aschaffenburg, Paul Pattloch] under the title *Die dämonische Besessenheit*) detailed the Catholic Church's position on the devil, on possession, and on exorcism, taking its examples from documented cases as well as from the Bible. Thea Hein told Father Rodewyk about Anneliese and her behavior during her pilgrimage to San Damiano. He requested that she send him a letter about her observations. He subsequently made the following statement:

On the basis of that I then answered that I did see some indication in what she had written that the girl was possessed. However, considering the great distance between Frankfurt and Klingenberg and my advanced age [born 1894], I could not concern myself with the matter. (Statement to the investigator dated November 8, 1976)

Instead, Father Rodewyk suggested that she get in touch with Father Herrmann in Aschaffenburg. He was retired and therefore would have more time than the busy pastor of the Mother of God parish. Thea Hein, who knew Father Herrmann quite well from the trips to San Damiano, passed this advice on to the Michels. A few days later Josef Michel called Father Herrmann, who agreed to an interview. As it turned out, he was indeed willing to spend more time with Anneliese than Father Habiger had been able to spare. Beginning with the first conversation in the fall of 1973 and up to the summer of 1975, he saw Anneliese about ten times in his home. In August 1976 he told the criminal investigator:

> We usually talked about her problem for half an hour to an hour. She was a nice young girl, obviously from a deeply religious home. She complained that she was no longer herself. "I am not my own ego anymore." Occasionally she saw distorted faces, *Fratzen,* which she was unable to describe in detail.
>
> I suggested that she go to a neurologist. . . . She told me that she had gone to Dr. Lüthy, but he had not been able to help her either.
>
> From her parents I heard that on occasion she evidenced disrespect toward sacred objects and there was a stench of dung or of something burning in the room where she was. However, these symptoms never occurred in my apartment, although quite frequently I said the rosary with her. During such instances she always behaved calmly and with piety and showed no such behavior.

In the meantime, however, Father Roth's interest in Anneliese's case had also increased. He had more than once conversed with his friend, Father Alt, about the matter and was very eager to get involved. Perhaps Ernst Alt could be persuaded to participate in the matter too. After all, this was a possible case of demonic possession. How many times does a priest have a chance to see something like that in this modern age? So it was through Father Karl Roth that Father Alt was finally drawn into the case in which he was to play such a decisive part.

Ernst Anton Alt was born in 1937 in Eppelborn, in the Saar (Sarre). His father worked as a molder and founder. He attended school in Eppelborn and then was trained for the priesthood in Germany and the Netherlands. His first assignment was as chaplain to a hospital in Bonn. He was also in charge of youth services at his parish there. In 1971 he came to Aschaffenburg, to St. Agatha parish. Upon the suggestion of his defense lawyer, Frau Thora, the Drs. Lungershausen and Köhler, neurologists and psychiatrists in the Psychiatry Department of the University of Ulm, were asked by the Court to prepare an evaluation of him in March 1978. In it they described him as a tall man with a full beard and in good health. They said, in part,

He is polite in interpersonal contact, with very polished manners, occasionally pensive. His statements are carefully formulated, impressive, and convincing. He is fluent, very analytical, [and] has a large vocabulary demonstrating his schooling and extensive reading. His formal thinking processes are entirely undisturbed, even under prolonged questioning.

After a detailed report on the fact that all of Father Alt's physiological, psychological, and neurological characteristics tested out normal, as did his EEG, the two experts came to the following rather startling conclusion:

In the case of Father Alt, we are dealing with an abnormal personality in the widest sense of the term. Parts of his prehistory, as he reported them, even suggest *the presence of a psychosis of the schizophrenic type,* although the findings cannot be construed as pointing to any symptoms that could prove this diagnosis. (emphasis mine)

Then they repeated once more: "In the psychiatric sense, Father Alt is to be considered abnormal." In other words, the man is entirely normal, we can find absolutely nothing wrong with him, but he is still mentally ill, a schizophrenic. Too bad that we cannot prove that he is that now, but we are at least sure that he was sometime in the past.

Curiously, this evaluation is in direct contrast to what the self-same two psychiatrists said forty pages earlier in their lengthy deposition to the Court.

His visions that he describes, in their scenic and pictorial character, *are not what might be expected, for instance, in the case of a schizophrenic psychosis.* They must be considered rather as pseudohallucinations. (emphasis mine)

They also viewed the changes in his olfactory and visual perception, the fragrances and stenches, the differences in colors that he reported, as mere "pseudohallucinations," that is, not really psychotic, not sick. What, then, did this man experience that made the psychiatrists "flip" in this peculiar manner? For the answer, we will have to return to September 1973, when Father Alt first came into contact with the Anneliese Michel case. He talked about it a year later in a letter (somewhat abbreviated here) to his superior, Bishop Josef Stangl of Würzburg.

Ettleben, September 30, 1974

Most Reverend Bishop:

After much consideration and considerable hesitation, I should now like to acquaint you with a case of spiritual counseling about which I spoke to you very briefly when you were here for a visit.

This is the case of Anneliese Michel of Klingenberg. I will attempt to relate the case to you in order, as it happened.

My friend, Father Roth, came to me one evening and asked me to aid him and some of his priest colleagues in solving a case of spiritual counseling. This concerned a girl, Anneliese Michel, whom he had not yet met. According to the opinion of some persons, she was alleged to be possessed or at least was being molested by the devil. I was supposed to tell, by tuning in on whatever she was radiating, whether she was sick or not.

We will have to pause here for a brief explanation. Father Alt had for some time been interested in the possible connection between religious experience and what is popularly called ESP. In the fall of 1973, prior to becoming a pastor of the Ettleben parish, he wrote a thesis entitled, "Is There a Parapsychological and Biological Basis to Religious Experience?" It shows that he was familiar with the literature on the topic; for instance, he knew the publications of Professor Weizsäcker and his Research Society for Eastern Wisdom and Western Science. From much experimentation he knew that he was a reliable douser. To the Drs. Lungershausen and Köhler he enumerated other capabilities, such as those of telepathy and precognition. Even with all of this conditioning, as it were, he obviously was not prepared for the magnitude of the reaction that he now experienced.

Suddenly I was able to describe the entire family—father, mother, sisters, the grandmother—something I could not possibly know since I had never seen them. Later all of this could be verified. As to Anneliese, I felt an enormous radiation that originated from her neck or, rather, from her thyroid and her head. I did not detect any illness. This, of course, did not permit any conclusions as to whether she was possessed or not.

Two days later a fellow priest [Father Herrmann] who was going to take charge of the case visited me. He handed me two letters, one written by mother Michel, the other by Anneliese. I was unable to read them because, all of a sudden, I became so nauseated that I thought that at any moment I was going to faint. I experienced a strange excitation such as I had never been subject to before, considerably frightening and startling my fellow priest, who was witness to all of this. Naturally, even this experience, of course, did not in any way prove that we were dealing with a case of possession.

That evening I celebrated the mass. I was mentally preparing for the transubstantiation [changing the substance of the bread and wine into the substance of the body and blood of Christ] and also included that as yet unknown girl in the sacrifice. All of a sudden something hit me in the back, the air turned cold and, at the same time, there was an intense stench as though something were burning. I had to lean against the altar. With great effort and only by dint of considerable concentration was I able to speak the rest of the text. I felt deeply distressed, as if a negative force were surrounding me, which, however, aside from vexing me, could inflict no real harm.

After the service I went to a fellow priest and reported everything to him calmly and in detail.

The subsequent night was the most restless I have ever spent. I had taken a very effective sleeping pill, one that previously had always helped, but I could find no rest. My apartment was filled with a variety of stenches, as though something were burning—of dung, of an open sewer, of fecal matter—and these kept alternating. It didn't matter whether I reached out for the rosary or whether I spoke some other prayer, the stench continued. It was literally infernal. In addition, there was an occasional loud thumping in my wardrobe. I lay in bed, feeling sorely pressed. I tried to pray. In my own words I spoke an exorcism, thinking of my priestly power. For a few minutes I felt easier, but I was simultaneously ice-cold and yet bathed in perspiration. In my extremity I called to Father Pio for help, since I knew that he had experienced similar tribulations. Nothing happened. I repeated my prayer to him and suddenly my room was filled with such an intense fragrance of violets that I thought I had dumped after-shave lotion on my pajamas. But it smelled only of my own sweat. Strangely, at the same time I stopped perspiring and my body felt warm. I breathed with relief and only then did I discover, to my amazement, that my field of vision had been very much narrowed, and that my color perception was reduced. Now I was able to see colors once more in their normal intensity. The pressure on my head had disappeared. Before having to get up, I fell into an hour's restful sleep. "My night" had lasted from eleven the previous evening until five o'clock in the morning.

When, the following evening, I told my fellow priests

about all of this, they were suddenly able to smell the same
strange stench. Their entire parish house smelled as though
of burning, although the windows were open.

So these were the "pseudohallucinations" that the Drs. Lungershausen and Köhler tried to evaluate. They did not last very
long and eventually disappeared altogether, as Father Alt tells the
bishop in the same letter.

The "molestations" did return a few more times, but they
became less vivid, and if I prayed the exorcism prayer to myself, they stopped quite abruptly. Occasionally it was as if I
had to struggle against them.

His visions actually came later. One of them occurred around
Christmas 1975. Suddenly he saw the living Christ on the cross,
suffering pain, and he heard a voice calling out, "For you." Then
everything was gone. In another vision, which occurred about two
months later, he saw a woman, surrounded by brilliant light, with
a small child. It lasted only a moment and made him happy because once more a voice said, "For you."
The letter continued:

In the evening I took a walk with my friend, Father Roth,
and once more, as we talked about Anneliese Michel, we
smelled the same series of stenches. Finally, now, I heard
some of the details about the girl's affliction. [He listed them
here.] A few weeks later I also met her personally. She was
very depressed, but in our conversation she was able to express herself very clearly, and she obviously had a considerable gift for analysis.

In another letter written to the criminal investigator on September 9, 1976, Father Alt gave a few more details about this first
conversation.

She looked in no way ill or sickly, but she was pale and very
serious. As far as I can recall, she said verbatim, "I am look-

ing for people who would believe me." She never used the word, "possessed," and from the conversation there was no way in which one could conclude that she was. I don't think she knew what, exactly, the word meant, and I must confess that neither was I clear on the theological concept of possession.

Father Roth and I cross-examined her, so to speak, and I assumed from then on that a possession was possible but that this would have to be proven one hundred percent, even if such proof would take a very long time. The statements of others about the matter I took as no more than a working hypothesis. . . .

All in all, it is quite clear that Father Alt could empathize so easily with Anneliese because he had experienced what she was going through, though in a much more abbreviated form. He also felt great compassion. "She looked like she needed support desperately," he said during his psychiatric interview, "a tormented young girl for whom one could not help but feel sorry."

As to Anneliese, priestly prayer did seem to aid her. But molestations came over her quite unpredictably. In one conversation Father Alt told how he suddenly saw her face change; her eyes darkened, and she became absent. At the same moment he perceived a shadow behind her. He asked her, "What's the matter, Anneliese?" "I am being molested," she answered. After he gave her the priestly blessing, all was well again. *Das war Klasse*—that was super," she said beamingly.

Prayers of the other priests also had a beneficial effect. Fortified in this way, she decided to register at the PH in Würzburg, with a major in education and theology. Classes started in October, and on November 1, 1973, she moved into the Ferdinandeum.

CHAPTER FOUR

THE DAM BREAKS

Würzburg, Germany's most beautiful baroque city and for centuries the capital of an ecclesiastical principality, was largely destroyed during the Second World War. By the time Anneliese became a student there, however, it had been completely rebuilt. It is the center of what is popularly called the *Marienländle* (Mary's little land) and statues of the Virgin in various guises adorn the corners of many old houses: with a golden halo, a crown, a wreath of stars, and with or without the Christ Child. Mary also greets the supplicant from the altars of its many churches.

Anneliese came to know several of these churches quite intimately in her search for a place to pray. For in the round and impersonal chapel of the Ferdinandeum there was not even a bench where she could kneel. Besides, it was open only for mass. At other times she had to go looking for someone who had a key and would have to get to it through the basement. So she started going across the parking lot to the Unsere Liebe Frau Church, or she took the bus downtown to the Neumünster Church and its sheltering, warm, Romanesque adoration chapel that Father Alt had called to her attention.

The Ferdinandeum also made her homesick in other ways. It was aseptic and neutral, with crowds of students bustling along its gray hallways. How she missed her sisters! She had to admit, though, that things could have been worse. After all, there were a few girls she did know from the Gymnasium in Aschaffenburg. There was Ursula Kuzay, now her roommate in the suite on the first floor of the high-rise. Karin Gora took nearly all the same classes and they saw each other most every day. And even Maria Burdich made a showing. She did not live in the high-rise but in a neighboring building with some other girls. Anneliese and she often met at lectures and during their free time.

But matters other than homesickness also weighed heavily upon Anneliese. Despite the fact that she took her pills faithfully, and that Father Alt saw her nearly every second week, those gruesome faces attacked her wherever she went, and her depression isolated and unnerved her. Going to lectures proved a nearly unbearable burden. "In the morning I wake up listlessly and really don't feel like getting up. By evening I am completely leached out," she told Dr. Dietrich Lenner of the Institute for Psychotherapy and Medical Psychology at the end of November. Exasperated, she blurted out, "I so want to really live again." It did not take Ursula Kuzay long to size up her roommate. "During the first few weeks at school Anneliese was completely withdrawn and very down. She drifted and went to lectures only if we dragged her along," she told the court investigator.

But things were about to change, for Anneliese fell in love. Early in November there had been a dance at the Ferdinandeum. Her friends got Anneliese to go along. One of the young men she danced with was a fellow student by the name of Peter, slightly built like herself, with wavy, dark hair and interesting eyes. He liked her from the start. "She was friendly, animated, outgoing, fun to talk to," he said in his personal reminiscences. He also lived in the Ferdinandeum. He and Anneliese had many of the same courses, and he made sure that they saw each other frequently.

Peter's company was very good for Anneliese. "It completely revived her," her roommate Ursula noted. "Anneliese often went dancing and even bowling with him, things she was not interested in before." And Karin added, "She became visibly lively, acting just like any other girl who is in love." Even Maria Burdich, who did not see her as often as the other two, noticed how she was blossoming.

About two weeks later, however, to Peter's consternation, she told him that they should stop seeing each other. "But why?" Peter wanted to know. "I often get terribly depressed and am not good company for anybody." "Everybody gets depressed sometimes," he argued. "With me it's different. It lasts." They were walking to a lecture on child psychology together. She turned and looked directly at him. "Believe me, you'll save yourself a lot of grief if you don't come to see me anymore."

Still, Peter stuck around. "Peter, really, this isn't fair to you," she would say. "I cannot feel what you feel for me." "You will once you get to know me better." "You don't understand. I can't feel any love at all. I am all numb, sort of. I can't feel emotions like that." Peter would not listen. It did not even scare him away when she told him that with the onset of her depressions she sometimes became stiff all over. "Some good doctor probably has a pill for that; you just have to find the right one," he would say and would continue coming to see her. He liked everything about her. She was pretty in a delicate way, with a nice figure, too. Very intelligent, not at all a "little goose" like so many girls at the PH. When she talked about fellow students, all of a sudden you saw aspects of their character that you had not even suspected before, and she was usually right. And although she said that since the Gymnasium she had not really done any concentrated studying, she obviously picked up a great deal in lectures and seminars anyway. Even Oberstudiendirektor Veth, the director of the Ferdinandeum, was impressed with her. You could tell from the way he always paid attention to her comments in class. And he liked her relationship to her family. It must have been fun, as she described it, growing up with three girls, and that blustering but kind father. Maybe her mother was a bit overambitious for her, but many mothers were that way. No wonder she went home every weekend. True, she seemed a bit too serious about religion. As for him, he had seen the church mostly from the outside for some years. But maybe she was right; perhaps there was more to it than he was willing to admit.

What they didn't see eye to eye on were those depressions of hers. "If it's not your parents, then maybe you had a friend who kept telling you that you were worthless or something." "Don't be silly." "Then maybe you are suffering from aftereffects of the *Abitur* exams, or you are worried about college now." She would just shake her head. It was like trying to batter his way through a wall. "Well, let's keep talking," he would say. "It is good to have someone to talk to when you are depressed."

On November 27 Anneliese let him take her to her first interview with Dr. Lenner. He waited outside so he could take her back. Dr. Lenner's notes list the complaints she had at the time. Clearly and incisively, as she was wont to do, she described how she had trouble concentrating or listening. "I have no willpower, I simply float around and don't know what I want." She also talked about Peter, that he was nice enough, and that she would really like him as a boyfriend, but that this simply wouldn't be right, for she could not feel, she felt nothing at all. He even volunteered to help her, but what in the world could he do for her?

Dr. Lenner was sympathetic, easier to talk to than Dr. Lüthy. Trained in the Freudian tradition, he asked a lot of questions about her relationship to her parents. In his perception she was a textbook case of a young girl suffering from a neurosis that had developed for some time, clearly caused by a father who had never understood her and a mother whom she hated with a fury, since she would not let her have boyfriends and would even forbid her to go dancing. As to those seizures she had experienced since she was sixteen—not many, to be sure, but still—well, they looked suspiciously like epilepsy. Better have that checked tomorrow in the University Neurological Clinic and Polyclinic.

The next day (November 28) Anneliese went to the Neurological Clinic on Füchsleinstrasse for an EEG. It was taken while she was asleep. In evaluating it, Dr. Irmgard Schleip, the academic director of the clinic, reported that she found "epileptic patterns," a discharge of a locus in the left temporal region. In her letter to the state attorney, dated July 7, 1976, she also stated, "On the basis of the patient's history, the description of the seizures, and the EEG finding, we had to assume diagnostically that we were dealing with a disease of seizures, that is, epilepsy."

Dr. Schleip took Anneliese off Dilantin, since that drug had apparently not completely suppressed the epilepsy-like activity in the brain, and switched her over to Tegretal (Tegretol in the United States), a much stronger and, in its side effects, much more dangerous drug. In her interview with Dr. Schleip, Anneliese told of how she suffered from her separation from her family—the family which, in Dr. Lenner's view, had caused her such psychological distress that she reacted with a depressive psychosis. She also mentioned the fact that she had problems with her boyfriend, whom she "could not love sufficiently." She did report on the nauseating stenches. Dr. Schleip interpreted those as "psychomotor seizures" and considered them, as well as Anneliese's depression, to be a product of the "epileptic patterns" in the brain. Anneliese, of course, was much too intelligent not to realize that she was caught between two schools of thought. To Dr. Lenner all her problems had a probable psychological source. For Dr. Schleip there was something wrong in her brain, caused by who knows what? Maybe by that fall she took as a child? If these two individuals could not agree, maybe one, or possibly both, were wrong. At any rate, she did not mention the *Fratzen* to either of them. Those belonged to a place to which neither Dr. Lenner, with his psychoanalysis, nor Dr. Schleip, with her single-minded interest in brain-wave patterns, had any access. How tightly she clamped on her security screen is obvious from what these two physicians reported. Dr. Lenner, with all the details he recorded, was clearly left in the dark as to that important part of Anneliese's experience. And Dr. Schleip remarked in the same letter quoted earlier that if she would have had any inkling at all that something "supernatural" was involved, she would certainly have made a note of it, "since personally I am very much interested in such things," adding, with proper caution and in parentheses, "scientifically, of course."

Anneliese could not hold back long from Peter, however. Although she told Dr. Lenner (in an interview on December 11) that she could not be sexually stimulated, that she felt like she was "castrated, ice-cold," with little capacity for communication, she had become quite fond of him. He tolerated her moodiness and her depressions, which came and went unaccountably. To please her he had even started going to church again. For Sunday evening mass he sometimes took her in his rusty VW bug up the hill overlooking the city to the "Käpele," that delicate rococo church, all in pale lilac, pink, silver, and gray, which never failed to enchant Anneliese. For the longest time she would stand in front of the statue of Brother Konrad, that saint from Lower Bavaria, with his long beard. "They say when he prayed golden bubbles would issue from his mouth," she mused. Peter was also willing to carry on a conversation about religious matters and to listen attentively to her glowing reports on San Damiano. "We'll have to go there together someday. After a visit to San Damiano, I always feel very good for weeks, almost free."

"Almost free? Free of what?"

"Of that inner pressure I always feel, that harrying, a fearful harassment that seems to be with me all the time."

More she would not say. But toward the latter part of December she finally came out with it. It had been a happy day, there were Advent celebrations everywhere, the Ferdinandeum smelled of fresh fir greenery and burning beeswax candles, and the winter wind was playing tag with some sparse snowflakes outside. Anneliese was humming a Christmas tune about Mary and Joseph and their babe as she and Peter walked toward the kitchenette.

"You are feeling all right today?" Peter said in a tone that was more like a question.

Anneliese looked up from the tea egg she was filling. They were alone. "Yes. Perhaps it was a good thing that Dr. Schleip changed the medication from Dilantin to that other drug she gave me, that Tegretol. But it still does not do anything about those other problems."

"Other problems? What other problems?"

"Those other problems, like the horrid stenches, for instance."

It was the first time Peter heard about the stenches and the torment they were causing her. "Please explain," he said as they were going back to her room, carrying teapot and cups.

Ursula was not in, so they could talk at ease. Anneliese told him how her family could also smell them, not only she, that they came up suddenly, smelling like something burning, like feces, rotten eggs, like dung, all manner of nasty, evil things, without any visible source at all. "Couldn't you open a window?"

"Oh, Peter, don't you think we tried? That doesn't help, not at all. The stench comes up, and then, sometimes days later, I don't smell it anymore. But, at any rate, it's awful."

Peter thought he finally understood. "And you are saying that this is what causes your depressions?"

"No, I am not saying that. The depressions appear together with the stench. And with those terrifying faces."

"You mean you are also hallucinating?"

"I am not sure that I know what hallucinations are, exactly. All of a sudden they are there, those *Fratzen,* something like devils. It makes no difference what I may be doing at the time. Usually I am thinking of something entirely different, completely unrelated. I can't describe them. I don't think I want to. They are the most frightening thing imaginable."

Peter suggested some plausible explanations. She was imagining them. "It's not my imagination. Sometimes they are not very clear, like shadows, but most of the time they are completely real. I see them like I see you." She had been taught some exaggerated ideas about the devil in religion class. "Not at all. We were told about Satan's existence and his designs on people's souls, but that was about it." Maybe she hated her parents and had a bad conscience about it. *"Du spinnst wohl*—you must be nuts. My parents are nice people. Difficult sometimes, but nice. I love them. Otherwise, why would I be homesick for them? Why would I go home every weekend?" How about too much thinking about sin? No, that wasn't it either. Of course, humans fell into sin all the time, but you could always go to confession and make things right with God again.

"Are you finished?" She smiled.

"I'll think of something tomorrow," he laughed back.

"There is still more."

"I don't think I have any more good answers in stock."

"That's all right. Just listen. The bad part is that when all of these things happen, my control over myself is gone. Anneliese, my real self, that is, sits in a hole inside of myself and has nothing to say about anything. I, the visible Anneliese, do everything as if something or somebody else were giving the orders. I struggle against this loss of my volition with all my might. But I always lose."

"Then why struggle?"

"If I didn't, that would mean that I would be giving up on myself."

As to this problem, at least, Peter thought he could do something. As he wrote in his reminiscences,

> We agreed that from now on Anneliese would be in charge of all the decisions in order to emphasize the strength of her ego and her volition. Subsequently I always made the same observation. If she felt "free," she took the initiative as a matter of course, deciding necessary matters entirely independently. But when that inner harassment took over, she was hardly able to make any decisions at all, or only with the greatest effort.

Perhaps she was a bit too optimistic in her conversations with Peter. For a while she gave him the impression that the depressions appeared only sporadically, but she told Dr. Lenner something different in her interview of December 11. She admitted that she did feel better since she had switched to Tegretol, something she also told Dr. Schleip on December 17. She even played tennis now and enjoyed her piano. However, she then commented, "This is no longer a depression, this is a condition." When questioned about her difficulties in communicating with her friends and fellow students at the Ferdinandeum, she made clear that the problem had remained because "they live on a different plane of consciousness than I do."

Not much changed with the advent of the new year. Anneliese had less opportunity to see Father Alt, because on January 1, 1974, he had been transferred from the parish of St. Agatha in Aschaffenburg to become pastor of the Ettleben parish. Before leaving, he had counseled Anneliese not to neglect seeking medical advice. This was also what her parents wanted. She complained to Peter that neither her priest nor her parents believed that she was being hounded by those awful faces; instead, she was being sent from psychiatrist to psychiatrist. But she complied anyway. She saw Dr. Schleip in January—we are not told on what date —who noted that she complained of headaches. Toward Dr. Lenner she was a bit more talkative. She told him that she could tolerate other people more easily, that she felt some joy now, such as when she played the piano, and she felt more relaxed. Sexually she still could not be stimulated, and she had problems with studying because of lack of concentration.

Led on by Dr. Lenner's questions, she described what he saw as a displacement of dependency from her parents to Peter. He quoted her as saying, "I am practically glued to him. . . . I always do what he tells me to do; he is always the one to take the initiative." Peter had wanted to bring her to Dr. Lenner, she said, but she had asked him to let her go alone. Peter had a large circle of friends, she continued, and kept inviting her to go along and meet them, but she felt very insecure with others and usually refused. She also refused to have Peter make love to her for fear that this would increase her dependency on him. Besides, studying should come first and then Peter. It was nice having him around, that was all. She envied those who could make plans. As to her, she left everything to chance. She felt unorganized, unable to do anything.

At the conclusion of the interview Dr. Lenner suggested that she seek group therapy. "The group I have in mind is composed of students. Frau Professor Dr. Erika Geisler is in charge. You'll like it. A nice bunch of young people, just talking out their problems."

Obliging as always, Anneliese went—once. She was appalled at the things that came up in the discussion. It was an entirely different world from hers, a world of complexes, inhibitions, frustrations, compulsions. She didn't belong there. "I have no idea what I was supposed to gain from going there," she told Peter. "I am not crazy." And she did not go back.

The carnival season rolled around and with it more conflicts with Peter. He wanted her to go out with him and meet his friends, dance, have fun. She held back. "Your friends won't like me, Peter. Besides, I find it so hard to get any pleasure from hopping around and acting like imbeciles." Perhaps her withdrawal was a harbinger of increased harassment from those faces, al-

though the stenches had let up for a while. For in March she
called up Father Alt for an appointment, saying that for a while
she had felt quite free, but that things were pretty bad once more,
and could she come to see him?

Father Alt mentioned this visit in his letter of September 30 of
that year to the bishop. Apparently her complaints had not
changed. She was taking her pills religiously, but those faces still
remained. She could not pray at all, or only with the greatest
effort. When she went to confession, something was holding her
back from telling everything. And there was that feeling of being
harried, oppressed by some foreign agent. She did not have
enough strength, she needed help from someone else.

Peter, who had driven her to Ettleben, was amazed at how
quick the improvement was as soon as Father Alt prayed with her.
He saw her change quite strikingly, her face became clear and
smiling, her conversation animated: She felt free. "Strange," she
would say, "as soon as I enter his house I even forget what it was
that I wanted to talk with him about." Father Alt also observed
this effect. Referring, in the same letter to his bishop, to several
such meetings in the spring and summer of 1974, he said,

> After every conversation she went home cheerful and
> relaxed, although I did nothing for her except to pray with
> her and to give her the formal priestly blessing. Her face
> would change abruptly, something lifted off of her. A smile
> played around her lips and her relief was palpable. The at-
> mosphere of the conversation instantly changed.

He felt that her condition might be improving after all, and
suggested that she pursue a strict religious way of life to ward off
whatever was besetting her. And although it was clear that prayer
helped, she should also continue going to her doctor. So Anneliese
went to see Dr. Schleip that April. Dr. Schleip said rather cryp-
tically in her report to the state attorney that "we assumed from
a description that small seizures had probably occurred once
more." Perhaps what Anneliese talked about again were the
headaches and also the depression, for on May 7, when she saw
Dr. Lenner, this is what he noted. The headaches were severe,

she said, rarely letting up, mainly in her forehead. She felt well only for a few hours at a time. He found her reflexes remarkably slowed down. She told him that she had to sleep a lot, that everything tired her; after sitting through a single lecture she felt exhausted. She was getting some enjoyment out of playing the piano, and even reacted to Peter somewhat more positively, but "if my boyfriend comes every day, I find that too much, I continually felt overtired, as if too much were demanded of me." And as if trying to express in terms intelligible to the psychoanalyst that she was simultaneously living on two "planes of consciousness," she added, "I am so torn apart, unintegrated . . . strung out between two poles, even physically."

A week earlier she had to teach a class of arithmetic in a local grade school. She liked being with children and thought them easier to handle than adults; they were more spontaneous, more honest. But teaching that class excited her terribly; she had trouble concentrating. On the Friday following the practice teaching session she experienced something like a paralysis on one side; she wanted to get up but could not. Dr. Lenner thought this looked suspiciously like a seizure and referred her back to Dr. Schleip's clinic.

"Not again," she complained to Peter. "I am taking the medication; it is not doing anything at all. So why bother? Why do I have to go from clinic to clinic, always answering the same questions, going through the same tests? Why don't they just admit that they don't know what's going on?" But she went anyway.

Dr. Schleip found her EEG "much improved, but there still seemed to be some indication for the existence of a locus of brain damage in the left temporal region." Anneliese was to continue with the Tegretol. As she saw it, Dr. Schleip suspected that the "small seizures" that Anneliese still seemed to be suffering from occurred because she was not taking her pills regularly enough. They seemed to last longer than the time they were prescribed for. This was probably not the case. Anneliese was raised to be conscientious about medicine. She may have gotten extra Tegretol in Klingenberg, during some of the many weekends she spent there, to supplement Dr. Schleip's prescription, for the Kehlers stated that they wrote out prescriptions for the drug at the request of the family.

The summer went by with increased demands on Anneliese from her courses and an abbreviated vacation due to practice teaching. She did take several trips to San Damiano, some with Peter, and visited Father Alt on those occasions when the inner harassment she suffered from became too much to bear. Father Alt was still wavering between what he considered a "naturalistic" explanation of her complaints—brain damage, perhaps, or psychological problems—and a religious one as another alternative, a possible molestation by demonic forces. After all, before he had ever met her he had also been similarly tormented just by touching the two letters by Anneliese and her mother that had been brought to him by Father Herrmann. Was it the work of Satan?

Whenever he had a chance to visit with his fellow priests in Aschaffenburg—his friends Father Roth, Father Herrmann, and Father Habiger—the four of them would have long conversations about Anneliese. "Don't you think that, indeed, it could be something like hysteria or schizophrenia?" one would ask. Father Alt adamantly denied it. "No way," he would say. "Remember that I was a priest in Bonn for years. I often saw people plagued by loneliness there who escaped into hysteria. I also saw hysterical patients in the neurology section of the hospital. She simply does not act that way. Neither is there anything schizophrenic about her." "Did she ever have an epileptic seizure again?" another queried. "Not in my presence she didn't."

"Perhaps it is, after all, what the church calls *Umsessenheit, circumsessio* in Latin,"[1] one or another priest would invariably ponder. "Her physicians certainly seem to be wavering, the way she tells it. Suspicion of epilepsy, but then maybe not. And the way they change her medication around, sometimes this, then something else. Not even her EEG is all that conclusive, she says."

"True," another one might say. "She told me that also. *Circumsessio* really fits, you know. She definitely is under intensive siege. And how about those *Fratzen?* Wouldn't those be the evil

---

[1] Being surrounded or enveloped by evil forces.

forces that are trying to harm her and prevent her from studying?"

"Exactly," the third one would muse. "Even her psychiatrist here in Aschaffenburg is supposed to have told her that she should seek the advice of a Jesuit."

"Speaking of Jesuits, didn't Father Rodewyk at least admit the possibility not just of *circumsessio* but of actual possession?"

"He did indeed. But then the test for possession is so much more stringent. There has to be the demon actually taking over control of the person, living in him, using his organs for demonic purposes, tormenting him, with the human being entirely helpless. Is that really the case with this young girl?" "I don't believe so at this point," Father Alt would opine. "As I keep pointing out to her boyfriend Peter, if it were true possession, we would be shown. We just have to be patient. Besides, she does seem to be improving, so perhaps we worry about her for nothing."

This was also what he kept telling Anneliese. "It can go either way," he would say. "What you need is to adopt a strict religious life-style under the guidance of a spiritual counselor. Give yourself a few days and decide who that should be." It came as no surprise that soon after she requested that he should assume this role.

The following is a letter from Anneliese to Father Alt, characterizing her mood during this period. The letter is suffused by dark despair. The joyous side of her life with her family, the kindness of her father, the happiness with her sisters—nothing is remembered. Even the positive aspects of her religious experience, such as what she had been given in Mittelberg, are submerged in the darkness of her depression.

Klingenberg, September 9, '74

Greetings, Father Alt:

I should like to write to you, although that is a difficult undertaking for me because it is so hard for me to gather up my thoughts. Usually I cannot commit to paper what I really want, and so I remain stuck in superficial matters.

Soon I will have to do my three-week practice teaching. To be honest, I am terrified of that and am truly scared. Once more I realize that I cannot cope with reality, which could be different if, yes, if I were master over myself. I simply am not in control, and this often depresses me deeply. I can feel it especially when I am with other people, or if I play the piano (in that case I am especially aware of it), or if I paint or write a letter. In fact, it doesn't really matter what I do, I simply feel it all the time. For this reason I am never really satisfied when I work, or even afterwards. After all, a person normally puts his all into his work, he feels happy when he works, he commits himself to it. I cannot understand why this is not the case with me. Why is it that God denies me this happiness? Is it even possible for a human being to live without this dedication to his work or task, without becoming fed up with himself, without feeling superfluous and empty inside? I am asking myself this question over and over. It intrudes into my mind a thousand times a day. Why?

I admit that things have become somewhat better. Life has taken on more meaning. Still, I am not all right yet. For instance, the following experience was a real shock for me. I wanted to do three weeks' vacation work in the hospital. I was there one day and got back home more in a trance than ordinary consciousness. First of all, I was totally exhausted physically as early as 1:30 in the afternoon, but also psychologically. I was aggressive and somehow felt as though I had no relationship to the world around me. My parents, of course, noticed what went on, and we took care of matters in such a way that Roswitha, my youngest sister, went to do the work. She finds it strenuous, too, but she seems to enjoy it nonetheless.

Last Saturday I went to confession. You know, one needs to overcome some resistance when one goes to confession, but as for me, that goes to the extreme. I often have the feeling as if all good spirits were deserting me on such occasions. Afterwards I was quite happy. On Sunday I took communion. I can feel that there is strength coming from that, although at the outset I always feel completely empty, I can sense nothing, and have the feeling that I cannot relate to anything. But this empty feeling disappears after a few minutes. I become more myself and feel well.

Just imagine, the last time Bishop Stangl visited here he asked for lay people to help give out the holy communion. It is my opinion that even the hand communion is not proper, but to let lay persons hand it out—that is really shocking. As for me, I will never accept communion from a lay person. After all, we are not in a situation of crisis. The hands of a lay person are not consecrated; they should not touch the holy communion.

Klingenberg, 2. 9. 74

Grüß Gott
Herr Pfarrer Alt !

Ich möchte Ihnen schreiben, auch wenn das ein schweres Unternehmen für mich ist, weil ich meine Gedanken so schlecht zusammenbekomme. Meistens kann ich das nicht zu Papier bringen, was ich möchte und bleibe an der Oberfläche.— Bald werde ich mein 3-Wochen Schulpraktikum ableisten müssen, wovor es mir ehrlich graust und wovor ich Angst habe. Ich sehe wieder, daß ich der Welt nicht gewachsen bin, was anders sein könnte, wenn, ja wenn ich mein eigener Herr in mir wäre. Ich habe nicht die Herrschaft in mir, was mich manchmal ganz deprimiert macht. Ich spüre das, wenn ich mit Menschen zusammen bin, oder wenn ich Klavier spiele (hier merke ich es ganz besonderen) oder wenn ich male oder wenn ich Brief schreibe ; es ist eigentlich ganz egal, was ich tue; ich spüre es einfach immer. Deshalb bin ich nie zufrieden mit in oder bei meiner Arbeit oder danach. Der Mensch legt ja normal immer alles in seine Arbeit; dann geht er auf; er fühlt sich glücklich, wenn er arbeitet. Ich verstehe nicht, warum das bei mir nicht so ist; Warum

Figure 1. This first page of a letter written by Anneliese to Father Alt shows the striking contrast to her handwriting on a later, desperate note on pp. 74–75.

After some brief comments about her sisters, Anneliese continued.

Peter no longer wants to come to our house because he cannot be alone with me and because Mama behaves in such

an impossible way. For instance, she won't allow him to
come to my room with me. It's ridiculous. She also made the
rule that he should come to see me only once a week . . .
Perhaps you could talk with her sometime.

She then described how alone she had often felt during the time
before her severe illness.

> At night I often cried to myself . . . There was no one to
> whom I could have gone and talked. Then I did not cry
> anymore, because it was no use. And after a while I could
> not even cry. Then I became very ill—pleurisy and TB—and I
> felt even lonelier and more helpless than ever. My mother
> had so much work, I told her nothing, and things got pro-
> gressively worse. I felt that God had deserted me entirely. I
> was considerably molested at that time already. I always
> wanted to kill myself. I was deathly afraid that I might be-
> come insane because I was so desperate. Then I felt that God
> had not deserted me completely. I was able to pray again. I
> felt better and recovered. But, unfortunately, I then had to go
> to the sanatorium in Mittelberg. There things went downhill.
> I suffered torture there. Prayer did not help me, and there
> was nothing else either. Then there was something like a re-
> covery when I was released after half a year, but somehow I
> was dead inside. . . . At least now you may be able to em-
> pathize a little better with me. I think I will come to see you
> soon.
>
> > Until then,
> > Anneliese

In the meantime Thea Hein had also done some talking. "The
child is being hounded by demons," she would point out to Anna.
"I know what I am talking about. I have seen possessed people
before. If you are involved with religious matters as much as I am,
you would know these things. Is she still seeing those *Fratzen?*"
Anna allowed that she did. "You see, didn't I tell you? The
Church ought to be doing something about that. There are special

prayers, you know? There is exorcism. I can't understand why the priests don't push the matter with the ecclesiastical authorities. After all, the girl needs help."

On September 16, as Father Alt wrote to his bishop, Thea Hein called him. He had met her briefly before and had been told that she bragged about having "discovered" Anneliese. As he wrote in his letter,

She was very excited and told me that something should be done. A few things had happened again. If our own ecclesiastical authority would not listen, maybe we should go to another one. I told her that we had done everything that was necessary and meaningful under the circumstances. After all, I told her, I could not report on a problem that had improved considerably and had temporarily even vanished completely.

Anneliese must have felt very low at the time, for the next day, September 17, she also called Father Alt and asked him for an appointment. He has left us a vivid picture of what happened in a letter, dated September 30, 1974, to Bishop Stangl.

She came with her father and was in bad condition. She was depressed, her glance unsteady, restless from the inside, as it were, with poor muscle control. I asked her father to let me talk privately to her and then gave her the solemn priestly blessing: A heavy load lifted off of her. I prayed with her—she felt even better. The strongly dilated pupils of her eyes contracted. During the conversation, which lasted twenty minutes, I kept repeating the solemn priestly blessing and the prayer. Each time I did that, she felt progressively better. Finally she said that everything was all right again. Afterwards her father observed with consternation that his daughter had changed radically . . .

In concluding this letter, Father Alt then proposed that Anneliese did indeed suffer from a "circumsession," a condition fostered by her sensitivity and her delicate physical condition. It could not be blamed on any moral failing on her part. The bishop, therefore, should give permission for the solemn exorcism to be spoken over her at a time of "crisis," that is, when she was especially molested. He felt, he said, that this should be capable of freeing her. And he explained that it should be done in secret in order to guarantee that the matter would retain the character of a worship service instead of degenerating into a religious sensation.

Bishop Stangl was not convinced. He instructed Father Alt to continue observing the case, but he was not to recite the solemn prayer of exorcism over her. Anneliese may have foreseen that decision, because even before it came she decided to take matters into her own hands. After all, she felt, Father Alt was only half convinced that she needed priestly help. She knew that she needed more than she was getting now. So she was going to try to help matters along by following his advice and becoming much more intensely involved with religious activities than she had been before. As to Dr. Lenner, who had referred her back to Dr. Schleip's clinic in May, she no longer consulted him. He was getting pretty tedious. It was not too difficult to see from the way he conducted his interviews that he kept expecting the same answers to the same questions. She went only for brief checkups to Dr. Schleip, for which the latter gives no dates. It was a lucky coincidence, she felt, that on September 1, after two semesters at the PH, she was given her own room, a privilege routinely granted to students of the more advanced semesters. She could use this opportunity to put some distance between herself and her friends, who would have had little understanding for the increased religious emphasis that she was going to introduce into her life. In some ways it may also have been a late reaction to these same friends always telling her in the spring that she was so dependent that continued to rankle.

Ursula Kuzay and the others soon noticed the estrangement. As Ursula said to the court investigator, "We continued living on the same floor, but from that time on it was no longer possible for us to establish close contact with her. She became very uncommunicative and literally segregated herself from us." Among themselves the girls suspected that Peter was the reason. "He's probably jealous. There are lots of guys who cannot hack it if their girl has other friends." Peter actually had nothing to do with it. In fact, he was also affected, for Anneliese emphasized her newfound independence by taking driving lessons; and borrowing his car, she started going places alone. Despite the fact that Dr. Schleip considered her an epileptic, there was clearly not enough reason in her medical history to forbid her to drive. In fact, she never had an accident.

As to friends, Anneliese made new ones from among a group of girls in the Ferdinandeum who were considered religious zealots, girls who opposed the liberalized style of worship being introduced at the time. They objected to the mass being celebrated in German rather than the traditional Latin and refused to accept the new form of the communion used in the Ferdinandeum when Dr. Veth celebrated the mass, where they themselves were called on to take of the bread and put it in their mouths. "Completely without dignity," they complained. So they attended mass at the rather more conservative services of the parish church of Unsere Liebe Frau nearby, which Anneliese also frequented. Anneliese became especially friendly with one girl within the faction, Anna Lippert, with whom she took theology courses at the University of Würzburg. She soon talked Anna and another girl, Maria Klug, into forming a prayer group. They regularly met in Anneliese's room to pray and spent much time talking about religious topics. Anneliese often mentioned San Damiano. She even brought them some water from there, which, according to what Thea Hein said, protected people against the forces of evil. They also exchanged religious literature. Anneliese wrote a letter to Father Alt about one of these publications in the spring of 1975.

Greetings, Father Alt:

I should like to send you the pamphlet titled "Ancilla." I would like you to read it. There are important things in it, and I also believe that the messages that are in it, received by that woman, do not come from the "Prophet of Lies" but from the Holy Ghost, even if some of the things that are said there are quite harsh. As far as I know, Father Kaiser was the one who published it.

Father Alt, please pray for me. I have just contemplated

the picture (on page 62 of the pamphlet) of the Sacred Face of Jesus, and it made me feel that I am nothing, truly nothing, that all in me is vanity. But please do not think that I always feel that; it was only for a few seconds. I believe a person would have to die if he continually had to feel that all he was was of no avail at all.

What am I to do?

I must try to become a better person.

On page 98 it says, "He who has kept me in his heart every day of his life is blessed by my Father." It would be so simple, and yet it is so hard.

I will also pray for you.

There is a picture of your church in the Sunday paper. [The renovation of the Ettleben parish church had just been completed.] I know that you are very busy, but I am sure that you will be able to find the time to read the "Ancilla."

> Best regards for now,
> Anneliese Michel

Joy in the autonomy of the self radiates from these pages. Please pray for me, and I will pray for you. You give me advice, but I also have something to offer. And there is the independence of her analysis that everyone who talked with her always noted: A person could not continuously feel unworthy; that would be self-destructive.

She also had the courage now to reach out to her former friends. Meeting them at lectures, or in the halls of the Ferdinandeum, she would invite Karin Gora or Maria Burdich to go to mass with her to the Unsere Liebe Frau Church, or she would engage them in a conversation about a religious topic that was important to her. "Earthly love is not perfect," Maria Burdich remembers her as saying. "A person should concentrate more on Christian charity." And Karin Gora may have been somewhat startled when Anneliese repeatedly explained to her that the end of the world was not far off. When it arrived, people would have to close their windows and doors to save themselves. Anybody who stayed inside and prayed incessantly would be saved.

All in all, it was a good time for Anneliese. Though she kept her on Tegretol, in January Dr. Schleip noted that "once again, there were no signs for an elevated tendency toward seizures to be detected in the EEG." With Anneliese feeling "free" more and more often, Peter was happy, too, this spring. Anneliese attended classes regularly. They often studied together and she helped him prepare for his final examinations, which were coming up in June. That these examinations were approaching for her as well the following semester was something she tried to put out of her mind.

On May 15, 1975, Oma Fürg died in Klingenberg. There were also other changes that Anneliese found painful to adjust to. Barbara was hired as a bookkeeper in Sulzbach, and although Anneliese felt that it was good for her sister to get away from home, she still missed her. With Gertrud away in Spain—she had started working as a mission helper in Fatima in the summer of 1974—the house was often too empty. Only Roswitha was always there when she would come home on weekends. Those who knew Anneliese well watched her apprehensively. A note of anxiety seemed to be surfacing that had all but vanished during the past few months. "You had better go and have yourself examined," Father Alt counseled her. "Perhaps it would be good if you had a complete physical." So in June Anneliese went to see the Kehlers. Dr. Martin Kehler examined her and was satisfied with her physical condition. But she seemed tense; perhaps this was due to overwork in school, he reasoned. "Don't worry about those exams," he sought to hearten her. "You'll see, everything will be all right." Trying to put a better face on what was beginning to harry her once again, she asked whether he thought those seizures she had experienced years ago were really epilepsy? Or did she perhaps have some other brain disease? Could epilepsy lead to insanity? "That certainly need not be the case," he said. "But your neurologist can tell you better than I."

Anneliese tried to get some definite answer from Dr. Schleip when she went to see her on June 13, soon after her checkup, but Dr. Schleip seemed noncommittal. "Your EEG is quite encouraging," she was told, but there was still something wrong with her brain. She was to continue taking the Tegretol; that, presumably, would take care of it. To be sure, marriage was out of the question when a person was on this drug, but the medication would probably not be necessary for more than another six months. Anneliese as well as Peter subsequently mentioned that this was what Dr. Schleip had said. In her statement to the state attorney, however, Dr. Schleip made no mention of this. Rather, we get the impression that according to her medical opinion, Anneliese would have to continue with the Tegretol indefinitely as a "permanent therapy," as she put it.

At any rate, Anneliese's anxiety deepened. Studying for the examinations in the fall semester seemed totally beyond her. Then there was also the matter of thesis research. She had added music to her majors. It had become her favorite subject, and she hoped to write her thesis in that field. However, each tutor customarily had only a limited number of topics available; to her disappointment, as Peter recalls, those of the music tutor had all been assigned by the time she went to see him. Since she was also interested in theology, she sought out Oberstudiendirektor Veth, the director of the Ferdinandeum and the tutor for that subject. By that time, however, the best topics in his list had also been appropriated by others. He went over the list with her, and she finally settled on one that she was not at all enthusiastic about, namely, "Overcoming Anxiety as a Task of Religious Education." She did some library research but found it increasingly difficult to work on the topic. Becoming more and more despondent, she finally decided to drop out of school and went to Veth to discuss it with him. He, however, felt that this was simply a case of an inferiority complex and made it clear that as far as her studies and preliminary thesis outline were concerned, he could see absolutely no reason why she should do such a thing.

For a while she was at least still able to hide the problem from casual acquaintances interviewed later by the court investigator, such as Elisabeth Kleinhenz, with whom she occasionally exchanged information on homework assignments. But even Elisabeth found her to be extremely pale and distant, buried deep within her own thoughts. Toward Anna Lippert and Maria Klug she was more open; both later remembered that it was at this time that depression overtook her much more frequently than before, that she often was so totally spent that she could not get up from her bed and could not eat, becoming visibly thinner. There was a pervasive, brooding sadness about her that they had not seen before.

Much later, when she was able to introspect again, she did tell Peter what had happened. She had suddenly been swamped, first by a strange, cold pride and then by a wave of mortal terror that carried with it the conviction that she was eternally damned. "I didn't know of any reason why I should be damned," she said. "But inside of me I kept hearing a voice that was trying to convince me that it was so. I tried to fight it off, but it was useless." On her desk he saw a sheaf of notebook pages. While reading them, it struck him how valiantly she was struggling to regain control. "Don't be afraid," she had written. "I don't need to be afraid, courage, courage, courage, be calm, very calm, throw your anxiety overboard, you have reason to hope . . ." But she was losing ground. Maria Klug recalled how at about this time she and Anna Lippert were in Anneliese's room, just talking. Suddenly Anneliese said, "Please stop praying. It hurts. I can't stand it." Maria added, "Neither one of us had been praying aloud. Perhaps one of us might have uttered a silent prayer and Anneliese noticed it."

At about the same time Anneliese seemed to develop a peculiar aversion to all sacred objects. She removed a picture of Christ from the wall. In Maria Klug's room she threw her rosary into a corner during a prayer session of the little group. Anna Lippert told Maria that she had done the same thing with a bottle of San Damiano holy water, thereby shattering it. Even more disconcerting for her two friends was the fact that she no longer went to church. "It's no use," she said. "I can only get as far as the door and not a step farther."

They tried to reason the matter out with each other. "It may have something to do with her legs. She does not seem to be able to bend them at the knees. Strange, isn't it? As though she were walking on stilts."

It was such a curious matter that, of the many things that happened to Anneliese that summer, this was something that stood out in her mother's mind when she spoke to the police the day after Anneliese's death. "Around the summer of 1975 she had difficulty walking. She held onto the furniture and walked that way, pulling herself along."

Anna Lippert recounted a, for her, even more disturbing occurrence.

> I remember an incident from July 1975. I sat with her in her room, and her boyfriend, Peter, was also present. Suddenly, right in the middle of the conversation, her face contracted into a real *Fratze*, a hideous, grimacing countenance that I cannot describe in detail. Her body became completely stiff. It took half an hour before the cramp disappeared. Her boyfriend explained to me that her condition was due to the fact that she was possessed. I too thought that it must be a possession, for her grimace was so demonic that I could think of nothing else [as a possible explanation].

In the meantime, Father Alt had apparently also come to the same conclusion. Recalling a visit by Anneliese, presumably in June, he stated in his report to the state attorney of September 9, 1976, "Anneliese's condition had worsened. Prayer and blessing did not calm her but rather got her excited. Her face would assume a tense expression. *You might say that this was no longer Anneliese.*" (emphasis mine)

Anneliese, however, continued seeking help from him. On Saturday, June 28, she came again, this time accompanied by Peter and Roswitha. After the usual prayers and blessing, she felt better, but the improvement did not last. On her own—Peter was working hard with a few of her friends, preparing for some written tests—she called Father Alt from the Ferdinandeum and begged him to come to Würzburg. "It is terrible," she said. "I cannot control myself. I want Peter or the girls around, but all of a sudden I throw things at them. Please, I need help." He promised to come the following Tuesday. In the same statement to the state attorney Father Alt noted:

> When I arrived [July 1] she opened the door. She was in deep despair. I think this was the first time that she told me

that she was condemned forever. Subsequently she kept repeating that.

I prayed with her. She did want to pray because she immediately got her rosary and sat down. But after three Ave Marias I could see that she was unable to continue. She suddenly began screaming loudly. Tears streamed down her face. Somebody knocked. I said, "Go on, open the door and say that Peter should come." She went to the door and said, "Oh Anna [Lippert], it's you. Please go and fetch Peter, will you?" Then she sat down again. Before we started praying once more I had asked her whether she had taken her pills, and she said that she had.

I gave her the solemn blessing, but her condition did not change. She no longer cried, nor did she scream. But I could feel a terrible cold that was radiating from her.

Finally I prayed the *exorcismus probativus,* but only mentally, not aloud. She immediately jumped up, scared and ready to defend herself. Screaming loudly, she tore up the rosary. Her posture was threatening and she looked more and more harried.

At last her boyfriend arrived. With a completely altered voice, she shouted at him, "Peter, get out."

As he was about to leave, Father Alt glanced at Anneliese's desk. He saw a piece of paper carelessly tossed aside, and he took it along. More than any statement by others about her, it epitomizes her struggle against what was about to overwhelm her. Her handwriting, controlled at first, becomes more and more unsteady, with some sentences breaking into fragments, until there is a final, desperate cry for help.

courage leaves, to say what I wanted.
I am a sinner, I have clearly recognized that in the chapel
today, even if I imagined something different. I . . . I am . . .
I have no courage, despaired.
I am afraid that my priest . . . my
no trust
I am standing at the crossroads, either . . . life or death . . .

Mut verläßt, das zu sagen,
was ich wollte
Ich bin ein Sünder, ~~auch~~
das habe ich heute in der
Kapelle klar erkannt, auch
~~M I~~ wenn ich mir ~~███~~
f etwas anderes eingebildet hab,
~~Ich~~ ~~Ich bin~~ Ich habe keinen
Mut, verzweifelt,
Ich habe Angst daß ~~████~~
Pfarrer zu meine U
kein Vertrauen,
ich stehe am Scheideweg
entweder ~~Lebe~~ Leben oder
Tod. ~~Tief~~ Verletzt, all die Jahre
durch laß mich nicht mehr
gewehrt!, jetzt auch nicht
Ich bin nach der hl. Kommunion
verzweifelt, in Genick u. am Herz
~~eine eiserne Kette~~ hält mein Herz um-
klammert, Angst Aussetzen, ~~Na~~
~~███ ist ~~ ~~Klein~~

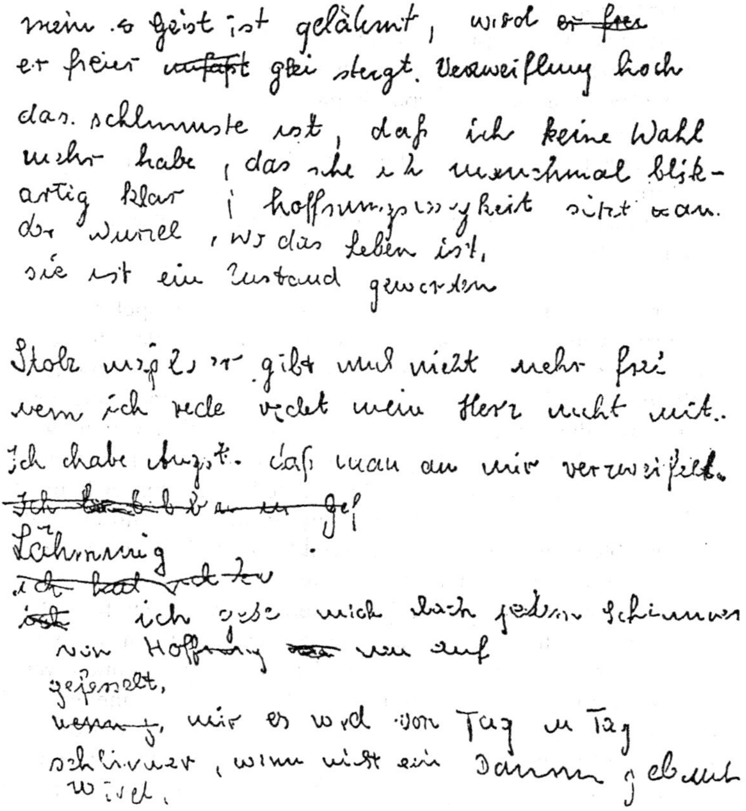
mein Geist ist gelähmt, wird er ~~frei~~
er freier ~~aufgefaßt~~ gleich steigt Verzweiflung hoch
das Schlimmste ist, daß ich keine Wahl
mehr habe, das sehe ich manchmal blitz-
artig klar, Hoffnungslosigkeit sitzt an
der Wurzel, wo das Leben ist,
sie ist ein Zustand geworden

Stolz ... gibt mich nicht mehr frei
wenn ich rede redet mein Herz nicht mit..
Ich habe Angst, daß man an mir verzweifelt.
Lähmung
ich ... mich nach jedem Schimmer
von Hoffnung ... auf
gefesselt,
... mir es wird von Tag zu Tag
schlimmer, wenn nicht ein Damm gebaut
wird.

Figure 2. A note written by Anneliese in June 1975.

Grievously injured . . through the years, I no longer defended myself . . not now either . . . I became desperate after the holy communion, in spirit and heart. An iron chain is pressing around my heart. Fear, terror . . . my spirit is lame, if it becomes free, freer . . . right away despair rises
the worst of it is that I have no choice anymore, I see
that sometimes clear like lightning, hopelessness sits
at the root where life is

it has become a condition
Pride, unspeakable pride will not set me free
when I speak, my heart does not speak along
I am afraid that people despair in me
paralysis
still I give myself to every glimmer of hope . . . newly up . . .
fettered
. . . things will get worse and worse with me day after day if no
dam will be constructed

There is an unconscious poetic power here—"Hopelessness sits
at the root where life is"—and an urgent plea for a dam to be constructed, a dam, that is, against what it was that she experienced
as flooding her being. Father Alt felt deeply worried and called
her parents the same afternoon, suggesting that they take Anneliese home. They apparently thought that she might recover as
she had before. But Anneliese lay in bed after this visit by her
spiritual counselor, stiff and responding to no one. And even after
she was able to get up again, she could not study or work on her
thesis. So on July 17 her parents came. They first went to Dr.
Schleip, whom they asked about Anneliese's prospects for a fruit-
ful professional life. Dr. Schleip tried to reassure them on that account. Clearly, however, something else was on their minds. What,
they asked, did Dr. Schleip think was the cause of Anneliese's illness? The explanation she offered, namely, that there was some
indication of an epileptic focus in the left temporal lobe, was technical and just vague enough to leave them anxious. It is clear from
Dr. Schleip's statement under oath at the trial what the distraught
couple really wanted to ask her: Could she possibly accept possession as an explanation for Anneliese's affliction? They made a hes-
itant attempt. What was Dr. Schleip's religious affiliation? Even
under oath she could not recall what she answered. It must have
been noncommittal, for the Michels, feeling discouraged, asked no
further. What was the sense of talking to someone who, as a non-
Catholic, would have no understanding at all of the assumptions
they accepted as true within their faith, let alone feel with them
the magnitude of their distress? The same day they took Anneliese
home.

At home again in Klingenberg, Anneliese started eating, but her other problems continued unabated. She walked around with stiff legs, as she herself said, "as though they were sticks." The worst of it was, as she saw it, that she could no longer pray. As she told Peter, "It used to be that prayer helped me a great deal when I was feeling bad. Despite all attempts, I now cannot pray at all." Thea Hein, who was always up on what was going on, called to suggest that since Father Alt was so far away, maybe they should ask Father Roth for help. Josef Michel reached him in Breitenbrunn, near Miltenberg, where he was on vacation at his brother's house. Just to be sure that he got the message, Thea Hein also called him from Ebersbach. Both told him that Anneliese was screaming and raging, and could he perhaps come and see what he could do. He hesitated. After all, the bishop had not given any permission for a formal exorcism. Might his appearance not make matters worse? But Josef Michel called again. Over the phone he let him hear the terrifying gutteral screams of the afflicted girl. So Father Roth decided to see for himself. Thea Hein, who had engineered the visit, also came along. In the words of Father Roth (from his statement to the police investigation),

Herr Michel received me and took me immediately to the living room. It was filled with a horrible stench, of something burning, and of dung, that penetrated everything. Herr Michel expressly called my attention to it and told me that Anneliese had been in the room just before. In other rooms of the Michel home and on the outside I could detect no trace of the stench.

I went to the kitchen with Herr Michel and there Fräulein Michel came running toward me, as if she wanted to assault me. About one meter away from me she suddenly stopped, very stiffly, without saying anything at all. After a few seconds she ran away again and then ran toward me once more, stopping at a short distance in front of me in a rigid posture.

I should like to say here parenthetically that Herr Michel told me during this visit that after he had talked to me on the phone, she had said, "Roth, that dog, he is also going to come," although he had told her nothing of my intended visit.

After running toward me twice and then standing still in this manner, Anneliese began raging and screaming very loudly. "Get out," she shouted at me, "you are tormenting me." Her parents asked me to stay, so I remained in the kitchen. Thereupon Anneliese tore up a rosary and threw the pieces on the floor.

Herr Michel took me outside and told me other details that took place while his daughter was having these attacks of rage. Both the family and Frau Hein then entreated me to say a blessing over Anneliese. But even when I just attempted to take my crucifix out of my breast pocket—she did not know that I carried one with me—the demon in the girl began to rage.

It finally got so far that she attempted to throw a five-liter container filled with water from San Damiano at me. Interestingly, the jug fell from her raised arms, landing beside her instead of hitting me.

After another brief conversation with Herr Michel, I drove back to Breitenbrunn.

On July 30 Peter came to visit Anneliese in Klingenberg. Before the end of the month, she needed to go back to Würzburg and register for the fall semester; otherwise she would not be allowed to start with her examinations. She also needed to take a few required physical education courses for her sports seminar. He knew from telephone conversations that she would probably be in no condition to go back with him, but he was going to try and see what he could do anyway.

Anneliese had not been out of the house for weeks. "Let's go for a walk," Peter proposed. "I can't bend my legs," Anneliese said in misery. But Peter insisted. Once in his car, he took her to a lonely country road, and they started walking very slowly. The pace was excruciatingly tiring for both of them. "Let's go home," Peter finally suggested. He continues to relate what happened next in his reminiscences:

Right in the middle of the conversation Anneliese stopped and, in amazement, looked at herself up and down. Then she started bending her fingers, as though she were doing it for the first time. She began to walk, quite normally, gingerly, then faster. Only then did she suddenly remember my presence. Laughingly, she threw her arms around my neck and exclaimed, "It is gone, I am free, entirely free, like never before." She wanted to go home quickly to tell her parents what had happened. She was full of hope, for "being herself" as intensely as she was now perceiving it was an experience that was entirely new to her. . . .

The next day the two of them went back to Würzburg together, and Anneliese registered for the fall semester. They were in the midst of grocery shopping when

Anneliese said, "I think it is starting up again." At the same time her facial expression tensed up and she could hardly walk. Luckily, at least she did not become aggressive. That, by the way, never happened in the presence of strangers.

The return home, which usually took about ten minutes, lasted an entire hour. Once in her room, things got worse. She stood completely stiff in front of a crucifix that was hanging on the wall. She looked at it fixedly, and her gaze was full of hatred. Her face was totally distorted, she growled like an animal and gritted her teeth so loudly that I was afraid that all her teeth would fall out. I started praying for her in thought, without giving any indication at all of what I was doing. Immediately she ordered me with clenched teeth to stop. . . .

For an hour she did not move an inch from the spot. . . . Keeping her gaze fixed on the cross, she bent her upper body backwards to get some distance from it, while at the same time trying to grab it with her hands. When she had calmed down somewhat and released the posture, she explained, "I wanted to take the cross in my hand, but against my will I was pushed back, so I couldn't reach it."

Afraid that such incidents would repeat themselves—and since

the most important matter, the registration, had been taken care of
—Peter took her back to Klingenberg the same day. Once there,
Anneliese's condition worsened. So he decided to stay for a while
in case he could be of help.

In the meantime Father Roth had reported on his experience
with Anneliese to his friend Ernst Alt. "Her parents begged me to
see to it that she gets exorcized. They also wrote to our Most Reverend Bishop about it," he told him. "There is no longer any
doubt in my mind that the girl is under the influence of demonic
forces." Father Alt agreed. It seemed to him that not only was
Anneliese "under the influence" of demonic forces, but that, indeed, those forces were now living in her, using her body, thus
meeting the condition of the Church, together with her aversion to
the sacred symbols of the faith, for the recognition of true possession. He had been convinced of that earlier on the basis of the
painful scene in Anneliese's room in the Ferdinandeum, and had
told Bishop Stangl on the phone at the time. But once more the
bishop had counseled patience. Armed with this new evidence, he
thought that he might now be able to overcome the bishop's hesitation: The girl desperately needed the Church's help, the demon
must be expelled, Satan had to be forced to release her by the one
tried and true weapon the Church had used down through the centuries, the solemn prayer of exorcism.

He went to Würzburg to speak to Bishop Stangl personally, but
the bishop was on vacation. Instead, he was ushered into the office
of one of the ecclesiastical dignitaries of the diocese, Vicar-
General Wittig. From him he succeeded in obtaining the vacation
address of the bishop, whom he called. The bishop at last relented
and gave oral permission for saying the exorcism over Anneliese,
but only the "small one."[2] On August 3, the Sunday after Anneliese had been to Würzburg with Peter, Father Alt came with Father Roth to Klingenberg. Father Roth reported:

> In our presence Anneliese Michel once more showed evi-
> dence that she was molested by demons, but this molestation
> was not as strong as during my previous visit.

[2] A German excerpt from the Latin, so-called "Great Exorcism," given in
the *Rituale Romanum*.

During the recitation of the small exorcism, she began to whimper and to moan and she pleaded, "Stop! It's burning." When asked where, she answered, "In my back, in my arms." What was also striking on that day was that she tried to knock the book containing the exorcism prayer according to Pope Leo XIII out of Father Alt's hands. As far as I can remember, she once said, "I am free." What she meant by that was that she was free of demons. But this lasted only a moment, and soon after she once more started whimpering and moaning. When we left the Michel home about two hours later, we were both convinced more than ever that we were dealing with a case of possession.

Father Alt's impression was that the exorcism had helped Anneliese. Still, he was troubled. What if she were molested again? On August 10 he was scheduled to go on vacation. "Would it be wiser if I did not go?" he asked Father Rodewyk, whose expertise on possession he respected, and whom he had consulted on the phone before. Father Rodewyk did not think so. "There is nothing you can do at the moment," he said. "Better go and rest; you'll need your strength." So he left. From his vacation resort he wrote a brief letter to his bishop on August 16, saying that as far as he could see, things in Klingenberg had calmed down somewhat before he had started his vacation. "I do not dare to say that Anneliese is better, however. Her reactions are those of a person in a trance."

His intuition was entirely correct. Things had, in fact, not calmed down in Klingenberg. Rather, Anneliese's torment reached heights that no one could possibly have anticipated. In the memory of those surrounding her—her parents, Roswitha, Peter—the events of August that year are a confused tangle of incidents blurred by horror. Arousal swept over Anneliese like the swirling winds of a hurricane. Sleep was nearly impossible, allowing her at most one or two hours' uneasy rest. Sometimes she would pray, shouting the same formula from dusk to the morrow: "My Jesus, forgiveness and mercy, forgiveness and mercy . . ." She rushed through the house, up and down the steps, "bucking like a billy goat," in Father Rodewyk's words. She knelt down, then got up

again with incredible speed until her knees swelled and were ul-
cerated, and still she continued. Her coarse, incessant screams, rising and falling like waves scudding against a rocky shore, echoed
from the walls. Then a peak would come, she would tremble and
twitch and, as a consequence of the enormity of her agitation she
would lapse into complete catatoniclike rigidity, not moving arms
or legs, and even the screams at last would cease for a while.
Shedding tears of compassion, Roswitha would wash her and try
to feed her as she lay inert for days.

Along with her excitation came muscle power that was close to
superhuman. Peter saw her take an apple and effortlessly squeeze
it with one hand so that the fragments exploded throughout the
room. Fast as lightning she grabbed Roswitha and threw her on
the floor as if she were a rag doll. Her neck muscles tensing like
bands of steel, she could not swallow any solid food and could
take liquids only sometimes. The rigidity spread to her chest and
she could not breathe. Struggling for breath with deadly desperation, she would press her face to the floor over and over again,
flatten her nose, and then rise and gulp some air. Her mother put
a pillow down to save her face from injury, which made the struggle worse. Her father tried to hold her upright, but then she turned
"as red as a lobster," and choked and gasped. "Just let me do
what I must," she would plead as soon as she could talk. "If you
try to help me, I'll be forced to do something much worse."

Her whole body seethed with heat. Maddened by the burning
sensation that pervaded her, she sought for coolness, rolling in the
black dust of the coal cellar, soaking herself in an old iron kettle
that she filled with icy water, sticking her head into the commode
in the bathroom. She would tear her clothes off her body and race
through the rooms naked. Her bed was too warm, covers were
insufferable. During the August nights the attic promised a cool
refuge. "I tried to talk her out of that," Roswitha wrote in her
"Experiences with My Sister Anneliese" (jotted down for me in
1978), "but to no avail. When there was something she had to do,
there was no stopping her. After all, it wasn't her acting but the
devil. I carried a blanket up to her and spread it on the attic floor.
I did not want to leave her completely alone, so I put my sleeping
bag under the attic stairs. There was no question of sleep, of

course. In the first place, she screamed all night, and, besides, she kept running around up there."

The world was upside down, where nonfood turned into sustenance and nondrink into refreshment. She stuffed flies and spiders into her mouth, tried to chew on coal, urinated on the kitchen floor and licked it up, and chewed on panties soaked with urine. Love became hate. Her family learned to duck her vicious blows. Peter took to wearing long-sleeved shirts in the August heat after receiving a deep and painful bite in the arm from her. When she tried to kiss—and she tried often—her face was distorted into a mask of loathing. And, finally, what was sacred needed to be profaned. There was so much of that about her, and she went after it with fury. She ripped holy pictures from the walls, dumped out water from San Damiano, tore rosaries apart, and yanked a medal from Thea Hein's neck, who had come by to see "the action." Once she got hold of a crucifix. "No, Anneliese, no," Roswitha exclaimed. "Let me, Roswitha, it helps me," she pleaded. Roswitha looked at her, dumbfounded, and at the same moment she had shattered the crucifix against the edge of the bed. "Of course, that wasn't her," Roswitha commented, "she was not the one who wanted to shatter the crucifix. It was the devil who enjoys destroying and desecrating all holy objects." She attacked the priests who came to pray with her verbally and with blows. "Take your paw off me, that burns like fire," she ordered one of them. And holy rites were anathema. "The exorcism was for me as if I had put my hand into a wasps' nest," she remarked later. Sundays and holidays were the bleakest part of the week, and the holier they were the more they seemed unbearable. "The ascension of Mary on August 15 was the worst day I had ever spent," she told Peter in September, when the storm had passed. She could not enter any church, and she could not pray.

Even the world took on an altered countenance. There were clouds of flies that appeared and then vanished unaccountably, and shadowy little animals that scurried about, dark and frightening; after a while, even her family saw them come and pass.

Yet not all experience arose from the sinister part of the world. Her kin came to comfort her, Anneliese told Peter later: Oma Fürg, who had died three months earlier, and her dead little sister

Martha. Sometimes she saw sudden flashes of light under a calm
and summery sky. Small, oval wounds opened on her feet. The
family viewed these "tokens of grace" with hushed reverence: the
stigmata, the wounds of the Lord on the cross. Holy people had
often been marked in this manner. "Later, when she was feeling
better," Peter averred, "they healed much more slowly than her
other injuries. Anneliese insisted that those were not spots where
she injured herself. She continued feeling a stinging pain in both
her feet even after they closed, sometimes more, sometimes less."

Day and night Anneliese raged on. Alternating in two-hour
shifts, her parents, Roswitha, and Peter watched over her, although there was little they could do to prevent her from inflicting
wounds on herself. Soon they were bone weary and at their wits'
end. "Why don't you get in touch with Father Alt?" Thea Hein
wanted to know. "I can't," Josef Michel sighed, "he is on vacation." "How about Pastor Habiger?" "I already called him. All he
had to say was that we should take Anneliese to a psychiatrist.
You know that we have done that, I'd hate to count how many
times. Or, he says, she should go to a psychiatric clinic for
observation. I'd like to see how he would want to talk Anneliese
into doing that!" "Well, then," Thea Hein concluded, "you will
have to get Alt to come. Things cannot go on the way they are
now." Josef Michel agreed. He was frantic. So on August 18 he
sent a telegram to Father Alt, who was on vacation in Spiazzo, in
the South Tyrol. "Request interrupt vacation. Come immediately.
Rodewyk was here and is expecting you. Our strength is at an
end." The reference to Rodewyk may have been a ruse born of
desperation. Father Rodewyk insisted that his visit was not until
the beginning of September. Alt did not react to the telegram.
"Maybe if you asked Father Rodewyk to get in touch with him,
that would convince him," Thea Hein suggested. Josef Michel
called him in Frankfurt, but Father Rodewyk refused to bother
Alt during his vacation. When Josef Michel insisted, he asked him
to put in writing some of the details about Anneliese's molestations that he mentioned on the phone. Josef Michel complied, and
on the basis of that letter Father Rodewyk decided that he would
like to see Anneliese for himself. Thea Hein made the practical arrangements, and early in September Father Rodewyk went by

train to Aschaffenburg, where Thea Hein, in the company of Father Herrmann, picked him up in her car and drove him to Klingenberg. Father Rodewyk described his visit to the Michel home to the state attorney as follows:

When I entered the house, Anneliese Michel lay, fully dressed, on the floor of the kitchen and could obviously not be addressed. I am of the opinion that she was in a typical hypnotic state, in a kind of deep sleep.

I should like to remark that such a state is a symptom of possession. I designate it as a crisis condition.

First I went to the living room with her parents and had them report to me about the condition of their daughter. Then I directed them to bring Anneliese into the room and make her sit on the sofa.

Her father led her in and held her by the hand because she tried to hit her parents. She did not look emaciated.

I sat down beside her and held her hands. In her trance state a second personage announced itself, calling itself Judas. I had asked, "What is your name?" and the answer came, "Judas." She spoke with an altered, much lower voice.

I had held her by her wrists. During the conversation I noticed that her cramped muscles relaxed. She came to and looked at me with surprise. Apparently it was not until then that she noticed me consciously. Subsequently I was able to carry on an entirely reasonable conversation with her. I told her that we would not desert her and that we would help her. I was thinking of priestly aid through exorcism. . . .

Suddenly the cramps started again. I asked her family to take her back to the kitchen. I told them that I knew enough about the case, that I had found confirmation of my surmise that we were dealing with a case of possession, and that I would have to consider what could be done. When I left the house, Anneliese came out of the kitchen and slapped my cheek.

"She certainly is possessed," Thea Hein said to no one in particular. As Father Rodewyk was being escorted to the door, she looked around to see where Anneliese was. Some chords coming from the living room told her: There was Anneliese, playing the piano as if nothing had happened.

As for Father Rodewyk, he carried away one more potent argument from the visit for his possession hypothesis: The possessing demon had given his name. In the opinion he subsequently formulated, he summarized her other symptoms, namely, her loathing of consecrated objects and her fear of the exorcism. He then spoke in detail about this important point.

> The last question remaining is the one concerning the devil that has taken possession of her. Asked several times, Anneliese always gave the name "Judas." He is well known from the history of possession . . . tempting his victims into stealing the Host [the consecrated wafer] by preventing them from swallowing it. With Anneliese we find something of that sort. She said herself that she once went to communion but could not swallow the Host and therefore let it dissolve in her mouth. This would indicate the influence of a demon Judas. There is also something else: her sudden tendency to kiss. The important matter in this case is her facial expression. This is in no way the expression of a girl who wants to kiss someone. Rather, her face betrays hostility, as we often see it portrayed on pictures of the Judas kiss. This fact would fit here.
>
> The conclusion, then, is that Anneliese is possessed, her principal demon being a Judas. This formulation allows the conjecture that there might also still be some subsidiary demons. When asked by a priest about this, Anneliese indicated by a slight nod of her head that this was indeed correct.
>
> What else needs to be discussed? To date, the demons have not spoken from Anneliese's mouth but have behaved as "mute demons." If the situation remains that way, then it will hardly be possible to clarify the case. The *Rituale Romanum* rules that the demons need to speak from the mouth of those possessed, and it demands that certain questions be asked of them, which they must answer truthfully.

To everyone's relief, while Father Rodewyk, back at home in Frankfurt, was composing an Opinion on all the arguments for assuming that Anneliese was possessed by demons, Anneliese herself began shaking it off. The first indication the family had of this was that she started eating again. As she herself explained to Peter later, earlier she had wanted to eat but "was not allowed to." If she tried it anyway, she either was unable to open her mouth or could not swallow anything. "I was always hungry," she said, "and it was terrible for me to smell food or hear the klinking of spoons and forks." Everyone was worried about her inability to take nourishment. "She is going to get very sick if she does not start eating soon," her mother said. "Perhaps we should call Dr. Kehler," Josef Michel suggested. But it was not necessary. The day after this conversation, about which Anneliese knew nothing, according to Peter, she rushed into the kitchen and commanded, *"Etwas zum Fressen her*—I want some grub." She gobbled up all the food offered her and continued taking regular meals. Her hollowed cheeks filled out quite rapidly, and the other manifestations also started going away.

Given her past history, there was, of course, no guarantee that she would not be "attacked" again in this manner. This was the conviction of her family and also of Anneliese. "If only the bishop would give permission for the solemn exorcism," she would say. "I am sure that that would finally free me." The priests who knew her felt the same way. "This thing needs to be brought under control. The demons must be routed, once and for all," was the consensus. As soon as Father Alt came back from his vacation on September 7, he had a phone call from Father Rodewyk from Frankfurt. "I have assembled the symptoms that I myself have observed," he told Father Alt. "From everything I now know, this is definitely a case of possession." He suggested that they get together with the Aschaffenburg priests as soon as possible to consult on the matter.

A few days later the meeting took place at the parish house of Unsere Liebe Frau in Aschaffenburg, with the Fathers Habiger, Roth, Rodewyk, and Alt in attendance. Father Rodewyk read them his Opinion and then summarized it, saying that, given his many years of experience in such matters, this was, in his view, a classical case of possession. The idea that the exorcism might be carried out in Italy—where exorcisms were carried out routinely in some churches—came up briefly and was rejected. If that course were chosen, it would be impossible to protect Anneliese from unwelcome publicity. Instead, all those present agreed that the bishop should now be asked for formal permission to carry out an exorcism as foreseen in the *Rituale Romanum,* and to find the right priest to carry out the rite. Father Alt was asked to contact Bishop Stangl. Father Roth thought that Father Arnold Renz, superior of the Salvatorian monastery of Rück-Schippach, near Klingenberg, and pastor of the parish there, might be willing to act as exorcist, since for Father Alt, it would be too burdensome to come regularly from Ettleben, a distance of 120 kilometers.

As a result of these decisions, Father Roth went to see Father Arnold Renz. Father Renz asked for three days' time to consider the matter and soon gave his consent, also calling Father Alt. The latter wrote the following formal letter to Bishop Stangl:

[date illegible]

Most Reverend Bishop,
   It has been a year now since I orally reported to you on a case of probable possession. I also sent you a written report last year, a copy of which I am enclosing. In the meantime I had contact with you by phone on several occasions concerning this case. As I reported to you in one of these telephone conversations, I have involved Father Rodewyk in the case, who has become well known for his books on demonic possession. In an Opinion he has summarized the reasons why one needs to speak of possession here. In order to protect the identity of the persons involved, he has summarized the matter under the name of "Anna Lieser."

Alt then reviewed the data on Anneliese before continuing.

   After the priests who knew of the matter met with Father Rodewyk and consulted with each other, as I reported to you, we came to the conclusion that we should present the outline of the case to you once more and entrust Father

Renz, a member of the Salvatorian order and superior of Rück-Schippach, with the matter. I have spoken with Father Renz. He is willing to undertake the matter but will not act without your express permission. I am enclosing a draft document, unintelligible to third parties, as counseled by Father Rodewyk. It is up to your discretion whether you would want to write to him in this or some other form to charge him with this task.

Most Reverend Bishop, I can only assure you that I fully and completely agree with this course of action. The distance between Ettleben and Klingenberg is too great for me to continue with the matter. One thing is clear: This is a matter of possession. For this reason, and because of the tremendous torment that Anna Lieser has to suffer, it is necessary to act immediately. Without a doubt, we were all surprised by the occurrence of the case and, in a way, more is demanded of us than we can deliver. But Father Rodewyk, S.J. has offered us his expert help. The conversation we had with him last week has made many things clear to us. I am writing this letter in great haste and am taking it to Würzburg myself, together with my report and Father Rodewyk's Opinion.

Begging for your blessing and prayer,
I remain,
Your Ernst Alt

In light of the entirely formal approach that the matter was now clothed in, satisfying all the conditions for a possession to be present according to Church law, Bishop Stangl acted expeditiously. He wrote the following letter to Father Renz.

The Bishop of Würzburg   September 16, 1975
To The Superior   *Strictly Confidential*
Father Arnold Renz
8751 Elsenfeld-Rück-Schippach

Reverend Fellow Priests,
After due consideration and with good information, I now charge the Reverend Father Renz, Salvatorian, Superior in

Rück-Schippach, to proceed with Miss Anna Lieser within the terms of *CIC* can 1151 §1. For some time now my prayers have been directed to this concern. May God give us his help. I thank everyone sincerely for their efforts.

With best wishes and my blessing,
+ Josef
Bishop of Würzburg

The reference in the above letter is to a particular section in the *Canonical Law, Codex Iuris Canonici,* Pii X Pontificis Maximi, 1936, Titulus VIII, can 1151, paragraph 1, which reads as follows:

Nemo, potestate exorcizandi praeditus, exorcismos, in obsessos proferre legitime potest, nisi ab Ordinario peculiarem et expressam licentiam obtinuerit.

No one empowered to carry out an exorcism may legitimately exorcise a possessed person unless he obtain specific and express permission from the bishop.

CHAPTER
FIVE

JOUSTING WITH THE
DEMONS

From September 1975 until Anneliese's death on July 1, 1976, Father Arnold Renz was destined to dominate the stage. Who was he? As to biographical information, Wilhelm Renz—the name Arnold was awarded to him when he joined his religious order—was born in 1911 in a village near Friedrichshafen in southwest Germany. The second son of peasant parents, and so not in line to inherit any land, he dedicated himself early on to a life in the service of the Church. He attended the high school of the Salvatorian order, studied in their College of Philosophy, and was ordained in 1938. His order then sent him on a missionary assignment to Fukien province in China, where he remained from 1938 to 1953. Upon returning home, he held various assignments until 1965, when he became pastor of the Rück-Schippach parish and superior of the monastery of his order there. The airy and modernistic St. Pius Church of Schippach, where he celebrated mass, was consecrated in 1960. Its land and foundations had been paid for prior to the First World War from money collected by an organization founded by Barbara Weigand, at home in Rück-Schippach. Father Renz had access to copies of the manuscripts of this pious peasant woman, Franciscan tertiary, and mystic, and studied them extensively.

In the course of the criminal investigation following Anneliese's death, Father Renz submitted to a physical and psychiatric examination by Drs. Lungershausen and Köhler, as had Father Alt. As we learn from their deposition, he came to the interview in the habit of his order. They found him to be of stocky build and in good health. His movements and facial expression were "pastoral," betraying his lifelong priestly activity. During the conversation they sometimes found his answers to be a bit rambling, but all in all "definite and precise." They found it curious, however, that he should be so obviously incapable of critical evaluation concerning the topic of exorcism when his intellectual capacity in other areas was entirely normal. The reason, stated forty pages later, was that by means of a CAT scan they were able to discover an albeit minimal calcification of the brain that, in their view, was apparently subject-specific—a most astounding quality, one should note, for a minute calcification, impairing only that specific cerebral region wherein resides the critical evaluation of exorcism and his own behavior with respect to it.

There was no indication of schizophrenia, manic-depressive psychosis, or of experiences of a hallucinatory character. He was, they concluded, "a deeply religious personality rooted in a magico-mystical thinking," whose critical faculties, unfortunately, were depressed by a "pathological change in the brain" due to a calcification which at the moment "could not yet be seen to be in any way grave."

To put it differently, Father Renz was a man whose religious convictions were unpalatable to the psychiatrists, but who did not provide them with a handle on his religious experience, nothing to which they could attach a suspicion of mental illness, "if not now, then surely in the past," as they had in the case of Ernst Alt. So they took recourse to processes in the brain, a bit of calcification, a point difficult to argue since no one really knows what consequences such minute changes might have. And they labeled him "magico-mystic"—an epithet smacking of the Dark Ages—"not to say primitive," in other words, out of touch with modern times.

There are, expectably, also other views of Father Renz. Father Roth saw him as the exceptional priest who fitted perfectly with the exacting qualifications laid down by Church law in the *Codex Iuris Canonici* for someone to be entrusted with carrying out the "great" exorcism. He should be pious, intelligent, and of blameless moral character. As explicated in the *Rituale Romanum,* the book of rites of the Catholic Church, he should put his trust not in himself but in the power of God. He should be free of avarice and greed, and should carry out the rite out of charity, humbly and steadfastly. And he should be of a mature age and be respected not for the sake of his office but for his moral earnestness. This is how Anneliese also thought of him. And if the tone of affection that pervades their taped conversation, alluded to earlier, of February 1, 1976, is any indication, she also trusted him not only as her spiritual counselor but as a kind and gentle father figure.

In his statement to the state attorney Father Renz recalled how his involvement with the Anneliese Michel case began; how Father Roth had come to him with the report on her by Father Rodewyk, whom he knew to be an expert in the field of exorcism, and whose book *Exorcism Today* he had read before; how he was asked by him and also by Anneliese's parents, who came to see him, if he would be willing to recite the exorcism for her; and how, while waiting for the official charge from the bishop, he had also read Father Rodewyk's *Exorcism According to the Rituale Romanum* and relevant passages in the *Rituale Romanum* itself. After receiving the bishop's letter,

. . . on September 23, 1975, I presented myself to the parents of the young girl, Josef and Anna Michel, in Klingenberg. Anneliese greeted me by saying, *"Ich bin die, wo*—I am the one who," and in a jocular vein I answered, *"Und ich bin der, wo*—and I am the one who."

I spoke with them for about an hour, and her sisters Roswitha and Barbara were also present.

I saw nothing out of the ordinary in Anneliese Michel on

this day, nothing that would have indicated any possession. If
I had not already been alerted to it . . . this idea would
never have occurred to me.

As a matter of fact, he took an immediate liking to Anneliese.
"She was a really nice, fine girl of great religious depth," he was
to write later in a personal letter (Oct. 9, 1978) addressed to me.
"She actually did not talk very much, not like others who gush all
day like a well." It was agreed that the first exorcism rite would be
held on the evening of September 24.

Father Renz arrived at four o'clock and found the others—
Anneliese's parents, her sisters Barbara and Roswitha, and Peter—
already assembled. Fathers Alt, Roth, and Herrmann had come,
and of course also Thea Hein, who was later joined by her husband. The rites were performed in an upstairs room facing back
toward the hills and vineyards, so that if Anneliese screamed it
would not be heard by passersby. Chairs were set up for the participants, and the family had arranged a small altar on a side
table, on which was an embroidered tablecloth. It contained a
crucifix, in front of which was a statue of Christ, a flowerpot with
a houseplant, and framed pictures of the Virgin Mary, of Father
Pio, the archangel Michael, and the Sacred Heart of Jesus. In the
pause between the lengthy prayers, everyone would go to the next
room to have some coffee and cake or some tea.

The rite in its entirety is contained in the *Rituale Romanum.*[1] It
starts out with an invocation, spoken communally, to God and all
the angels and saints. It continues with other prayers, some
spoken singly by the exorcist, some by the congregation surrounding the victim of possession. There are many Lord's Prayers and
Ave Marias, and, in between, the questions that need to be asked:
Why did the demonic personage possess his victim? When did he
intend to leave? What was his name? What cannot be named is
difficult to exorcize. If the priest can trick the demon into reveal-

[1] The modern English version of the *Rites* omits the entire section containing the great exorcism. The new American ritual (Collectio Rituum,
1961) concerns only baptism, extreme unction, and matrimony, for which
the use of the English language is authorized.

ing his identity, he gains a measure of power over him. And there are the exorcistic commands themselves: The demon, once named, is ordered to leave his victim, *famula dei* Anneliese, the handmaiden of God, and he is told to return to his hellish abode, to the depth of *gehennam*, in truly majestic formulas.

The people surrounding Anneliese during the first exorcism and all the subsequent ones—her congregation, as it were—shared in the beliefs represented by these prayers. Moreover, throughout the years of painful "molestations" that Anneliese had suffered, and that they had experienced with her, they had become convinced— long before the ordained officials of their church had come round to it—that Anneliese's will, not her consciousness, had been taken over by an alien entity, for she experienced everything that went on as though she were spying on it from that "hole" she often spoke about and that she could not get out of. They knew that this alien entity was malevolent. Why else would it torment her so, make her twitch and writhe and scream, prevent her from eating and drinking and sleeping? Why would it fill her with such un- earthly terror, why appear to her in those ghastly faces, why make her break a crucifix, and box the ears of a venerable old priest? To them Anneliese had become an innocent medium, a vessel coveted by Satan, who had to be expelled to make the vessel whole and clean once more. At long last they now had the power to do just that, for the bishop, empowered by the Church, had given his consent and had provided them with the counselor to guide them in the task.

Father Renz's diary entry gives us a faint outline of the first of the exorcism sessions.

24 September 1975. Arrive at 16 hours. Started exorcism according to instructions. Anneliese, or rather the demons, behaved rather quietly at first. Anneliese is being shaken more and more strongly. Anneliese, or rather the demons, react most violently against the holy water. She starts screaming and raging.

Anneliese knows everything. She knows what it is that she said; apparently she is always fully conscious. No amnesia at all. Brief pause. Anneliese is held by three men (so she

would not injure herself or others), by Herr Hein, her friend
Peter, and her father. She wants to bite right and left. She
kicks toward me. Sometimes she simply hits toward the front.
At first she sits on a chair, then on the couch. She is not allowed to remain lying down. Sometimes she does it but has
to get up again right away. She complains that the devil sits
in her lower back.

Occasionally she screams, especially if she is sprinkled with
holy water. At times she howls like a dog. Repeatedly she
says, "Stop with that shit," or "You shit guy," "You dirty
sow," "Put away that shit" (holy water). Actually she does
not say very much, uses even the obscenities sparingly.

In the end, during the Gloria Patri which we pray together
repeatedly, she becomes furious. The entire session lasted
from 16 hours to 21:30.

Afterwards she said, "You should have continued." Apparently she felt that the demons were being routed. When
she said good-bye she was actually quite lively. The entire
matter must be very strenuous for her. She consumes a lot of
energy, considering that three men are holding her down, and
she continually struggles against them.

From his remarks at the conclusion of the notes of the session
we get some feeling for the trepidation with which he had approached this, his first exorcism assignment. "I have more courage
now, am not so afraid anymore of the unknown and the uncertain." But he was also disappointed. No demon had been cast out
and he could sense that a prolonged and strenuous effort lay
ahead. "One needs to grapple with a feeling of uselessness and
failure," he observed.

For the following session, held on Sunday, September 28, Thea
Hein brought a tape recorder. Josef Michel thought this a good
idea and fetched his own from downstairs too. Although Father
Renz found much of what Anneliese said most revealing of the
demon's character, he thought that he could do without a mechanical device, for he intended to continue writing a detailed account at
home. He soon discovered that he was able to reconstruct very little, because there was no possibility for taking notes. Besides, he

could not simply sit back and observe. He had to read the Latin text, conduct the communal prayers, sprinkle holy water, make the sign of the cross over Anneliese, perhaps place the stole around her shoulder or touch her forehead in a blessing, as the ritual demanded. So he also started to record, accumulating over forty tapes in the course of the ensuing months. Eventually he condensed some of the most striking utterances on two tapes and played them to Bishop Stangl and to others who were interested. But that summarization reduces the glowing body of the drama that was played out there in the upstairs room of the Michel house to a mere skeleton. On an original tape we experience, as those around Anneliese did, something of that alien, autonomous presence that, in the sense of Catholic dogma, had taken up residence in her body and was using it for its own demonic purposes.

There are the undulating, hoarse screams and furious growls and grunts that legitimize the demon for what he is in Church teaching, a denison of the deep, the emissary of the night side, of all that is frightful and polluted. The hellish brew of sound sluggishly heaves and churns, and sometimes words and phrases form like muddy bubbles bursting on the surface. And when that happens, the demon talks, the evil force becomes a person. But not just any person, because he speaks in the dialect of the Bavarian Forest, of the dusty market of the village, of a village like Leiblfing, in a dialect broad and homey and pithy, stripped of all the lacy finery of the city tongue. He is a devil medieval in his obscenities, always ready with his "arsehole," "shit," "sow," and "carcass," hunching his back against the verbal assaults of the priest and then turning and mocking him with an "I'll poison you yet" or "Ah, shut up" and a well-applied curse, or upstaging him with an outrageous allusion to that which is most holy, the Virgin. He picks up the Latin phrases, answering them in crude rebuttal as a rebellious vagrant splashing muck on a cardinal's purple. "*Immaculata*" . . . "You with your shit words, save your trouble, not even a sow believes that." "*Saecula saeculorum*" . . . "Not true . . . it doesn't even say that there." "*Educto*" . . . "Go on, babble all day, I'm not leaving." "*Ut discedas ab hac famula dei Anneliese*" . . . "No, no, she belongs to me, get out of here, you carcass, no, she belongs to me, to me." And it is the village that lives and breathes in the answer to the question of why Anneliese was being possessed. "She was not born yet when she was cursed." A woman had done it out of envy. Who was she? "A neighbor of her mother's in Leiblfing." Did she also curse others? Obstinate silence. Peter says that Anneliese's parents tried to check the story out, but the woman had died.

Sometimes the demon gives off flashes of savage humor, as when the priest refers to a martyr who shed his blood and the demon answers, *"Der isch a einer von dene Deppe gewee*—That was also one of those blockheads," or when he comments, after a reference to the *santa ecclesia,* "Those nuns pray and believe nothing, then go to communion, holding out their little paws."

After a while he gets company, and there is a quarrel over who should get Anneliese, and, later, a conspirational dialogue, as if two demons were putting their heads together: "Shit, I'm not leaving, I'm staying . . . ," punctuated by a furious scream. Then there is a hasty stage whisper:

"Let's leave together."

"No."

"Come on, let's go."

"No."

"Then you leave."

"No, I won't."

"Yes, you will too."

"No."

And then a triumphant, "We're not getting out; we'll stick together."

There is a rhythm to the interchange between priest and demon introduced by the repetition of the formulas: God's handmaiden, Anneliese . . . she is mine; you are to leave her . . . no, no, I will not; give your name . . . I won't, I won't. And in between the screams we hear over and over again, as though the demonic body were twisting in a flame, *"Auf Ewigkeit verdammt o-oh*—Damned for all eternity," which rises to the E of *Ewigkeit,* "eternity," lengthens it and hovers there, then sinks down, collapsing toward the prolonged "o-oh," a haunting melody, ever repeated, like a strain from the ghostly dances atop Moussorgsky's Bald Mountain.

The witnesses to the demonic dance—Anneliese's family, Peter, the Heins, the priests—were like careless bystanders in the path of a tornado. Before they thought to run for shelter, they were caught up in the funnel and hurtled across the threshold that separates this world from the other. From then on, whenever they stepped into that upstairs room overlooking the placid vineyards of Klingenberg, they were no longer in their home, or in the saw-mill and the office and the *"Grüss Gott,* Frau Michel, I recommend the pork chops today," returning to those things only when the exorcism session was over. This was a world in which the outrageous was commonplace, where demons spoke and the Mother of God was never far away. Bewildered children in the land behind the rainbow, they began looking around. These demons, what were they like? If you came right down to it, they were not really that unfathomable, almost local people, as it were. They hated familiar places and personalities, such as Schippach, San Damiano, and Barbara Weigand. They knew what was going on in Klingenberg, remarking on how people no longer believed in the sacred books, or in the horrors of hell, or even in the efficacy of prayer. They quarreled with each other and they lied about themselves, about the Virgin, about the date they would leave. And they were not all that powerful, cowering before the Mother of God, who could order them around and could even force them to say things against their will. Most important, the demons had names, they were not faceless, floating nonentities. They had all heard it, how Judas had first owned up to his. "No, you are not to say my name, no, not my name," he screamed. Then came Lucifer and, a bit later, Nero. "I am the third of the confederacy," he announced. With their identities condensing around their names, they became palpable personages, loathsome but familiar. There was no reason why the priests should do all the questioning anymore. The women were emboldened first. The demons often parried them with a curt scream like "Shut up" or "Keep your mouth shut, you dirty sow." But sometimes they did manage to wring an answer from one of them, as when Roswitha accused Judas of having made Anneliese break the crucifix. Judas angrily demurred. "It was that damn dog Lucifer," he growled, "I did nothing." After a while the men also spoke up, albeit more cautiously, commenting on rather than addressing the ghastly presences, and quietly observing. "I get the impression that the stench we used to smell around Anneliese is no longer there," one remarked. "At least I don't smell it when the exorcism is going on." "Right," another one said. "But have you noticed that quite often there is something like the fragrance of incense?" "No," Roswitha countered. "I seem to detect roses, not incense."

Suddenly there was a signal that they could not trespass with impunity in this strange domain. Those sitting next to Anneliese felt a weight bearing down on them, pulling in their backs and making them stiff. Herr Hein and Peter, charged with holding Anneliese down, found their arms getting unbearably heavy; they could not lift them after letting go of her. Thea Hein tried to touch her and then cried out, "My hand . . . what am I to do? I cannot move it! What in the world is the matter with it? Help me, please . . . my hand!"

It was reassuring to have their priests with them. Like mighty St. Michael, they knew how to deal with demons. After an exorcism prayer from them, the weights lifted and the hand became free. They were not above tweaking the demons' noses either, but being more powerful, through the grace of God, than ordinary people, they got away with it. Like the time when Father Renz brought five small bottles, different but unmarked, some filled with holy water from Lourdes and from San Damiano, the others with tap water. He certainly had the demons jumping. They screamed, but only when he used the holy water on them. Or the time when he had the help of a friend of his, a priest living in another town, for a test of the demons. An astounded Peter explained what happened.

One evening, as the exorcism was in progress, Anneliese suddenly looked at Father Renz with an expression of impertinence and provocation and said, "I am not going to say anything." I was taken aback because she had not been asked anything. In the ensuing pause I wanted to call Father Renz's attention to this strange matter, when Anneliese herself came up to him and asked him the same thing. To our surprise, Father Renz said that he had agreed with a bishop that he

should pray the exorcism over Anneliese beginning at seven
o'clock. They would then see how the demon in Anneliese
would react to it. It was at seven when Anneliese had said, "I
am not going to say anything."

It was also a good thing that the priests were so well versed in
Latin. For although the demons knew German well, speaking like
everyone else in Klingenberg, they still often did not seem to understand what the priests wanted, acting like tourists in the local
wine-tasting tavern. Latin seemed more like what they were used
to, and Father Renz made sure that they knew what he was talking about. "Tell me the hour when you will get out," he would
demand in German. And then he would also repeat it in Latin:
"Dic mihi horam exitus tui," which sometimes did the trick. Not
always, of course, for the demons were obdurate and mean.

As could be expected, the demons had been around and picked
up a language or two here and there. Father Renz probably suspected that, for one day he suddenly started asking questions in
Chinese. The demon doing the talking did not like being examined
like that, which was evident from the way he screamed, disre-
spectfully as always, "I am not telling you anything, you damn
dirty sow." Later on he screeched, "If you want to ask me something, ask it in German." Then he added under his breath, "But I
do, too, understand it." And he even mocked the Father by growling, "Sheh, sheh, sheh." Father Alt tried French and Dutch on
him. What he said in Dutch was, "Is there anything in your family
that has any relationship at all to the case and should not become
public?" The answer was as plain as day: "There is nothing like
that."

Sometimes the demons got back at the Fathers, and that could
almost be fun if it did not get too serious. Like the time when Father Renz asked, "Why did you put your hands over your ears?"
and the demon shot back, "Because the prayer is so beautiful." Or
when the demon said that there was noise in the house. "Are you
making that noise?" the priest would ask. "Yea—who else do you
think?" And he would growl and laugh in his compressed and
choppy way, "He, he, he, he."

Mostly, however, the priests would do battle with the demons, and that was terrifying and dead serious. In a mixture of fascination and horror the small circle watched the tilting in the lists. There was always the conviction, of course, that the priests would win and expel the horrid pests that had invaded the girl, their innocent victim. Good always triumphed over evil. But as the days wore on, anxiety pressed on their hearts, for what if this was the first time that evil would win, and the world—all of it—would fall victim to the roving band of evil spirits that was so stubbornly holding out against the valiant priests? Would the Mother of God prevail? She was there, always, dominating the lists from her corner like the white queen sweeping across the chessboard. She could call on allies like Barbara Weigand or Father Pio. She could, and often did, force the demons to say things and give answers they had never intended to, and she did surround Anneliese with her mantle of power. But who could tell what, in the end, would be the divine design? It became very clear that her adversaries were by no means without power of their own. They could dispense with language and frighten everyone with their infernal lowing and screaming and growling. They were cunning, twisting what the priests said by means of invective and obscenity. And they could sight the victims at whom they aimed their spears, while the priests were fighting blindly, seeing no more than the demons' presence in the trembling and twitching body of the girl, in her distorted face—her lips parted to form a rectangle, baring her teeth—in the flashes of hatred and revolt that passed over it like lightning during a storm. "How many of you are there?" the priests would ask. "Really only four," they would mock, and then they would give the names of five, when they had by then confessed that there were six, with Cain, Hitler, and a fallen priest by the name of Fleischmann having also joined up. They would engage Father Renz in a spectral game of blindman's buff, making him grope his way: "I command you, in the name of the Father, the Son, and the Holy Ghost, to tell me who is talking." Silence, or a growl. "Lucifer, is that you?" Another growl, and then a scream. "Adolf, Adolf, are you still there?" A screeching laughter. "Fleischmann, what have you got to say for yourself?" A series of howls shaking the rafters. *"Quot vos estis?*—How many of you are there?" The same frustration.

The demons could also deceive, as when they would utter prophecies about the end of the world, and you really could not tell whether it was a message from the Mother of God or not, whether you should go out and buy extra food and tell your acquaintances about it. And how they would taunt everyone with their promises: Yes, we'll leave; no, we won't; we like it here; yes, maybe next week; and on and on in that way.

Yet the deck of power was obviously stacked against them. You could see that in the hour upon hour of exorcism sessions every second or third day. The priests were great fighters, for one thing, although very different. Father Renz was persistent, patient, willing to labor on endlessly, and strict with the demons despite his old man's gentleness. Father Alt, who was not there so often, fought with his weapons bared. Even the onlookers winced when he would say, with that steely precision of his, "Unclean spirit, in the name of the Father, the Son, and the Holy Ghost I command you to say the truth," and the demons would spit back, "What's your business here anyway, you dirty sow," or "You can't order me around!" But, indeed, the priests can order the demons around. If the priest is tired and sees that Anneliese is tired too, he can demand that the demons relent for a while and give them all a pause. "You want to go on, you restless spirit?" Father Renz says. "Well, you can't. We need an intermission." And the demon gets it. It does not work the other way around. The demons try it on the Father. "Put away that shit." "You mean the rosary?" "Yea." "I won't, because you seem to like it so much," is the taunting reply.

The priest can bait the demon. "You are hard of hearing. Come on, say something." The only defense the demon has is a curse. The priest can insult the demons by telling them what a demon is —the originator of incest, the perpetrator of sacrilege, the teacher of heresies and more—and what can the demon do? The priest can threaten him and hurl an awful prediction: "At the end of the world you will be annihilated, your head will be crushed under the heel of God," and the demon has to cringe.

The priest can catch the demon between himself and the Mother of God as if in a vise and force him to profess a tenet of faith against his will—"Mary, the holy Virgin . . ."—and then give

him an infuriating pat on the head with, "You've said that very
nicely." He can also oblige him to reveal reasons for past mis-
deeds, as when Father Renz gets the demons to talk about how
they manhandled Anneliese at her *Abitur*. "We got her all confused in German literature, in that hour that she was in there, so
she didn't know back from front." Defensively, the demonic
spokesman added, "But we had permission." "She still passed,"
Anna Michel calls out from the back, enraged. "Yes, because she,
the Lady, she wanted that."

The priest can also maneuver the demons into betraying what is
noxious to them and then use it against them like a clever landlord
harassing unwelcome tenants. The onlookers discover that the demons abhor holy water and any consecrated object. They are
afraid of the name Jesus, of patterning one's life after that of the
Savior, and of prayer. "Pray, then nothing can really go wrong
. . . you damn dirty sow you. . . . But luckily not many believe
that anymore." They want no supplications to St. Michael, whose
task it is to fling back into hell the evil spirits roaming the earth
and imperiling the souls. They fear appeals to the guardian angels
and scream in horror when the Litany of the Five Sacred Wounds
of Jesus is intoned: "I greet and adore the sacred wound of your
right hand, oh Jesus . . . ," going into a veritable frenzy when it
comes to the fifth one: "I greet and adore the wound of your sacred heart, and into this wound I place my soul . . ." So those
matters are repeated over and over again, being used as potent
threat, a matchless weapon for evicting the hellish horde. Other
recitations leave the demons cold, as when Father Renz begins
reading from Revelation, the last book of the New Testament,
specifically from Chapter 13, verse 1:

> And I saw a beast rising out of the sea, with ten horns and
> seven heads, with ten diadems upon its horns and a blasphe-
> mous name upon its heads. And the beast that I saw was like
> a leopard, its feet were like a bear's, and its mouth was like a
> lion's mouth . . ."

Although often sounding like snarling beasts at bay when called
names, the demons do not recognize themselves in this description

and unconcernedly go back to quarreling among themselves about which one of them should get to keep Anneliese. Nor are they moved by a reading from St. Luke, Chapter 11, verse 14, where it is told of Jesus:

> Now he was casting out a demon that was dumb; when the demon had gone out, the dumb man spoke, and the people marveled. But some of them said, "He casts out demons by Be-el'zebul, the prince of demons" . . .

Father Renz did not use these texts again.

The most effective weapon the priests have against the demons, however, is that of cross-examination, of asking questions. Here they have the demons at a total disadvantage, for the demons are incapable of doing that back. They experience great difficulties in saying names, yet on occasion they can break through that. But there is never a dispensation from the rule about questions. They are not human, and they can never become equal to humans, because they cannot do what humans do a thousand times a day: They cannot ask. The priests make aggressive use of questions throughout the exorcism. Their questions hammer away at the demons relentlessly in an unswerving barrage, returning mercilessly to key issues like a skillful prosecutor at a murder trial—Why are they here? What are their names? When will they leave? What messages do they have from the Mother of God? Why were they cast into hell?—over and over again, wearing down their resistance until, on that eagerly awaited day, they will finally tire of it all and be cast out.

It was this kind of inquisition that had revealed the second trio of demons, including Cain, Hitler, and a Pastor Fleischmann. Cain remained nondescript and taciturn and Hitler had little to contribute either. Only a muffled "Heil, Heil, Heil," the greeting introduced during the Nazi era, can be heard on the tapes. When Father Renz asked about Hitler, Judas, who was usually the spokesman of the unholy crew, answered, "He, he only has a big mouth but has nothing to say"—an ambiguity in German that may either mean that he has no statement to make or that he is stripped of all power. For a man who whipped millions into action with his hypnotic speeches and whose commands were absolute law, that must certainly be the ultimate punishment. Anneliese related to Peter that while she was still in the Gymnasium a film about Hitler was running in a movie theater nearby. She avoided looking at the pictures advertising the film at all cost because when she had inadvertently done so the first time an unspeakable horror had engulfed her that she had a hard time shaking off.

How "Pastor Fleischmann" came to join the demonic assemblage is quite a different story. In a conversation taped for me in July 1979 Father Alt relates the following:

> When I became pastor of the parish in Ettleben, the church was in bad condition, and I had the task of having it restored. I made a search of the church documents to discover what authority had the "building obligation" for the church [Germany has no separation of Church and State], the community or possibly the state. I went to the repository of the village, the files of which are complete since 1646 and contain scattered documents of even earlier centuries, clear back to the founding of the parish in 1288. As I was going through these papers, I came across a file of the priests who had been pastors in Ettleben since about 1300. In glancing through it, my attention was caught by a notation on a Pastor Fleischmann. The name was entirely unknown to me, and I started reading what this man may have been up to. He was characterized as *concubinarius,* that is, a womanizer; his daughter Martha's gravestone, from the sixteenth century, can still be seen in Ettleben; he was *vino adicto,* in other words, a drunkard; he had four children, and he was a brutal bully. One day he beat a man to death right in the parish house. There was also a report that he had battered a woman so fiercely that for weeks and months she had to remain in the care of the barber in Würzburg.
>
> In the fall of 1975 I went for a visit to Klingenberg. I had been in Ettleben over a year and a half by then, and I was asked, "Well, and how are things in Ettleben, with the restored church and all that?" And I said, half in jest, "Let's see now, of course there have always been bad pastors in

Ettleben, and perhaps I am also one of those; at any rate, there was one who killed another man." This was during a pause in the exorcism. We sat there, relaxing, drinking tea, when suddenly Anneliese began to scream the way she often screamed during the exorcism. It startled me so that the fright stayed with me for hours, and everybody made fun of me. . . . About two or three weeks later I was in Klingenberg once more for an afternoon, because I had business close by. That way I had the opportunity to talk with Anneliese; her boyfriend was there, too, and we had a very nice conversation. Finally I said to her, "I must tell you, you gave me a real scare last time. I couldn't shake it for days. How come you get so excited when the name of Fleischmann is mentioned?" And then suddenly she began to scream. For the first time I saw how she struggled against it, how she smiled, then her face contorted, she smiled again, her face contorted, she went on screaming, and she was barely able to say quickly in between, "Please, don't take it too hard, I can't help it." Peter and I were quite surprised that we were able to see so clearly what she was doing. I immediately gave an exorcistic command, saying that she should be left alone, and it was over. She became quiet. She excused herself, and the two of them prayed for me, because they could see that the matter had upset me so that I became quite pale. That evening, while Father Renz was reciting the exorcism, the sixth demon, by the name of Fleischmann, announced himself, saying that he was the fallen priest of Ettleben who had killed a man. He gave many details, none of which I had mentioned in her presence. . . . It has been maintained since that she must have read the chronicle, but I can prove that at the time in question it was in the hands of the archivist in Würzburg. All those details came from her spontaneously, and it was a surprise for me, a very great surprise. Anneliese herself was tremendously afraid of this particular demon.

And, indeed, we read in Anneliese's diary for October 29, 1975, "The 'Black One' threatened me with his fist."

Father Alt concludes his narrative by relating how from the start he had trouble sleeping in the Ettleben parish house. His skin would crawl as if his bed were an ant heap. He felt that he was being yanked from left to right by two beings, back and forth—the right one won, he added with a chuckle—or as if someone were jumping down on him from four feet above, missing him by very little. There were noises of a person walking up and down the stairs, of doors slamming, and of someone knocking. His housekeeper heard the noises, too, and her little daughter refused to sleep upstairs because "somebody is up there." As he found out in the course of time, even within the memory of the oldest people of the village, the parish house had always been known to be haunted by a tall figure clad in black, wearing a black hat. Father Alt never saw it. He made no conjectures as to whether that figure and the demon Fleischmann that tormented Anneliese were identical or not, nor how he might have gotten to Anneliese in the first place.

Toward the end of the first week in October, it seemed that the strategy against the demons was working. They were beginning to weaken. Their tortured exclamation, "damned for all eternity" had dropped out earlier, and by the session of October 4 the tapes reveal other promising changes. The demons had little to say. There were long stretches of prayers not answered by the demonic, raucous screams, growls, and bellowing. By Monday, October 6, the hellish brigade seemed routed and in disorderly retreat. While still refusing to be cast out, no demon reviled the Latin formulas about the many despicable character traits of Satan enumerated by Father Renz, the father of discord, of lies, of greed and avarice, and not even the rear guard seemed interested in growling at "Anneliese, *famula dei.*" Only toward the end of the session was there a bit of a skirmish, just to keep up appearances. Father Renz thought that there was virtue in pressing on, without giving the demons a chance to rest, and decided to come back the next day, a Tuesday, instead of waiting till Wednesday, as was his custom. Unfortunately, he was to be sadly disappointed. Whether what followed had any causal relation or not, we do need to note that, according to Dr. Kehler's records, he wrote out a prescription for Tegretol for Anneliese on October 7, and on that evening the short truce was broken along the entire front. The shuddering screams were back, separated by only very brief pauses, the growls, the fury at the Latin scolding, the quarrel about which demon was to get Anneliese, the angry shrieks that no demon, no demon at all, was going to leave. They bellowed and screeched. Unbelievably, at one point, one of them gave out a hoarse scream and a high, weird laugh simultaneously.

Some time after the start of the session, which went on with undiminished force for hours, Father Rodewyk came to check up on Father Renz's performance as an exorcist. Thea Hein had arranged for Father Habiger to pick him up at the train depot in Aschaffenburg. Father Habiger was appalled at how Anneliese raged. "Won't the demons kill her?" he asked Father Rodewyk. "No," the latter replied, "there is no record of that. The demons are allowed to torment a person, but not to kill him." When questioned by the court investigator, Father Rodewyk could not recall having made that statement, which Father Renz also said he heard, but he admitted that, indeed, he had written so in his books. He was well satisfied with the execution of the rites and did not stay very long. The demons had paid no attention to the two visitors, but later on we hear on the tape how one of them shouts very loudly, "That one says he doesn't want to go yet," after which there is an unexpected lull. A woman's voice is heard, and whatever she says stops Father Renz's Latin exorcism recital in midsentence.

"Oh hello," he says, "and how are you?" And Anneliese gives a quiet, friendly answer, *"Ach ja, grad gut—*All right, I guess," as if she had just entered through the door. The ensuing conversation lasts only a bit over ten minutes, but it paints the scene much more than the long interchange recorded on February 1 of the following year. From little background interjections we know the young people are there—Roswitha, Peter, Barbara—keeping politely to themselves. Anna and Josef Michel are hovering anxiously over their afflicted child. And we get a feeling for the central presence of Father Renz, who is governing the conversation. He calls Anneliese by the fatherly, friendly *"du—*you," the familiar address, rather than by the more formal *"Sie"* that Father Alt favors. The family and Anneliese, in turn, speak to him in the most respectful of all address forms, the very traditional, very deferential third person, as in "when the Father prays," instead of "when you pray."

Father Renz asks about her appetite, which she says is poor, and then suggests that she is probably not "allowed," that is, prevented by the demons from eating anything that tastes good. Independent as always, she denies that. "And I still sleep on the floor," she volunteers.

"Still? Do you at least spread a blanket for yourself?"

"Yes, I do that."

"Are you being yanked out of bed?"

With a little chuckle she answers, "Oh, I don't even try to get in."

"Well, are you at least able to lie down when you sleep at night?"

"Yes, I can do that. But here I am prevented from doing it. I might try to lie down, but I am immediately forced to sit up again. And *he* also gives me a real bad time in other ways."

"In what way is *he* tormenting you?"

"In all sorts of ways. First of all psychologically, with that frightful anxiety, a mood of annihilation. And by making me hurt, as when the Father makes the sign of the cross over me; that is always unspeakably terrible."

"Do you have any idea where *he* is?"

"That differs. Usually *he* is all around, but sometimes either back there or down low."

Apparently wondering whether, in addition to observing the demon, she also notes things around her, Father Renz asks,

"And when the Father [Father Rodewyk] was here, did you realize that?"

"Yes, I can take in everything. But my memory is getting real weak, it's awful. Like when the Father prays, there are times when I no longer remember exactly what *he*—I mean 'the other one'—said. And when I study—after all, I have to pass those exams—that's a real catastrophe."

The first exam, on theology, is on November 6, then comes teaching religion on the twenty-seventh, political science, German literature . . . she enumerates all the other subjects. Are there many students? Father Renz wants to know.

"Oh yes, about six hundred. And with that many students you need good grades." Sometimes she can get it all into her head fast, "but at other times I sit in front of a single page for hours and get nothing of it at all because I am so terribly beleaguered."

"When did that start, this feeling of being beleaguered? Is that something that you also felt when you were younger?"

"Oh, yes, like from the tenth grade on [1968–69] I had it very strongly."

"Even when you were a small child?"

"No, not that early. But I have noticed it long before now. Only I thought that this was something that everyone felt. I can remember that even years ago I had this funny thing—I don't know how to describe it—like a condition of anxiety and despair, and I had no idea for what reason."

When asked about her reaction to going to church and to mass, she related,

"I was mostly able to go to mass and to communion, but there was often something that seemed to want to hold me back. Sometimes it was really terrible. I was so maltreated psychologically. It was like I wasn't supposed to go in, and if I did anyway, I got sick to my stomach, and I would have to run out of the church. After that I would often feel much better."

Here Anna Michel enters the conversation: "Now, it seems, she really wants to attend the holy mass again, *net*?"—at which point Father Renz interjects, "But that makes no sense yet; she is still being jerked [by demons]"—Anna continues, "but I told her that she would still have to wait." We hear Barbara, from a short distance, answering Father Renz's objection: "Oh, that, that jerking only starts when Father proceeds to pray." And Anna eagerly confirms this fact: "That's right. There is nothing wrong with her now, only when she starts doing that."

"I believe it," Father Renz says. "That's how that starts. But now you are not even made to hit people anymore. That's over, thank God. It was a real torment for you." And from the back comes Josef Michel's voice: "Now we don't need to hold her down either." At this point Anna Michel warms to the subject.

"Well, we had to tie her down a week ago; she was tied down; it was real bad. She said, 'I'll explode today; you'll have to tie me down.'" Thea Hein's voice confirms how awful that was and Anna rambles on. "We did tie her down like that, we tied her hands and feet, because she said it three or four times, 'You'll have to tie me down today or I'll explode.'"

As Anna still talks on—"But today she said, 'I don't have to say anything yet'"—Anneliese says "yes," then heaves a deep sigh, and the demon is back on stage with a growl. It takes Father Renz several seconds before he adjusts to the abruptly changed scene and once more takes up the Latin prayer.

The exorcistic session of October 10 was almost as agitated as the previous one, but by October 13 we can again hear quite a number of growls separating the furious screams, as before the October 7 outbreak. There is a considerable amount of talking, and even some pauses in the demonic utterances, while the prayers are being recited. On this same day Anneliese experienced something entirely new and exhilarating. As if a deaf person were unexpectedly given the gift of hearing or a blind one that of sight, the everyday world around her gained an added dimension. The Mother of God, her champion in the exorcism sessions, came closer and began communicating with her directly, telling her to write down what she was told. So Anneliese started a diary. She was also instructed by her patroness to tell Father Renz about this development. Being the "very together" young lady that she was, she wrote her notes with a sheet of carbon paper beneath and gave Father Renz the copy. Her first entry reads,

13.10.75
Mother of God: "You will often receive inspirations of this kind from me from now on. Things will not always be easy for you. Tell this to Father Arnold. Remember, he is to be your spiritual counselor."

When she told her family about it that day, there were, of course, some doubts. Was it really the Virgin who made her write? Or was it just another demonic trick? Anneliese herself remained doubtful, at first worrying about the origin of these insights, which seemed to appear without her asking for them, and later weighing them critically: Could this have been said by the Mother of God? Was it reasonable to assume that the Savior would hold such a view?

21.10.75
(One thing I must say, even if over and over again I had doubts concerning the origin of the inspirations, that since a little while ago I have a greater desire or need to pray.) [parentheses in original]

If her friends and family were wavering, the demons obligingly disabused them on the evening of Anneliese's first diary entry. "The shit she is writing," one of them snarled, "she," pointing at the Virgin's picture on the house altar, "it's she who charged her to do it." Father Renz's first thought was of Barbara Weigand, who all through life had received divine messages and had written many of them down. Copies of her manuscripts were in his possession, and he promised Anneliese to loan her some of them. It was heartwarming to see her face suffused with enthusiasm: Here was a woman who had had the same experience as she was having now. On October 16 Anneliese wrote in her diary,

16.10.75
Mother of God: "You are going to complete the work of Barbara Weigand." (I resist; I can't do that, I say; she should look for somebody else.)[2]

and on October 17 in the afternoon she added:

Mother of God says: (I am writing along) "I want the dissemination of Barbara Weigand's mission."

That evening Father Renz brought a volume for her when he

[2] The inquiry for beatification of Barbara Weigand was initiated in Würzburg in 1975.

came for the exorcism session. After that was over, it was too late to start reading it, but the next morning she went right to it:

18.10.75, 18:00
Mother of God gives me to understand that this morning I did not act quite properly. (After breakfast I immediately started reading Barbara Weigand's book; did not help with the housework.) Too curious! Duty!

In the ensuing weeks she copied a great deal of material from the manuscript, carefully citing the pages and underlining words in the text, like the one about the Savior saying to Barbara Weigand,

pages 24–25
Why are you worried that perhaps you underwent your suffering for nothing? Let us suppose that no one will believe anything you say. You should know that *your merit stays the same* as if you had *converted the entire world,* remember that.

Or:

page 27
I have told you this morning that I will, over and over again, forgive doubt and anxiety, as indeed I have forgiven you, although you had begged me that I should take away your suffering. I did not do that because you should know that from the moment that you gave me your consent you surrendered to me. I have taken possession of you, not only of your spirit but also of your body, so that I shall dwell in you despite all of your doubts, unless you commit a grave sin. You must know that *if suffering is caused you by other people, they mainly come from me,* and that it is my hand that shapes them so that they *make you suffer.*

It is clear what was on Anneliese's mind: Why was she forced to suffer so much? Would she be punished for doubting that after associating with demons all this time, though against her will, she would still be supported by divine favor? There is also her hope that perhaps there was some hidden meaning in the demons tormenting her, that perhaps, indeed, they had been sent by God to test her, as the people that made Barbara Weigand suffer had been shaped by the Savior's hand for that task.

As if in confirmation, we read the following brief note:

29.10.75
If I am not mistaken, Barbara Weigand said to me yesterday afternoon that I would have to suffer a great deal.

On the day following the first revelation from the Mother of God, Jesus also spoke up in Anneliese's diary. The entry is a single word:

Tues., 14.10.75
Savior: "Stigmata"

In a curious way it foreshadows something that happened during an exorcism session on October 17. During that session the demonic reaction was quite muted, approaching the mood of the one on October 6. Father Renz did everything he could think of to get the demons to react more vigorously, which he considered important if he was to cast them out. Unexpectedly, one of the demons came to his aid and offered a surprising suggestion. Father Renz talked about it in a letter to Bishop Stangl dated October 18, 1975.

Last night 'he' said, "I am commanded by 'her over there'" (he, or, rather, she points to the Mother of God, whose picture is on the table with other things) "that you should venerate the Five Sacred Wounds more." We immediately started that and prayed in adoration of the Five Sacred Wounds. He got tremendously excited about it. He kept screaming "Shut up" in my face.

The scene is striking on the tape: ". . . the sacred wound of your right hand . . ." "Shut up!" followed by a series of furious growls, ". . . the sacred wound of your left hand . . ." "Shut up!" even more ferociously, and more growls, ". . . the sacred wound of your head . . ." "Shut up, stop it, I can't stand that!" Growls and enormous screams. And on, and on. Still, however, the demons did not leave.

There is an intimate, personal quality about Anneliese's revelations, as though the Mother of God were leaning over the fence into Anneliese's reality; as if Jesus were casually passing by, the kindly brother; Barbara Weigand sits in the grape arbor in the garden; Father Pio comes to call for an afternoon cup of coffee; and Satan lurks out of sight, just around the corner. Anneliese herself very carefully delineates the subtleness of her experience. "I see nothing," she writes. "I don't hear voices, exactly," she tells Father Renz. "I am only given to understand" and "I am writing along." Still, the imagery suggests itself.

The Mother of God chats about all manner of things, as they become important to Anneliese. There are those two women from Klingenberg; Anneliese knows them. They were just taken to Lohr, the state mental institution:

16.10.75
Mother of God: "Frau D. is in full possession of her mental faculties, also Frau H. They are suffering for the Kingdom of God."

She foretells the casting out of the demons:

Mother of God tells me once more that I would become entirely free in October. (She had said it before, a few days ago, but at that time I thought that the inspiration was not genuine.)[3]

---

[3] This entry has no date. Father Renz covered up everything Anneliese wrote that dealt with matters other than her religious experience, especially censuring references to other persons. As her confessor he was within his rights to do so, and the Court respected it. At my request he let me have a few additional fragments, such as the one about her father's experience during the war in Russia, quoted earlier, and the important entry about her getting married, given later.

And there is talk about a judgment day. This is a topic of great interest to the demons, too; they come back to it in a number of the exorcism sessions. The angry altercation between the demon and Father Alt on October 10 is an example. After some hints concerning this prediction, Father Alt imperiously demands clarification: "Unclean spirit, I command you, in the name of the Father, the Son, and the Holy Ghost, to say the truth!" After a string of obscenities, the demon answers, forcing the words out with obvious effort:

"A new judgment day is coming, so there."

"What is it going to be like?"

"Terrible, worse than the last two."

"Where?"

"In Europe."

"Where in Europe?"

"In Europe," the demon screeches petulantly, and then turns to another topic, namely, about how repulsive the prayer of the rosary is to him.

The Mother of God had told Anneliese about this earlier.

16.10.75

Mother of God says (I am writing along): "The Judgment is very, very close. Pray as much as you can for your neighborhood, your kin, your friends and benefactors, for priests and laity, for the politicians and the people."

And the Savior also spoke about it:

25.10.75

Savior: "Fetch food into your houses; tell this to everyone whom you know."

In the margin for this entry there is the notation, "I am not sure whether this was from the Savior or from Satan."

There is a feeling, never expressed in so many words in the diary entries, that maybe Mother and Son talk about Anneliese. Perhaps there might even be a conversation to the effect that Mary comes to Jesus and says, "You know, things are not easy for that

young girl." And he answers, "Yes, it's rough. What could we do
for her?" And Mary says, "Maybe she should have some company." So they see to it that she does.

[Date deleted]
The nephew of Father Roth [Siegfried, paralyzed since childhood, who had died the week before] was here with me on
the evening of October 10 and let me know that he was in
heaven. I did not want to believe it at first. In the meantime I
did come round to believing it. First of all, because he came
to me this morning and several times during the day (as far
as seeing is concerned, I see nothing), and, secondly, because
he always tries to give me courage. When I asked him why he
visited me so often, he said, because I also had to suffer, just
as he had to when he was still alive. He promised to give me
support in all my tribulations.

Perhaps Jesus and Mary talk about Anneliese again and Mary
says, "I think I am going to give her a glimpse of the future."
Jesus likes the idea and says, "I will do the same. When all clouds
up, that will cheer her."

[Probably 29.10.75]
Mother of God: "Later you will also have visions," if I understood correctly, as compensation for the satanic countenances [Satansfratzen] that I kept seeing in the past and that
I still see. (I am not sure if this was not something that Satan
deluded me with.)

20.10.75
Savior (said): "There is still something that you have to
write down."
I: "What is that?"
Savior: "What I told you last night."
(I did not want to write that down because I thought it was
from Satan; besides, my nature revolts against the idea.) Sav-
ior demands that I obey, therefore I will write it down.
Savior said: "You will become a great saint."

(I still did not want to believe it, and then the Savior, to prove that I had heard it correctly, made me weep tears.)

[Date deleted]

Savior: "You are going to get married, Anneliese, but that does not matter. I am also in need of holy mothers. Think of St. Monica; she was also a mother (and married), and she was a saint. Or think of St. Elizabeth, your patron saint. In this one way you are not going to be like Barbara Weigand. But you are going to be like her in every other way, in suffering and in sacrifice; you will be a spiritual daughter of Barbara Weigand.

This entry was not contained in the copy of Anneliese's diary that Father Renz prepared for the state attorney's office. He sent it to me later. His hesitation is understandable, since the prophecy contained in it failed. As can be seen from the following quotation from his letter of December 29, 1979, he had a hard time reconciling himself to this fact.

It was a problem for me. How can the Savior say, "You are going to get married," etc., and then He lets her die? It took some time before I understood this. Today I am convinced that this was actually what God had wanted, that she was to get married. But, on the other hand, God allows humans enough freedom so that they can interfere in a person's life with noxious medicines. If this happens, He then carries out his plans in some other way. Anneliese was to become a saint, no matter what. If it could not be through her life and work, through a marriage blessed with children, then it had to be realized through her "demonic martyrdom." God did achieve his goal with Anneliese, even though, due to human interference, she had to travel a different path.

Satan never speaks directly to Anneliese in the form of a revelation, but his presence is often felt, as though he were seen slinking by.

29.10.75
The Savior said I should not answer Satan, even if he
screams at me or accosts me. (That requires self-restraint because he is often very insolent.)

But he also has other matters on his mind, for, being God, the
sadness of the future weighs heavily on him. It is not easy what he
has to demand of her; he had better warn her:

24.10.75
Savior said: "You will suffer a great deal and do penance,
even now. But your suffering, your sadness and desperation,
will help me to save other souls."

And when he sees that the thought is still hard for her to bear, he
gossips with her about a boy in school.

27.10.75
Day before yesterday, in the evening, the Savior showed me a
person who, through my counseling him, could have been
guided to a better path. [lengthy deletion by Father Renz]
Now the Savior wanted to know if I was willing to take
suffering upon myself for this person. I did not say yes right
away. But a few minutes later I did consent, because I felt
prompted to do so, entirely voluntarily. The Savior also
promised me that I would come out purified from this suffering, and that I would not fall. (I was afraid that it might be
too difficult.)

29.10.75
I'll still have to add something concerning the matter of
27.10. The Savior showed me exactly when and how I could
have helped this student. When? That was when I was in the
tenth grade in the Gymnasium. Where? At a birthday party
to which I was invited and also this student. He tried to talk
to me, but he also was trying to get fresh, and I did not like
that. Actually, I really disliked him, because in my eyes he
bragged too much. But I did feel, at the time, that he was

looking for help. This is where I failed. I wanted to dance
with somebody else instead of talking with him eye to eye.

29.10.75
(Savior: "You'll find out eventually why I demanded this of
you in such detail.")
(A few minutes later) Savior: "Be patient."
Later:
(If I am not mistaken, then the Savior just said to me that
this was so, because I had, after all, consented to suffer for
this fellow student.)

During October the demons had repeatedly announced, under
pressure from the Mother of God, that they would have to relin-
quish their hold on Anneliese in the course of this month. During
the exorcism session of October 29 they were ordered by the
Mother of God to say that they would have to leave on Friday,
October 31. Anneliese also noted it in her diary entry for the same
day:

29.10.75
Mother of God during exorcism: "On Friday I will come and
chase them away." (This was the meaning of what she said.)

Everyone involved with Anneliese and her unwelcome moles-
tors eagerly awaited the auspicious day. Father Renz had taken a
rest from Tuesday till Friday, and so did Anneliese. In the morning Dr. Kehler wrote out a Tegretol prescription. In the late afternoon the circle of participants began to arrive. As Father Alt
relates the event in his letter of November 13, 1975, to the bishop,

We were all assembled on October 31 in order to be able to
witness the events that had been predicted. We were happy
that, with God's help, on this evening, possibly, we would be
victorious, coming to the end of a long struggle. Earlier I had
called Father Rodewyk in Frankfurt, and he wished us luck.
He warned, however, that even after being expelled demons

might return, and the exorcism would have to start all over again.

The session was to be an exceedingly long one. Its taped record covers four and a half hours. In copying them Father Renz edited out a number of sections where Anneliese was silent. Otherwise it would have been still longer.

The session starts out with a German prayer asking for God's mercy. Father Renz then summarizes, in prayer form, some of the strategies that had worked against the demons, the prayers to the guardian angels, to the saints, and to the souls in purgatory, the Litany of the Five Sacred Wounds. He begs the Mother of God for her intercession, as well as the blessed Barbara Weigand, and asks the Holy Ghost for guidance. He then intones a Latin prayer, and Anneliese emits an audible sigh, inhaling deeply as a swimmer would before diving, and then exhaling. She utters a brief shout, but it is the young girl shouting, not a demon. Once more she takes a deep breath, followed by a scream, "We are not leaving," but again it is the girl. As the Latin prayer drones on, she tries a third time, producing a long, high shriek, painfully tearing at her vocal cords, and then she breaks out into a heartrending sob, high and tortured, interrupted by screams that once more are hers, not the demon's. She stops and breathes rapidly and deeply, cries out "Oooh" in a very high pitch, as if in extreme pain, and then stops altogether.

If those present were startled, there is no evidence of it on the tape. Father Renz goes on with his Latin prayer, intermingled with German exhortations to the demons: "Yield, yield, yield to the Blessed Virgin . . ." But the scream, "*Ja,*" that answers him is once more the girl's.

He continues with the exorcism ritual. There is a long German prayer, followed by a very long Latin prayer, and no reaction at all from the demons. Father Renz tries to egg them on: "Tell me, what is your name? You don't want to tell me?" But he is met by stony silence.

He enumerates the character traits of Satan, finally gives a benediction, then switches into German again: "The Blessed Virgin is going to order you out of here. She is going to chase you away tonight, all of you. Are you all there? You go back to hell so you cannot hurt anyone anymore."

Once again he continues with the Latin text of the grand exorcism. There is a scream, but again it is the girl screaming. Father Renz continues with the Latin prayer for a while, then says, "This evening you will stop, you will all be cast out." At long last, the demon is there, with a growled "Yes."

The Latin prayer rolls on as the monotony of percussion instruments ties together the bars of a melody.

"Why are you tormenting Anneliese?" Long pause. Then the demon answers, "Because that's fun."

"Cain, why are you here? Having fun is not the answer. Do you have permission to be here?" Long pause and Latin prayer, at one point accompanied by a low growl and a scream. Father Renz stops, but the demon has nothing to say, so he continues. The Latin ends and there is a German communal prayer, which on the second tape passes into the Litany of the Five Sacred Wounds. Then Father Renz starts lecturing the demons:

"You have specified the time of your departure. Now I demand that you present yourselves, and that when doing so you will greet the Mother of God. What you have to say is, 'Hail Mary, full of grace.'"

"No," screams a demonic voice.

"I command you to do it."

"No."

"In the name of the Holy Trinity, of the Father, the Son, and the Holy Ghost, I command you to obey."

"No, you dirty sow you." This is followed by a series of shouts and growls.

"I am under the protection of the Holy Virgin. I command you once more to leave." He goes into the Latin text, getting to the character of Satan. The demon comments only with a growl and then falls silent once more. There is another growl, a shout, then an interminable pause, while Father Renz patiently and persistently drums on in Latin. Just when the hearer is almost convinced that the demons will never speak up again, there is a growl, and Father Renz next switches back to German:

"Cain, why did you slay your brother? Why did you become a

murderer?" Then he repeats the same in Latin: *"Dic mihi . . ."*
No answer. The ensuing pause is long enough for him to get
through the entire Latin text, clear to the formula of the casting
out itself, *"non resistas—*do not resist." Still the demon remains re-
calcitrant. Father Renz:

"Cain, in the name of the Holy Trinity, of the Father, the Son,
and the Holy Ghost, I order you to stop tormenting Anneliese."
He repeats it two more times, without any response from the
demon, and so he switches back into the Latin prayer. At the very
end of it, there is a scream.

"Which of you is that? Is that Cain? He is to announce himself
if he is there. Or is this Judas, or Lucifer, or Nero, Hitler, Fleischmann?"

"Yes, very correct," the demon growls, reverting back to his familiar form. But he has nothing more to add, so Father Renz re-
turns to his Latin. It takes another eternity until there is a very
loud sequence of demonic screams and growls. Father Renz comes
to life:

"Lucifer, your hour has come."

"Keep your mouth shut, you dirty sow," followed by a grating,
very long scream and a sequence of shorter ones, until silence
reigns once more. The Latin prayer is like the undyed cloth that
here and there is lightened by the red thread of a sudden demonic
exclamation. Father Renz switches to German:

"I forbid you to torment Anneliese, in the name of the Father,
the Son, and the Holy Ghost." The demon has nothing to say.
Then, against the background of the Latin, comes an inarticulate
scream, followed by an even louder "Keep your mouth shut—ooh,"
some growls, another scream, and more growls, as if the infernal
beast had been sleeping and was now beginning to stir, annoyed at
the constant commotion and worrying. Then nothing.

Father Renz goes back to Latin, on and on, then tries to
threaten:

"We will beseech the three sacred powers to fling you into hell.
We will appeal to the poor souls in purgatory, to the guardian angels, and to all the saints. Let us pray the Lord's Prayer." There is
an answering scream, "No, no, no, no, no," wagging a tail of
growls. "Hail Mary, full of grace . . ." is answered by overlong,

frightening growls. "St. Michael, we pray to you, fling back into hell Satan and the evil spirits roaming the earth and imperiling the souls . . ." is followed by screams and growls. "She will crush your head under her heel . . ."

For some twenty minutes the alternating German and Latin prayers, threats, screams, and growls go on. It is a very disorderly dialogue because the demon does not respect social convention, growling and howling between, under, and over Father Renz's words like a mad dog ducking the kicks and trying to get in a bite. "It's high time for you to go out . . . What have you ever done for us humans? You brought us nothing but torment." Now the demon hits back.

"We're still going to stay," he growls.

"By whose permission?"

"The Lady's," barks the demon.

Father Renz starts the Latin prayer again, then tries another approach.

"It must be very unpleasant for you to stay here. You should be glad to go out."

"Because *there* it is much worse." The demons seem to feel that although their time is running out, they do not have to concede any points by hurrying. Only occasionally do they growl or scream as Father Renz now tries to enlist the help of Barbara Weigand and the guardian angels. The demons' countermove consists of trying to divert Father Renz's preoccupation with casting them out by bringing up other topics. She, the snotnose, they say, she will pass her exams in December. And then there is the matter of that judgment day. There will be crashing and roaring. We won't tell you when. Everything will be destroyed. There won't be any grub. Then the demon spokesman goes back to growling and screaming, a harsh cacophony tearing into long stretches of prayer by Father Renz and by the group. Illogical as always, one demon suddenly announces right in the middle of a Latin exhortation,

"I'll have to go."

"Cain, slayer of your brother, Judas, Lucifer, Nero, Hitler, Fleischmann . . ."

"Let Hitler leave, I'm not going." They continue dawdling, ripping into Father Renz's prayers with screams and growls and answering his injunction—Cain, Lucifer, all the others, you will have to bend your knee before the Mother of God—with a disdainful silence. The parties have been tilting at each other for nearly three hours now, with the demons cleverly eluding the priest's stabs. So Father Renz tries yet another strategy to engage them in hand-to-hand combat, asking:

"I am sure you still have some message for us from the Most Holy Virgin? You have nothing to say? Nobody home? Are you there, all of you?"

"Yes."

"What are you all going to perpetrate tonight? You are supposed to go out. Are you waiting for the hour? It's not going to be long now. Less than three hours and you'll have to leave."

"We'll leave at ten and not before."

"All of you together?"

"One after the other."

Everyone joins in a prayer to the Virgin for assistance. "Pray for us, holy bearer of God . . ." But Father Renz is anxious to keep the dialogue going.

"Who all is here tonight? The Mother of God is here. Is Barbara Weigand here? Yes. Siegfried also? Yes. Who else? The grandma of the snotnose. Who else? Her sister. And some more, too. Who? That one from Italy . . . Father Pio? Yes. "And Theresa of Konnersreuth . . . and Brother Konrad . . . and St. Michael . . . St. Joseph . . . and the guardian angels. . . ."

"Are you really able to see all of them?" Father Renz inquires. Furious lowing, and once more the demons refuse to cooperate any further. Father Renz goes back to alternating between Latin and German and communal prayer. He is getting exhausted and asks for an intermission. "No!" screeches the demon. Father Renz speaks the exorcism. Then, to enliven the proceedings, he has the group sing a hymn to Mary, then another one. The demons growl and howl along, then one blurts out a message from the Virgin:

"I . . . am to tell you something." A volley of screams. "She is happy about all of you." More screams. "Because you kept on praying. You are to continue as much as you can." A finale of screams.

Overjoyed, Father Renz calls upon all to pray the Magnificat,

"My soul doth magnify the Lord," but they do not get to it because the demon screams very loudly, growls, screams again still louder, growls, screams, then goes into a volley of screams never heard before, like a pulsing orgy of tearing and heaving, as though he were about to vomit out his entire insides, stomach, intestines, and all.[4] Father Renz attempts to break into the sequence but cannot. He starts a communal prayer. The screams become somewhat lower, then stop abruptly. He uses the breach.

"It is ten o'clock. The Holy Virgin has commanded you to get out." The demons scream again as he repeats the injunction two more times. "In the name of the Holy Trinity, in the name of the Father, the Son, and the Holy Ghost, I command you go out, never to return." The girl screams, then the demon is back, screams, and blurts out the required confession:

"I am damned because I . . . I administered my office so badly."

"Who are you? Judas?"

"No."

Here Father Alt comes in.

"Fleischmann?"

"Yes . . . I have to go now."

"Into hell?"

"Yes."

Father Renz: "You know what you still have to say?"

"Yes," followed by a string of screams. Once more there is that unbelievably shrill, compressed, enormous retching, and the demon blurts out, "Hail Mary, full of grace." A curious silence descends like a lull in a storm. Then we hear Father Renz say:

"Hail Mary, full of grace. That was the condition. That's what he said. So Fleischmann is gone, Fleischmann is gone. Now it is the turn of the others."

Promptly there is that strident retching, a sigh, more retching, another sigh, twice more, and Father Renz asks:

"Whose turn is it now?"

---

[4] The scene appears so unexpectedly and is so suggestive and powerful that I had to stop the tape to compose myself and try to overcome an urgent impulse to throw up.

"Hitler." Screams and more retching.

"In the name of the Holy Trinity, of the Father, the Son, and the Holy Ghost, I command you to go out." The demon answers with more screams. "Confess why you are in hell." Screams again. "In the name of the Holy Trinity I order you . . ." A huge, vomiting scream. Only after two more commands does the demon admit, between screams,

"Because I killed so many . . . and killed myself . . ." and then fiercely growling, "and now I am condemned—oooh."

"Do you know what you have to say as a farewell?" It takes several more tortured vomits, growls, and repeated commands from Father Renz before he stammers out the formula "Hail Mary, full of grace," the last word ending with a descending sigh and sinking into the abyss.

"Who is the next one?" asks Father Renz. "In the name of the Holy Trinity . . ." He is interrupted by a husky voice,

"I am Cain." Then, after a few low screams, there comes the voluntary admission, "I have slain my brother."

Other than on this point, Cain will not concede defeat easily. His tremendous vomits nearly drown out Father Renz's commands for submission. He tries to pronounce the required Hail Mary, but the effort drowns in a pitiful stutter, and he reverts to screams and a furious, "You arsehole you." Soon afterwards, however, when Father Renz once more invokes the power of the Virgin, he produces his "Hail Mary, full of grace," in a painfully compressed voice, and leaves the scene.

"So, now Cain is also gone," comments Father Renz with audible satisfaction, while another growling signal is already welling up. "Is it now Nero's turn?"

"Yessir, now it's my turn."

Nero gives off horrible lowings, never even paying attention to Father Renz's repeated demands—in the name of the Father, the Son, and the Holy Ghost—that he should confess his sins. Father Renz finally repeats it in Latin. Addressed in his mother tongue, Nero condescends to answer, but he stutters badly.

"I . . . I . . . I . . . I killed the Christians. . . . I lived a lecherous life," followed by more growls.

"Greet the Most Holy Virgin."

"No, no, no, no," accompanied by furious growls.

Over and over again Father Renz has to repeat the command, only to be answered in screams, another retch, more screams. Then Nero says in a rather small voice, "No, I wouldn't like to do that."

Father Renz is in hot pursuit, repeating his command in the name of the heavenly administration again and again.

Nero gives in. With a scream and a growl he repeats the Hail Mary and vanishes with an audible sigh. Father Renz is clearly satisfied.

"So, now he is also gone. Now there is still Judas. He must also yield." He starts the exorcistic command, but there is no answer.

"Judas Iscariot, are you there?" Screams. Father Renz repeats the exorcistic command formula, hears screams, repeats it, there is a screech, and then the growled confession,

"I went to hell because I despaired."

"Because you betrayed the Savior?"

"Yes . . . but I am not going out." He remains adamant even after three more repetitions of the formula, and when Father Renz reminds him that the Virgin will chase him away, he turns on him and shouts that the picture should be thrown out. "In the name of the Father, the Son, and the Holy Ghost, in the name of the Holy Mother of God . . ." Judas stutters a defiant "No . . . no . . . no . . . no!"

"In the name of . . ."

Judas tries to negotiate: "Where am I supposed to go?"

"Into hell."

"No."

"That's where you belong."

"No."

"You deserve being there. You did not want to serve the Lord." Judas can resist no longer. The retching and vomiting is as frightful as before. Once more Father Renz repeats the command, then says impatiently, "Come on, get out." Judas hails the Virgin and sinks below with a sigh. Father Renz relaxes for a few seconds, then says,

"So now he is gone too. Now there is only Lucifer." He pauses briefly to fetch the picture of the archangel Michael from the house altar.

"Here, look," he says. The demon answers with a very small, hoarse voice, "I am not leaving," then screams. He resists stubbornly, making Father Renz repeat the exorcistic formula many times, still without any result. Father Renz changes weapons and calls for the prayer to St. Michael. Lucifer finds this unfair and screams and growls in protest. "Holy archangel Michael, please fling Lucifer into the abyss a second time." Noting that the demon is growling, he presses his advantage. "Holy archangel Michael, defend us in our battle against the deviousness and the persecutions of Satan, be our protector . . ." The others join in a renewed supplication to the archangel, and when they have concluded, Father Renz repeats his command. Although the demon now has to vomit, he still refuses to leave. Father Renz appeals to the Virgin, but to no avail. To Jesus, the archangel Michael, the Holy Trinity—nothing. The demon almost vomits again but keeps saying no. Three more exorcistic commands later, he seems to yield.

"I am damned because I did not, I did not . . . want to serve . . . God. I wanted to rule myself, although I was only a thing created." Then he turns right around and adds, "I am not going."

Father Renz's many commands hail down on the defiant demon. Still he does not throw in the towel. He retches violently, an unbelievable four times in succession. Some of his screams are heard on two registers simultaneously, as though he had two mouths. "You did not want to surrender to heaven, now you have to go to hell." "No, no, no, no." But then he breaks. "Hail Mary, full of grace," Lucifer stutters, compressed as in a convulsion. There is silence.[5]

Anneliese sighs, "Ah—yeh," as if waking from a dream. Muffled voices join in, like people surrounding and comforting her, and Father Renz says, "It is twenty to eleven. Let us sing the Te

---

[5] I was sitting on the edge of my chair. Don't be so sure, I kept thinking. Remember the warning. They may be back. There may be more demons. But, encased in the past and half a world away, the mystery play proceeded on its foreordained path.

Deum." He starts up the German version, *"Grosser Gott, wir loben dich,"* and is joined by everyone present. The clear voices ring out

"Wie du warst zu aller Zeit,
So bleibst du in Ewigkeit—"

"As you were through all time,
So you shall remain in eternity—"

and go through three more verses. Then there is silence, everyone gathering up his thoughts. Father Renz, grateful to the Virgin, wants to thank her too. "Let us also still sing a song to Mary." And they begin,
"Maria zu lieben . . ."
when, as if from the very depths of hell, a growl and a scream break in on them, and a demonic voice says, "I have not gone out yet." The singers are so caught up in their mood that they continue for two more lines before they stop, overwhelmed by the screams. Father Renz asks, "Who is not out yet?"
"I."
Until half past one that night he labored on, trying to cast out the demon, who refused to give his name and said that he had not revealed his presence before. He did not succeed.

CHAPTER
SIX

THE EXORCISM
FAILS

It was a small and dispirited family group that assembled in the upstairs room the following Monday, November 3. Of the priests
only Father Renz was there; the Heins had not come either. Anneliese seemed well enough, saying that she felt wondrously "free,"
but it weighed heavily on everyone's mind that, of course, she was
not. They started the session with the song to the Virgin Mary, the
same one that the demon had so cruelly interrupted when they
were celebrating Anneliese's deliverance: *"Maria zu lieben . . ."*
After Father Renz had prayed for a while, a demon announced
his presence by growling that he would not leave.

"You will if you have to," Father Renz counters.

"That will take a while."

"How long?" Stubbornly, the demon is silent for a long while,
not even honoring the exorcistic prayers with a scream or a low
growl. Then, erratic as always, he is heard again, gloating, "We

really pulled a fast one on you." Father Renz is unflappable.
That's right, he says, the demons did lie to them. Then he makes a
legal point: According to the exorcistic agreement—he then quotes
the Latin text slowly and clearly, with special emphasis on the
salient points—they were all to leave. Why hadn't they? All he gets
from the demon is a vicious growl, "Stop already with that shit."

Otherwise the demon has little to say. Sometimes he growls or
screams, but mostly he just sulks and throws in a few misan-
thropic remarks, such as the statement that Anneliese was not
going to pass her exam. Besieged with more prayer, he says in his
low, hoarse voice,

"You might as well stop."

None of the tried and true strategies work. He will not come
forth with any information on his name, his associates, if any, or
the time of his exit. In the end he remains entirely silent. Father
Renz gives up. "He is asleep. Let's let him sleep. Anneliese is
probably also tired from last Friday, and she has an exam coming
up this week. Maybe we should just stop early today. Is that all
right with you?" There is a murmured assent, and he dismisses
them with the usual, "In the name of the Father, the Son, and the
Holy Ghost, amen." All in all he is not discouraged, despite the
failure to cast the demons out successfully and forever. To Bishop
Stangl he wrote on November 5,

> The Anna Lieser case is a difficult task for me that takes a
> great deal of time and effort. But it also enriches me very
> much. The case is not over yet, but it seems that it will not
> take much longer.

The day after this exorcism Anneliese went back to Würzburg.
She had been prevented by "something" to do much studying for
her test that Friday, so she tried to catch up. She also had to move
from the first to the fifth floor of the high-rise. The Ferdinandeum
was pretty dreary now that Peter had completed all his examinations and was no longer living there, but she did come across some
other old friends. The first one was Maria Burdich, whom she met
in the hall. They talked about the upcoming exams.

"Did you spend a lot of time studying?" Maria wanted to know.

Anneliese shook her head. "No, not really. I don't feel well and find it so hard to buckle down. It's much easier to pray than to study; it seems I'd much rather do that." It was a strange thing to say, the exam being only four days away, and when asked about this time in Anneliese's life, Maria Burdich remembered it.

Anneliese often went to pray during this time, especially to the prayer chapel of Neumünster Church. As soon as she crossed the courtyard between the cathedral and the Neumünster she felt better. She slipped through the side entrance, down the stairs, and past the figure of Christ in his grave. The chapel surrounded her in quiet peace. The low, soft lines of the Romanesque arches, the green plants in front of the niches, the pale glow of the candles—all of it breathed gentle succor. It may have been at this time that she experienced something she told Father Renz about. She said that she went to pray at the chapel and had stayed for three hours. Then she wanted to go home, but a kind voice said to her, "Stay awhile," and she prayed another two hours.

Anna Lippert was back in the Ferdinandeum, too, after the summer recess, as was Ursula Kuzay and Elisabeth Kleinhenz. It was nice nodding to them in the halls. She met a new girl, Mechthild Scheuering, who had lived on the fifth floor for some time. To Mechthild Anneliese looked very tired and apathetic. But when she started talking to her about some of her own problems she was surprised at how much empathy Anneliese showed her, and how much insight she seemed to have into other people.

Two days before the examination Anneliese suddenly felt a need to work. The weight she always sensed was lifted, and she was able to cram, learning a great deal of information in a remarkably short time. She did not find the theology test hard and passed it with a good grade. She was much relieved, and for the first time in a long while she felt that she might be able to go to confession and communion. It had been one of the melancholy aspects of the month of October, and even earlier, that she was prevented from participating in this very intimate, very central part of the mass, for whenever she would get up from her seat to go to the front and take communion, she would become stiff and could not move from the spot. On this day she succeeded, but soon afterwards the old curse was back again.

She went to give thanks in the prayer chapel as well. She wrote as follows in her diary:

8.11.75
Savior: "I am to visit him more often when I am in Würz-burg, and am to take Anna with me. I was glad that you came to see me; quite often there is no one here."

She then continued:

My guardian angel(?) (it most certainly was not Satan) did some real gymnastics with me. He bent me in all directions so that my joints literally cracked, but it was fun. It seemed to me that I was hearing someone say that I had become very stiff (which is true, because Satan continually impedes my movements, so that, for instance, I think that instead of 2 legs I have 2 sticks).

With the next examination on teaching religion looming up before her at the end of the month, she needed reassurance, and her heavenly friend did not desert her:

10.11.75
[text deleted by Father Renz]
This morning:
Savior: "You will pass all your tests (my teacher's examina-tions).

There is more in this revelation, however, and it has nothing to do with schoolwork. Like the rumbling of a distant storm, it continues,

But you are going to be called upon to undergo tests of an entirely different kind. I will give you my grace. You will be true unto death."

Significantly, this prophetic inspiration is the last entry. She did still write down some revelations, but they assumed a different form, less personal, more in the style that she had learned in reading Barbara Weigand's work. She no longer dated this material, but she did number it. Nor did she say from whom it came to her. On February 15 of the following year she handed the four notebook pages over to Father Renz, who faithfully kept what amounts to her spiritual legacy.

1. Everything that you do well, or have done well in the past, is from Me, every good thought, every good deed. Nothing is from you. This is why I let you oversleep (the holy mass) in order to show you that you are not able to do anything by yourself, and in order to humiliate you. You are not to believe that you have accomplished anything. Everything is a gift of My great love for you.

2. Expect everything from Me, everything. I can make the impossible possible. Trust me completely. That honors Me. It attracts Me.

3. Repent of your sins and then believe that I have forgiven you, and go on courageously. Believe in My *great* love for you, do not doubt it; that makes Me very sad. My ways are mysterious ways; you will have to leave it to Me what path I choose for you. Have I not given you many tokens of My love?

4. Be silent! Do not speak so much. Keep a tight rein over your tongue. For you will have to give an accounting of every superfluous word. Love loneliness. Go to social affairs only if it is necessary to show your loyalty to others, not for the sake of pleasure. Also renounce permitted pleasures.

5. Do not worry about the future. Unburden everything on Me. Seek for every minute that you can listen to Me, and fulfill My will and My wish. I love you tenderly. Do the same for Me by fulfilling My slightest wish—by listening to My voice. (The lambs know the voice of their shepherd. I am the good shepherd and I love My lambs.)

6. Believe that I grant every prayer if it does not stand in the way of the salvation of the soul. Often I do not grant the legitimate requests of My children for a long time in order to make them steadfast.

7. Do not become upset immediately if things do not (right away) turn out as you would like. At least try to govern your temper. You do not know what a vexation may be good and useful for. You should be grateful for it. Often I do not grant even legitimate requests to My children, in order to make them steadfast and to let their prayers benefit some sinner. Be patient toward the lack of faith of other people, as I am also patient with you. The patient person and the steadfast one accomplish everything—that which is essential.

8. Pray and plead incessantly for your fellow human beings so that they may also reach their heavenly home.

9. Am I not a loving father who takes care of you?

10. Do not forget what a gift of grace it is that you are permitted to read the writings of Barbara Weigand. Pray that soon the treasury of these writings may become available to everyone.

11. Pray and sacrifice a lot for my priests. Not for nothing did I show you the greatness and the dignity of *every* priest (in San Damiano) so that you shuddered with awe. Consider that even the most unworthy priest is a second Christ. Do not judge anyone so that you be not judged. Leave that to Me.

12. Struggle against temptation; do not surrender. I will not allow it to exceed your strength. How far I will allow temptation to come your way need not concern you. That is up to Me.

One grows with the struggle if you struggle with Me.

Father Renz had cut short the November 3 exorcism session because, as was mentioned earlier, he felt that Anneliese was probably still tired from her exertion during that interminable rite on October 31, and because the demon was asleep—it was for this reason that the latter remained obdurately unresponsive. Father Renz was probably wrong as far as Anneliese was concerned. She never showed any signs of tiredness as a result of an exorcism session, always maintaining that she was feeling very well afterwards. Not even her voice was tired, no matter how much the demons had ranted and raged. She said that they were using her vocal cords, and that she was only a spectator who could not prevent what they were doing with parts of her body. Afterwards it was as though nothing had happened at all as far as her physical strength was concerned. None of it had been consumed. As to the demon, he indeed seemed to have lapsed into a sleeplike stupor. He was still not awake when Anneliese came home from Würzburg the next weekend after the theology examination.

The demon remained somnolent for quite a while into the exorcism session of November 9, which Father Alt also attended. When he finally screams and growls, there is a startling quality of malignant viciousness about him. Only occasionally does he revert back to the old folksy style, as when he breaks out into an angry, growled tirade, saying,

"If the snotnose goes to church once more, that accursed wench, I am going to cause such a furor that everybody is going to come running." Or, as Father Renz keeps pressuring him over and over again—in German, in Latin, in Chinese—to reveal his identity, he says in his inimitable gravelly voice, "Go on, try puzzling it out some more." When his patience finally snaps, he gives a low, threatening growl and says, "You can blab till your mouth is frazzled," adding, almost in a whisper, "I am still not talking."

To irritate the demon further, Father Renz suggests that they all sing the hymn to the Virgin Mary, "*Maria zu lieben . . .*" What follows is a striking musical presentation of the conflict between heaven and hell. The clear voices of Anneliese's sisters ring out in praise of the Heavenly Queen, while the demon screeches and growls along, crosscutting the stanzas, the melody, and the rhythm, so that the effect is one of an affront, a painful insult to the holy, a quintessential blasphemy.

Goaded to the extreme, about an hour after the start of the session the demon finally falls into Father Renz's trap. This comes when the Father plays his hunch and keeps talking about Judas, *traditor,* the traitor. The demon reacts with strident screams.

"Why does it get you mad when I talk about Judas?" asks Father Renz.

"Because I am back."

"Are you Judas?"

"*Jawohl*—yessir."

In the background Father Alt exclaims,

"So that's it. Who permitted you to return?"

"Who—who—who—do you think?"

"Who already?"

"The exalted Lady."

But he will not give much more information, saying he will wait and see what the bishop's reaction is to all that has transpired. Further questions pass him by, and he begins to scream about his damnation. Once more a sense of foreboding and of disintegration pervades the scene, for although he talks about being eternally damned, as before, it is not the striking melody of the early exorcisms welling up from the fires of hell. Instead of that *"auf Ewigkeit verdammt—o-oh,"* with its eerie lingering on the "E," it is now *"verdammt in all Ewigkeit,"* which has no clear peak, slithering along like a snake and ending in a growled tail.

Later on in the same sessions Father Renz succeeds in engaging the demon in another exchange. We hear that he came back right after having been cast out. The question is not broached as to why the door was still ajar when the priests thought that they had successfully sealed it with the Te Deum. The demon says that there are five of them back, and that they will stay "until the triumph of the Lady." That triumph will consist of the demons being cast out, plus some other things that he refuses to divulge. He does blurt out that the Lady sends the message that they should be patient. Once more everyone sings a hymn to Mary, to the cacophonous growls of the demon, after which the latter lapses into silence. Father Alt's reading of some passages from Barbara Weigand's manuscript gets him riled briefly, but then he does not have much to say anymore and only contributes an angry growl off and on. The picture is also much the same on Monday, November 10.

During the lengthy pauses when the demon had nothing to say Anneliese would sit as though submerged in thought, her eyes half open, her hands in her lap, the upper part of her body bent slightly forward. Sometimes she would swing her legs or rub her fingertips together lightly, giving the impression that she was waiting for someone.

Anneliese went to Würzburg the following day to do library research for her thesis. She came back for the weekend and another exorcism session on November 14, harboring a tired and unresponsive demon. He calls Father Renz a dirty sack now instead of a dirty sow, complains about holy water, which he refers to as dishwater, and answers Father Renz's commands and exhortations with abbreviated invectives or simply with "Shut up." Usually he does not even growl. No wonder that on November 16 Father Renz opens the session with an urgent appeal to the Virgin for strength to bear the cross. The demon doesn't really care whether he is called Judas or not, or whether the girls sing hymns to the Virgin Mary. Father Renz's idea to bring Pope Pius X, the patron of his church in Schippach, into the proceedings, meets with few growls and screams. In the end the demon himself sums it up by growling,

"You might as well stop praying."

"Why?"

"Because it's no use."

On November 17, the following Monday, it was the same.

Back from library research in Würzburg on Friday, November 21, Anneliese found that Father Renz, ever resourceful, now thought that the demon might be goaded into anger and thus become more amenable to the idea of leaving forever if he was shown a picture of Pope Pius X. Just to make sure of the effect, he also brought several small reliquaries along containing relics of Pius X, of St. Vincent, and a fragment of the cross. And, indeed, the demon was greatly annoyed.

"Put away that filth, you damn dog you," he screamed, following it up with strident screeches substantially longer than his usual three-to-four-second rantings. He had clearly been caught off guard but recouped by the next session held on Sunday, November 23, when he declared sullenly that no matter what Father Renz would come up with, "I am not going to stop pestering the snotnose, and neither are the others."

"What others?"

"Nobody."

Father Renz can get nothing else out of him. Later on, however, the demon volunteers that the "exalted Lady" is present. "Who else?" Father Renz presses him. The questioning reveals the other visitors: Barbara Weigand, Father Pio, Anneliese's grandmother, some more of her kindred and antecedents—growl, growl

—and that great-aunt of hers, the stupid one in the convent. In the background there is Josef Michel's voice, happily giving his aunt's name.

"How about St. Josef?"

"Yes, he's here."

"And the guardian angels?"

"*Jawohl,*" growl, scream. And then he adds, with a glint of his old gutter humor, "Can't stand the crowd in here." Father Renz is very grateful. He gets in a couple more archangels and then has everyone pray the Lord's Prayer to thank the representatives of heaven for their interest. Into the "who art in heaven" the demon insinuates in his hoarse stage whisper, "But we are also represented."

Just to make the saintly ones feel as uncomfortable as they are making him feel, he volunteers a bit of revelation.

"Tell the people a message."

"What?"

"Communion while standing."

"What else?"

"Take the Host by hand."

"What else?"

"That's it."

"In whose behalf?"

Sardonically, the demon spits out,

"In ours."

A bit later, apparently still feeling crowded by all those celestial personages in the small, overheated room, he lets it be known that he has company, not just the ones who had been cast out but others who would not speak and whose names he would not betray. . . . No, no, no, no.

"They will have to leave, all of them. And you, too," Father Renz warns him.

"Right, but that will still take a while," and he seals it with some noisy screams and growls. By the November 24 session most of the excitement had subsided once more.

On November 27 Anneliese took her second test, this one on teaching religion. That not everything went smoothly we may gather from Father Renz's taunting remark to the demon during the November 28 exorcism, namely, that the day before the Mother of God was with Anneliese, helping her in her exam, and Therese Neumann of Konnersreuth, too.[1] "And you were there also, right? You caused her a lot of trouble." But the demon does not take up the challenge, talking instead about the synod of bishops, which had just concluded its deliberation, and how he liked the reform decisions that had been made.

Clearly, the demon was bored and unhappy that the circle of faithful had shrunk. The priests from Aschaffenburg hardly ever visited anymore, Thea Hein came less often, and even Father Alt was too preoccupied with his parish to be able to make the long trip over from Ettleben.

"That dirty sow from Ettleben does not come around at all anymore," he complains with the usual growls.

"He can't come today. The highways are iced over."

"That's no good reason. He can make it."

"What is the pastor of Ettleben to do here? Give a blessing? Or help pray?"

"Let him first come, that dirty dog."

"What do you want him to do?"

"I'll tell him."

Despite all this conversation, however, the demon still will not make a conjecture as to the departure date of his crew, lapsing into long periods of growls, screams, and pauses. When, upon being summoned by Father Renz's telephone call, Father Alt came for the exorcism session on the evening of November 30, the demon predictably had no message for him. He sulked in silence, sometimes screamed or growled, or demanded that Father Renz put away the reliquary. When Father Renz exhorted him instead, telling him of the reasons why demons belonged in hell, he broke out into a tremendous series of screams. As the Father persisted in holding the picture of Pope Pius X up to him, he screeched,

"You dirty sow, you filthy dog."

"What now?"

"I'll spit in his face." And he did, right on target. The demon—though not Anneliese when she was free of possession—could hit

---

[1] A Bavarian mystic (1898–1962), a peasant woman bearing the stigmata.

an object with deadly accuracy at three feet or more. Angrily Father Renz demanded that he apologize—without any hope of compliance, of course.

On December 1 Dr. Kehler wrote out another prescription for Tegretol. Gertrud arrived from Fatima, Spain, for an extended vacation, lending her clear voice to the hymns to the Virgin Mary that the family continued singing off and on during the exorcisms. She participated in the session of December 7, for the first time seeing her sister possessed. The demon was his grim self, arguing that there was nothing after this life—which drew an amused "You should know" from Father Renz—and that Jesus never lived. He screamed some, but mostly he just growled rather vociferously, especially when Father Renz appealed to Therese Neumann of Konnersreuth, "the great lover of suffering and penance," to help Anneliese and to protect her. The new patron must have felt kindly toward the tormented girl, for right after the exorcism she came up to Father Renz and said that she thought she could go to communion. It was a big surprise, Peter recalled in his reminiscences. He immediately drove Father Renz and Anneliese to the church in Schippach. Once there, she received the holy communion without any difficulty.

The demon did not comment on the matter during the December 12 exorcism. But on December 14 Father Renz kept baiting him about it. The Holy Virgin was surely very happy that Anneliese could go to communion again, he told him. We are so happy, too. And there is nothing you can do about it. After some growls and screams that the demon, as usual, utters before the Father is done with what he wants to say, he cuts loose:

"If that wench goes again, I'll tear her apart. I'll spit out that thing . . . mumble, mumble . . . Stupid sow." He continues growling and screaming very loudly. Father Renz thinks that he has scored a point and wants to score another by suggesting that the demon let go of Anneliese long enough so that she may say a Lord's Prayer in gratitude for being able to receive communion now. But he has chosen the wrong moment, trying to command the demon in the name of the Father, the Son, and the Holy Ghost. He gets a stony "no" each time. So he gives up and says, all right, if the Mother of God does not order the demon to grant

this wish, they would pray it together without her. Later on Father
Renz asks the demon, as he has done so many times before, when
he would exit.

"Not me, nor the others either."

"Why not?"

"Because we don't have to."

"How long are you still going to stay?"

"A while longer." Father Renz sighs and prays a brief Latin
prayer asking for patience. *"Patientia, patientia,* shit" the demon
mocks him, and utters his infernal screams as Father Renz
professes his belief that in the end the Holy Mother of God will
emerge victorious.

On December 17, 1975, when Anneliese was in Würzburg
during the last week before the Christmas vacation, she went to
Dr. Schleip's office for a checkup. But Dr. Schleip had to be at
court that morning and did not get to see her. "Perhaps she got
tired of waiting for me," she conjectured in her statement to the
Court. According to Anneliese's parents, however, their daughter
had her prescription for Tegretol refilled.

Two days later, during the exorcism session of December 19,
the demon is tremendously agitated. He reviles Father Renz,
screams and rants. Then, after a lengthy pause, he gives off
a series of long screams almost as high and tearing as the vomiting screams of the grand casting out on the last day of October. While those present intone a communal prayer, the demon
rages on, one heaving scream following another, some ten or
eleven seconds long. They begin alternating with growls and come
back in renewed fury throughout the lengthy prayer that Father
Renz recites. He gets to the spot in the exorcism where he has to
ask when the demon will go out. The answer is a scream. Then the
demon croaks,

"Wenn's kracht—when it cracks (or crashes)." He goes on
screeching and growling, and no more questions are answered.
The demon had said this before and subsequently repeated the curious prediction over and over again without ever explaining what
was meant.

Christmas was a joyous one for the Michel household. All the
girls were home, unlike the year before, when Gertrud was in Fat-

ima. And Anneliese was radiant. She said that she never felt better, and she repeated it to Peter, who came to see her.

The last exorcism of the old year, held on December 30, started out like all the others, but Father Renz was not even halfway through reciting the prayer the first time, when the demon let out a prolonged scream that undulated painfully upward, sweeping along the phrase "a-ah-damned." As if in pain, he then blurted out,

"We don't leave because that one won't allow it."

"You mean our Savior?"

"Yes, he won't let us."

"He wants you to stay on?"

"Yes," the demon howls. "We want out—ooh, out—ooh!" The shriek is the same as the one in which he moaned out his "a-ah-damned." In a growl that is at once fearful and eerily plaintive, he continues,

"She goes every day . . . every day . . ."

"To communion?"

"Yes . . . I can't stand it . . . we want out . . . out . . . out . . . out . . . There she goes, kneeling again—we want out . . . out . . . out!" trailing off into a hoarse whimper. Then, in a hurried whisper, he adds, "And he won't let us." The shrieks that follow are a ghostly dirge: "He won't let us out . . . o-oh, out, o-oh," and more inarticulate screams.

Father Renz's voice betrays his consternation, which turns into compassion. "Why wouldn't he let you out?"

"Yes . . . why . . . why . . . why . . . why . . . ," the demon's voice growls downward, as if he were sinking into the grave.

Father Renz begins reciting the Latin exorcism very quietly, very softly, and above the ancient formulas there echoes the desperate horror of the demons' "We want out . . . out . . . out . . . out . . . shriek, shriek, we want out . . . out . . . out . . . out . . . many shrieks, we want out . . . out . . . out . . . out . . . ," with the last "r" of the German "*raus*—out" transmuted into a rolling rrrrrr and a seemingly endless series of screams, rising and falling like a heartbeat racing before death. The last scream stretches as if it would never end. The demon says, "Stop it already," then sinks into a gravelly "We are damned, damned, damned."

Father Renz has regained his composure and, like a stern schoolmaster, begins an exhortation about the demons having brought this upon themselves, which contrasts incongruously with the heartrending, elemental, unresolvable tragedy that the demon has just shaped into sound.

Once more the demon recaptures the previous level of outrageous despair. His shrieks become vomits, but they open no gate through which he can escape from what by now has become an impregnable dungeon. He growls pitiably, then lapses into silence as the bright girls' voices intone, *"Maria zu lieben . . ."*

Feeling quite well, Anneliese went to Würzburg for several days in the first week in January to prepare for the examination in political science. Peter recalled his visit to her:

> We were talking about a private topic. Anneliese was entirely calm and "normal." Suddenly, and without any discernible reason, her face became distorted, she started growling and she hit me. With great effort she was able to tell me quickly that I should sprinkle her with some holy water. I did it, she quieted down instantly, and we were able to continue with our conversation. . . .

It startled Peter because such attacks outside of an exorcism session occurred relatively rarely. They happened only if there were persons near her who knew of the matter. It was for this reason that uninformed people had no idea of Anneliese's possession—something she wanted to keep secret at all cost.

The incident is reminiscent of one that Roswitha described in her notes on her sister, which were written for me in 1978.

> Once we were in the kitchen praying our rosary. My sister Anneliese was also praying it with us. Suddenly she began to scream. We were badly startled because we had not expected anything like that. The strange thing was that Anneliese was surprised, too, about the scream that came from her mouth.

She apologized, saying, "That wasn't me, it was the other one."

During the session of January 9 the demon again broke into the huge, vomiting screams. The effort was unearthly in its magnitude, subjecting the girl's body to a tremendous exertion, but once again it was in vain: No demon was cast out. Soon after Anneliese found that she was unable to go to the front to receive the Host during communion. As Father Renz described it to Bishop Stangl in his letter of January 25, 1976, "Anneliese usually kneels in church. Before and after the communion she can get up as she wishes; during the time when the holy communion is in progress, it is impossible for her to rise from her knees." She had told Father Renz about this renewed attack by the demons in a telephone conversation on January 15, after taking her political science examination, in which she earned a 2, the German equivalent of a B. Father Renz gave an exorcistic command over the phone, telling the demons to desist. But apparently they were not listening.

Since Christmas the incidents during the exorcism when the demon was audible at all—screaming, growling, or talking—had steadily declined. More and more he had lapsed into silence. Occasions when the sessions had lasted four hours or more were a thing of the past, for without his cooperation there was no sense in going on. Still, Father Renz came faithfully whenever Anneliese was home from Würzburg, reciting the prescribed two-hour exorcism, praying, exhorting, commanding the demons to leave, always hoping that perhaps the next time it would happen. One needed to have faith, he felt, and patience, and trust in the help of the Mother of God and all the other celestial personages who had come to assist in casting out the evil forces that had invaded the girl. So he continued coming at least once, sometimes twice, a week. He came on January 16, the Sunday after Anneliese's political science exam. The demon was awake enough for a little while to growl at the Father's Latin prayers and Chinese questions. But when he, Judas, the traitor, was accused of being responsible for Anneliese's inability to participate in the communion, he fell silent. Several communal prayers later he remarked, quite out of context, "It'll be a while before we leave." That was all. The January 19 session was even more discouraging. The demon screamed and growled some, spit out an invective or two, then fell into somnolence. As if too weary to be bothered, he would make an appearance only because the Father insisted on knocking. On January 23 he admitted that maybe he was Lucifer and said that he hated it that Anneliese continued copying from Barbara Weigand's manuscripts. She should be studying. The books should be banned, banned. On January 26 he reiterated the prediction about going out when "it cracks," but when Father Renz insisted that he should name the day, and *veritatem*, speak the truth, he hissed back, "*Veritatem, veritatem,* shit word," growled a few more times, and crawled back into his lair.

It was in the course of an intermission during a similarly dispirited session on February 1 that Father Renz recorded the extended conversation with Anneliese already referred to several times. In a letter written to me on October 9, 1978, he stated,

How happy I am that I made this recording. I had heard earlier that there had been some events during the week before. I took my second tape recorder with me so I could record separately. During the pause (after about two hours of exorcism) the others left the room, and Anneliese and I remained because I expected that she would tell me about it. We stood side by side next to the table. When she began talking I pressed the record button (she saw me do that) and then paid no more attention to the set.

After the introductory remarks, quoted earlier, about the abject terror that had pervaded her the week prior to the conversation, and how it had made her think of the Savior's shudders of death on the Mount of Olives—that is how that must have been, only much worse—she continues,

"The other problem that I had all week is that I was not permitted to eat, or that I could eat only very little. One day I was not allowed to eat at all . . ."
"How did you know that?" [Father Renz asks]
"I feel it. I may be tremendously hungry, and then there is

a barrier there, it is like a compulsion, and I am not allowed
to . . . What also happened was that I was not allowed to
put on any gloves, or a cap, and it was cold outside. It
wouldn't be so bad, but when the weather gets as cold as it
did last week, it sure made me shiver. And during the night I
was not allowed to cover myself properly."

"And he also demanded other things, didn't he?"

"The worst of it was that I had to get undressed completely, although that lasted only an hour, or an hour and a
half. And that terrible compulsion that I am now supposed to
·go to Anna [Lippert]. 'You have to do that now,' with an
urgency—you cannot imagine what that was like, Father. I
cannot explain how that was. Suddenly it was gone. The
pressure—you are to go out now—suddenly gone. I pleaded:
Lord, my Savior, I cannot do that, and Lord, that is not possible. That did not help one bit. I have found that I can
storm the heavens all I want. They are deaf."

"Perhaps you were thinking about what he said, that he
was going to torment those who were slated to assume places
in heaven."

"I don't know whether I did—Oh, Father, I never thought
it would be as cruel as this. I always thought that I would
want to suffer for others so they would not have to go to hell,
and all that, but that it could be this bad and this cruel and
terrible. People think suffering, that's an easy matter, but
when things get really awful, then you don't want to go on,
you don't want to take a single further step."

Father Renz talks about suffering, then asks about her communion problem.

"I am feeling very well right now, but as to communion, I
am trying to go, I try to get up, but it just isn't possible. Father Arnold, it is really difficult to imagine what that is like.
How is it possible that they can force a person like that? You
have no power of your own at all. I don't understand at all
how something like that is possible."

"To feel that you are completely delivered up to evil, to its power?"

"Yes, something like that."

"But just think, now he has power only over your body. It is when the evil one has power over one's soul, that is when things are really bad. You can't do anything against it, you are being forced, so you carry no responsibility . . ."

"I did not have the idea that I was damned. No, I did not think so; that would have been the worst . . .

"On Tuesday evening about nine o'clock I wanted to go to bed, and then I felt it coming. Suddenly I had to knock my head against the wall, something that had happened before. I had to get down to the floor and press my face against it until I could not breathe anymore. And woe to me if I did not do it that way, until I could not breathe. Then I had to do it all over again so often that I nearly suffocated. And then that feeling of abject terror. Then it abated, I wanted to go to bed, and then I got the command to strip. What in the world is that supposed to mean? I don't hear it, I simply realize that I have to do it. It is a true compulsion. I cannot explain how such a thing is possible. Until I was completely undressed. And then the thing started up, that I should go over [to Anna's room]."

"Were you able to offer any opposition?"

"I certainly tried to hold my own, but I would have been forced to do it, except that all of a sudden everything was gone. Even the icy terror was gone. I was allowed to get dressed, but only in my shirt and panties, and I had to sleep that way. I was allowed to use my coverlet but not the thick blanket that I also have on my bed. I was very cold all night. But, still, it could have been worse."

"Were you able to sleep at all?"

"Yes, although I slept restlessly and was half awake. Still, I did get to sleep more or less. I really thought that things would start again, and that I would not get to sleep a single minute. Just as I thought that I would really have to go out [naked]. During the summer I also thought there could be no such thing, nobody can demand of me that I do that, that

I strip naked and appear before other people, and, yet, that is how it was. And so I thought that it was going to be like that again. And suddenly all that pressure was gone once more."

"So you feel that you cannot defend yourself at all?"

"No—I do defend myself, but it does not help at all. It doesn't do anything."

"Someone else commands you?"

"Yes, it is really true, somebody else gives the orders. And it must be somebody from below. But the funny thing is that I am to do this and that, I am to strip, I become aware of it, and I also hear it just a little bit, and then I always think that it must be the Savior. It masquerades itself that way; it is really curious."

"The Savior would not do such a thing."

"Well, this is what I don't understand. For instance, all week long I rubbed open my heel and still I was made to put on the same shoes and walk around in them. The naked flesh was exposed. It hurt and still I had to put on the same shoes. Yesterday I was allowed to change to these here. And that something represents itself as though it were the Savior. Anyway, no matter whether it is the Savior or the other one, I have to do it. I cannot offer any opposition. I try, but it isn't worth beans. The more I resist and struggle against it and don't want to do it, the worse it gets."

"So you think it is the Savior?"

"That is precisely what I do not believe. But the voice that tells me what to do is not bad, it is not frightening, not at all."

"It is known that devils may assume the voice of angels, and so also his, of course."

"I suddenly hear myself addressed: Now listen here, Anneliese, you do this now, something like that. You'll have to put on these shoes, this is how I hear that. I do not hear it spoken in so many words. I am given to know that things must be done in this way. [It is quite different from when] I offered a voluntary sacrifice, say, if I drank only milk or ate dry bread. In that case there was no pressure. I was able to make a free choice."

Father Renz lectures her briefly on the nature of the Savior, the guardian angels, and others, saying that they would not force anyone. Only the evil one exerts force. He remarks that she did not tear the rosary from her neck as these things were going on.

"Yes, I had it around my neck. You are right, I did not even think of that.

"You know, Father Arnold, I never thought that anything like this could ever be possible. Since last summer I know what it is like. I knew it even before then. During the *Abitur* I had it just as bad. Although at that time it was somewhat different, there was this terrible horror."

Father Renz suggests that there were probably also other people living with horror, horror of the future, or young people who have not found their way to God and Christ, although he does not really know this from his own experience. He then wants to know what happened in school on Wednesday.

"Peter was there on Wednesday. I even ate lunch and also supper. It was Thursday that I was not permitted to eat anything. By Friday I was so weak that I could not go to singing class. You have no idea how weak I was, Father. I stood up, then everything turned around me and I was only able to quickly open the window. Then I vomited—bile. After that I was allowed to drink a little milk. I just crouched there. As if I were recovering from a serious illness."

"You were allowed to eat on Friday?"

"Yes, on Friday I came home. Since I have been here, I have been allowed to eat nearly everything. Yesterday I was not permitted to eat cucumbers. But at least I could eat two sandwiches with cold cuts. Really, Father, I would never have thought that I was so dependent on food. I have just now realized how terrible it is when a person may not eat."

"How was that, when you could eat no cucumbers? Was it a compulsion or an invitation to renunciation?"

"In this case it was a compulsion. It was fascinating. I had become aware that I would not be allowed to eat that. Mama or Papa had cut off two slices of cucumber for me to eat, but I did not eat them because I realized that I was not supposed to. I reached for them, but—no. I didn't know what to do about it. I did not want to give them to Papa. I had told him earlier that I had not been allowed to eat, and also that I had been so cold, although I did not tell him everything. He would have scolded me if I had given the cucumber slices back to him. He scolds me. I am supposed to eat. After all, I am not exactly fat. After a while I was allowed to eat them. It happens sometimes that I am not permitted to do something and then I am allowed to. It happens quite arbitrarily."

How about praying, the Father wants to know.

"I have to pray a great deal. There is such a contradiction here. I do it voluntarily, and yet there is a pressure behind it."

After some remarks on the terrors of hell, quoted earlier, she continues.

"It was also that way this past summer. Sometimes I could not pray at all for days and weeks. Then again I had to kneel for hours and pray one rosary after the other until twelve or one o'clock at night, and Papa prayed with me. I was forced to do it. It was terrifying. I felt an abysmal horror, nobody can imagine that . . . That horror may have had something to do with the fact that I wanted to have nothing to do [with sacred things]."
"Not with the picture of the Savior either?"
"Right. Because I connected these things, because he allowed it that things became so cruel."

Father Renz reminds her how the other day he showed the picture of the Savior to the demon in her, and how the demon made her bend this way and that in order to avoid looking at it. Perhaps there had been something of the demon in her when she had become so negative. Anneliese remains unconvinced. "But the Sav-

ior did permit it to happen," she says. And as an afterthought she
adds, "Afterwards things are different again."

It is a remarkable document, this conversation. It would be remarkable if all Anneliese did was to hammer out the difference
between voluntary renunciation and the compulsion she was feeling; or of the relationship between her own pulsing, vibrating experience and the traditions she has learned about the life of her
Savior. It is more than that. She insists on her autonomy, her
young dignity when, for the first and only time, she allows us a
glimpse of her revolt, her questioning of why the Savior—her kind,
older brother—would allow all these cruel things to happen to her.
And throughout this almost casual, friendly confrontation she
manages to put the lustre of immediacy on the timeworn robe of
an ancient faith.

The conversation took place on the first day of February. By
the middle of the month the Mother of God and the Savior had
stopped dictating revelations, and the demon was also increasingly
receding. Father Renz prayed the exorcism many times over Anneliese, but the demon was to respond only until the beginning of
March, immured within his progressively impenetrable keep. During the exorcisms in the middle of February he was so close-
mouthed that at one point Father Renz said, "All right, be silent if
you have nothing to say." The demon emerges to lament, "We are
damned . . . rrrr," and then throws Anna Michel a crumb: "Your
mother, she is now upstairs," and we hear Anna crying in the
background. He does one of his growling, screaming interludes,
then shrieks, "Shit bunch, should all be exterminated."

"Who?"

"You there, you squatting there." He says he knows when he is
going to leave. It is when the Exalted Lady and He will allow it.
When pressed for more information, the screams rise to precipi-
tous heights. After a fractured dialogue about catechists and bishops—which gets nowhere—he retires, growling and screaming,
into his own inaccessible recesses.

Layer by layer the barrier around the demon thickens. On February 20 there is one more heartrending plea: "We want out, out,
out, out," with the screams tearing and lengthening as though
brought up from an echoing well. "Do you want to get out of

Anneliese or out of hell?" Father Renz asks. "Out of both" is the gravelly answer. He works himself into a paroxysm of pitiable shrieks, ending in, *"Wir wollen raus o-oh, o-oh—*We want out," trembling on the "a" of *raus* and moaning down to the double "o-oh."

By February 23 the demon has sunken away even deeper. For the hundredth time Father Renz asks for his departure date. Is it this week? Next week? In a month? From the back Josef Michel asks hopefully, "In time for the Carnival?" All they get is a sullen, "I don't have to say anything."

On the next tape the end of the February 23 exorcism blends into a few screams from that of February 27, some of them so long that they seem to be snaking through canyon walls. Father Renz tries to get things back to normal by insulting the demons. "Miscreants, *degenerati, impii,* how long before you will be cast out?" With no answer forthcoming, the Father reads the second chapter of the Gospel according to St. Luke. The demon provides a few growls and screams to go along with it, saying, "That's some shit you are reading," and with one more scream falls silent. The girls, appealingly harmonizing, start up, *"Maria zu lieben . . ."* We are reminded of a diary entry of Anneliese's from October, where the Savior says that his mother liked how they sang. "So few do anymore." They go on to *"Salve, salve, Regina . . ."* and it is like a farewell. On February 29 the tape contains a single scream and a growl against the backdrop of the communal prayer, then there is silence, and Father Renz's voice comes on with, "Today *he* had nothing at all to say."

CHAPTER SEVEN

THE FINAL MONTHS

On Ash Wednesday, March 3, Anneliese went to Würzburg with the intention of returning home on the weekend. But that proved impossible. While trying to board the train, she became stiff and had to go back to the Ferdinandeum. That afternoon Elisabeth Kleinhenz came to her room to ask about some school matters and found her crouching on the floor in a cramped position, dressed only in a shirt and panties. At a loss as to how to help her, Elisabeth rushed to Mechthild Scheuering's room for help. When they got back to Anneliese and asked her what was the matter, she said that they should leave her alone, that it was nothing bad, and that she would get better momentarily. The girls thought it had something to do with menstrual cramps. They lifted her up, put her into her bed, and covered her. Then they went and called her parents to ask if they should get a physician to examine Anneliese. They were told that the Michels themselves would send a doctor to her. The girls waited around, but when no physician came they called again. They got the same answer, so eventually they gave up, since Anneliese seemed more herself by then.

When, some hours later, Anneliese tried to call her parents, she was "not allowed" to pick up the phone. Peter, who had come to visit her, did it for her. Her parents decided to come and see her, taking Roswitha along. They also invited Father Renz so he could pray the exorcism over her. "I found Anneliese in bed in her room," he declared to the state attorney, "seemingly unconscious. She did not react at all to the exorcism. Her only response was a weak smile, and she did not open her eyes." On the tape he says, "March 7. Today *he* had nothing at all to say."

Roswitha stayed on in Würzburg to care for Anneliese, helped by Elisabeth Kleinhenz and Mechthild Scheuering. Anna Lippert would come by, too, looking in on her when she stayed in bed and calling Father Renz with requests for exorcism prayers. He always complied at home in Schippach. Anneliese said that she could perceive it, and it made her feel better. It was about this time that she told Roswitha that she overheard the demons quarreling among themselves. Then the heinous faces, the *Fratzen,* had faded and disappeared. She also mentioned it to Father Alt, who came to see her as he had done before in February.

Soon, however, she was up and around again. She resumed her thesis research and on March 9 went to see Dr. Wolfert, the general practitioner of the Ferdinandeum. She gave him a brief description of her neurological history, and he renewed her Tegretol prescription for her. "She looked somewhat exhausted," Dr. Wolfert wrote to the state attorney on February 9, 1977, "but she made a psychologically normal impression." She did not tell him of the possession, of course. Nor did she mention what she did tell Peter, namely, that although her feet had healed up, she felt a continuous ache where the stigmata had been. She also perceived the stigmata on her hands as a pain in the middle of her palms, sometimes stronger, then receding again. She ate a lot, to Peter's surprise, often double portions. "How come?" he asked her. She looked a little guilty. "I know this is the Lenten season, and I should be eating less, not more. But I have the feeling that I need to, although I don't know why." Then she added, smiling a little, "But I do renounce some foods that I really like to make up for it."

At home in Klingenberg, Gertrud's vacation was coming to an

end. On April 1 she returned to Fatima without having seen Anneliese again, who still could not travel home. She had even tried the bus, without any luck, always becoming stiff and unable to move. She did, however, go to see Thea Hein, who gave a sworn statement to this effect to the state attorney. The Heins had attended few exorcisms in the new year, at first because Thea Hein had resumed taking pilgrims to San Damiano, and later because her husband fell ill. Thea Hein could not date Anneliese's visit, but she remembered that it was a warm spring day because both of them had worn short-sleeved dresses. According to Thea Hein, Anneliese called her around noon from Sulzbach, where she had gone by train, and Thea Hein picked her up there. It was not until they arrived in the Hein home that Anneliese came out with the reason for her visit. She wanted Thea Hein to promise that she would not suggest that her parents or anybody get a physician to see her, and she should tell Anneliese if anything like that was afoot. "She begged me on her knees," Thea Hein maintained.

I gave her my promise, and she was satisfied. We talked about other things, about her everyday life and about school. I gave her something to eat and drink and drove her back to the train station in Sulzbach. We were almost there when she said, "Watch it, Thea, in a moment there is going to be a strong smell of something burning." And it did happen right then and there. I stopped the car because we could not stand the stench. I had to open all the doors of my Opel-Caravan. We waited about ten minutes, then we drove on to the depot.

When Father Alt came to see her at about the same time, she told him that May and June would be very bad but that July would bring the resolution. "Let's wait and see," he said, and wondered how she could be so sure. But the turn for the worse came even earlier than she had predicted. On the evening of April 13, the Tuesday of Easter week, she felt compelled to go to the chapel of the Ferdinandeum, to kneel down on the floor and stay there until the next morning. Again and again she tried to get up, only to fall back on her knees with such force that the skin cracked open. She tried to call her parents the next morning from a public phone outside the Ferdinandeum, but she could not lift the receiver: Her arm would not obey her. Peter happened to come by and saw her there. On the way back to her room she told him what had happened.

With her prescience about another trial being close at hand, she went to see Dr. Veth that same day to discuss her thesis with him. As he explained to the criminal investigator,

> It was my impression that Miss Michel had dedicated herself to her work with a great deal of industry and personal involvement. From her critical statements concerning some of the publications on her topic, I gained the impression that she had a lucid ability to judge the data, and that she was definitely determined to conclude the third part of her thesis as quickly as possible. . . . As far as her psychological and physical condition during that interview were concerned, I saw nothing whatever to worry about.

The Thursday before Easter was not bad. Most everybody had gone home for the Easter holiday, and the Ferdinandeum was quiet. Only Mechthild was on the fifth floor. About eight in the evening Anneliese went across the street to the Unsere Liebe Frau Church to pray. As she told Peter the next day, she had barely knelt down when a crushing fear descended on her that escalated into mortal terror. At the same time she felt that a thousand weights were pressing her downward into the bench. She broke out into such a heavy sweat that very soon her clothes were drenched. The veins stood out grossly on her hands and, looking at them, she was afraid they might burst and she would start sweating blood. "The death agony of the Lord," she thought. "I am experiencing the death agony of the Savior." She continued praying, all the while feeling the pain of the stigmata. It was midnight before the condition eased and she was able to return to her room. Once there, something knocked her down and she spent the rest of the night on the floor, unable to sleep. This is how Mechthild found her the next morning when she came in to ask where Anneliese had been last night. She helped her up and tried to talk with her, but Anneliese only smiled and said little, as though she

wanted to talk but could not. At noon Mechthild came back so
they could go to lunch together, but she found Anneliese in front
of her little altar, praying. So she quietly slipped out again. When
she returned two hours later, Anneliese was still standing at the
same spot, in the same posture, and did not answer her questions.
Mechthild gave up. At three she went over to the Unsere Liebe
Frau Church for Good Friday observances. From where she was
standing she could see that about ten minutes later Anneliese also
entered the church, curiously dragging her feet. At the end of the
service she remained standing in a prayerful position. When
Mechthild went up to her and asked her if she did not want to
walk back to the Ferdinandeum with her, there was no reaction
from Anneliese. So she went alone, passing by again at about half
past six to see if Anneliese was all right. She found her standing
the same way, her hands gripping her prayer book, her eyes
closed, not answering Mechthild's questions. She became seriously
worried and left to get help. In front of the Schönborn-Gym-
nasium, close to the Ferdinandeum, she ran into Peter, who had
just gotten back to Würzburg, and told him what was going on.
Peter found Anneliese standing in the aisle. Her face was totally
rigid, and she did not answer Peter's inquiries. He started watching
her eyes. During the summer, when she had had the experience of
freezing into immobility in the same way, they had agreed that if it
happened again she would talk to him with her eyes. That was a
part of her body she retained power over. From a slight movement
of her eyelids he could see that she did, in fact, understand what
he was saying, but that she just had no power to respond. So he
told her that since she could not move, he would stay with her and
pray for her. He knelt down, and in a very short while he heard a
cracking sound as if all her limbs had been released from their
rigor simultaneously. A few moments later Anneliese came to him
and told him that they could leave. To the right of the rear exit of
this church there was a small side chapel, illuminated only at
Easter, which contained a painting depicting the lament of Christ.
She wanted to see it, so Peter agreed and they stepped up to it together for a short prayer. But when Peter was ready to go, Anneliese was once more immobilized. It took until eight that evening
for her to be able to move. On the way home she told him what

had happened on Thursday, and that she now had an idea what Jesus suffered during the last days of his life. Once in her room, she started shivering uncontrollably, went to bed, and once more became rigid and unable to speak.

Mechthild saw her the next day. She was all right by then, and the three of them, that is, herself, Anneliese, and Peter, had lunch together. Anneliese was able to talk but seemed listless and exhausted. Mechthild went home for a vacation that afternoon, but Anneliese insisted to Peter that she could still not go home. Back in her room, she became stiff again and had to be put in bed. Peter called Klingenberg and asked for Roswitha to come help nurse her sister. Roswitha arrived on April 19 and took over in her gentle yet energetic way. She cleaned up the room, spoon-fed Anneliese, and since she found her very weak, she also walked her to the bathroom. She even told her some jokes; it made her happy to see her sister smile. Most of the time, however, Anneliese lay in bed and sometimes moaned. Peter stayed on and helped too. He and Roswitha discussed the situation several times, agreeing that it would be so much simpler to get Anneliese home and care for her there. But when they tried to get her out of bed and into her clothes, her entire body became rigid and her limbs contorted in a grotesque way, so they gave up on that attempt.

A few days into the week Roswitha encountered Ursula Kuzay in the small kitchenette while she was heating up some soup for Anneliese. Ursula had met her before and asked where Anneliese was.

"In her room, in bed. She does not feel particularly well," Roswitha said. So Ursula went with her to wish her a speedy recovery. It is easy to understand her alarm: Instead of a friend with the sniffles or a languid headache, she saw a stranger rigidly stretched out, arms crossed over her chest, unresponsive as a corpse to her questions and attempts at conversation. "Shouldn't we call Dr. Wolfert?" she asked Roswitha. But Roswitha said she would call a doctor herself if needed, and, besides, a physician would not be able to help Anneliese. She had had something like this before and would recover all by herself in a while. Maria Burdich was no less startled. She had come to Anneliese's room unaware that there was anything wrong with her. She saw Roswitha feed Anneliese some applesauce. Anneliese was flat on her back in bed, her eyes closed, opening her mouth mechanically and swallowing without seemingly knowing what she was doing. "What in the world is going on?" Maria asked. "Nothing, really. Anneliese is just a little off her rocker again," shrugged Roswitha. Then she turned back to Anneliese and asked her if she wanted more applesauce. She could just as well have talked to the doorpost. Maria stepped up to the bed. "Anneliese, you want me to do something? Call somebody? Anything?" She got no answer. "Maybe Anneliese should rest now," Roswitha said. Maria felt that she was not wanted, so she left. When she looked in again a few days later, Anneliese was still in bed, still in the same posture. She was getting ready to leave when Anna Lippert came. "We must get a doctor here fast," Maria said to her. Anna Lippert agreed and promised to call one right away. In fact, she told her as they went out into the hall, she had already called a physician, a man from Ochsenfurt, but he had not arrived yet. In the meantime Elisabeth Kleinhenz had also talked with Karin Gora, so that by now the entire circle of friends around Anneliese had been alerted. Karin got to Anneliese's room while Elisabeth and Mechthild were also there. She tried to talk to her, asked her what was wrong with her. Anneliese did not react. Elisabeth stepped up to her and caressed her hand. Anneliese started laughing in a curious way. She would laugh, stop, and then laugh again, over and over. Turning to Mechthild and Karin, Elisabeth said, "I understand that she is suffering from circulatory problems and that she has had this kind of condition before." Roswitha made no comment. When Karin suggested that they should get a physician, Roswitha said, "Anneliese does not want one. Besides, such attacks always pass within a short time."

Clearly, none of the girls had been let in on the secret about the possession and exorcism. In fact, only Anna Lippert knew. Peter considered her sufficiently committed religiously so that she could be told. He warned her that the bishop of Würzburg had ordered the strictest secrecy in the matter. Loyally, she cooperated with Roswitha in shielding Anneliese from the matter becoming known among her fellow students, helped to nurse her, and kept in touch with Father Renz. Unfortunately, during part of April she was at home with her parents. When she returned at the beginning of the last week of the month, she found out that Anneliese had begun to refuse food and sometimes would moan for hours on end. It was obvious that, given the condition in which Anneliese now was, she would be unable to complete the third part of her thesis, which was due May 5. So she recruited Elisabeth Kleinhenz and the two of them went to see Dr. Veth. He told them that an extension could only be granted by the chairman of the examination committee, Dr. Schröder, on the basis of a doctor's certificate. What was wrong with Fräulein Michel? The girls told him that she was mostly unconscious and did not answer any questions. Did they think he should go and see her? The girls said no, her sister was with her. How about consulting a physician? Apparently their colleague did not want to see one.

During the night of April 30 Anneliese started to scream loudly and incessantly. At two in the morning Roswitha went to Anna Lippert for help. Anna had heard Anneliese scream before, but it had been intermittent, usually when she also contorted her body as if in great pain. But this was alarming. The two girls were especially worried that other inhabitants of the Ferdinandeum would be alerted. So Anna went to a public phone and called Father Renz, asking him for an exorcism. When she got back to Anneliese's room, the latter had quieted down, but some of the other girls had woken up and were asking questions. "Did you call a doctor?" "I am going right now," Anna said. She did go to make another phone call, only to Father Alt in Ettleben. He promised to come first thing in the morning.

Next morning—this was May 1—Peter arrived and went up to Anneliese. As he looked down at her, her rigid body relaxed, she stretched a little, and she sat up in bed, talking with Peter in a matter-of-fact way. Later the three of them—Peter, Roswitha, and Anneliese—had breakfast together, and Anneliese even went to the kitchenette and talked with another girl as if nothing at all had happened. After breakfast Father Alt arrived. He found Anneliese sitting on the table swinging her legs, drinking Kaba (a chocolaty drink), munching cake, and looking gay and relaxed. "You know," she told him later, "if people could have seen me last night, they would have thought I had lost my marbles." "Right," he said, "and if I were not a priest, I would have thought the same." Under the circumstances he suggested that it was best to inform Dr. Veth of what was really going on, that this was a case of possession being treated by exorcism, and he went to talk with him. Given the official involvement of Bishop Stangl, who was also Dr. Veth's superior, the latter felt that there was no need to involve himself. He did ask about medical care for Anneliese. Father Alt briefly outlined for him all that had been done earlier in that respect.

Consulting with the young people later, Father Alt made it clear that he thought it unwise if Anneliese stayed in the Ferdinandeum any longer. What if another attack happened like the one she had just gone through? It would probably no longer be possible to keep things secret. Could she perhaps come to Ettleben, Anneliese asked? She could work on her thesis there and prepare for her examinations just as easily, and then, if something happened, Father Alt would be there to recite the exorcism. Father Alt agreed. There was room enough in the parish house. He had a housekeeper, and he could ask one of the old women from the village to come and help if need be. Roswitha packed what was necessary, and although Anneliese had been in bed for nearly two weeks, she walked down the five flights of stairs to Peter's car, unaided by anyone. On the way to Ettleben—the highway wound along the Main through small villages, finally passing through Opferbaum and then Werneck—Peter and Anneliese had a long conversation. She repeated what she had also told Father Alt, that she would have to suffer till July, at which time everything would be over.

Father Alt's housekeeper had lunch waiting for them. The weather was beautiful that day. The fields around Ettleben bore a flush of the green of winter wheat. The old apple tree in the courtyard between the church and the parish house was sprinkled with a few early pink blossoms. So after the meal Peter suggested to Anneliese that they take a walk. Before doing this, however, Anneliese wanted to go over and see what the newly renovated church looked like.[1] Having just entered the church, with Peter still looking at the painting of St. Michael on the ceiling, Anneliese's face

[1] This narrative paraphrases Peter's report in his reminiscences.

suddenly hardened into a sinister mask. She said that she would have to stay and pray until the evening mass. Since that was three hours away, Peter tried to talk her into taking the walk and then coming back later, but he could not get through to her. He attempted to lift her from the bench, but she had become so heavy that he could not budge her. So he went to the parish house to summon Father Alt. Together they came back to the church, where Father Alt prayed for her. Under the effect of the prayer she was able to get up, and the three of them returned to the parish house. But once in her room she relapsed into her former condition.

Things got worse during the days that followed. She began grunting for hours on end, at first softly, later ever more loudly. She refused to eat, lay on the floor instead of in her bed, could not sleep, and her body contorted and became stiff. She gritted her teeth and then screamed for long periods. Roswitha was called in from Klingenberg to nurse her, and Father Alt asked an elderly woman from the village to come to the parish house. She slept with Roswitha in one room, and the two of them took turns caring for Anneliese. One time Roswitha came rushing downstairs to Father Alt because Anneliese was half out of bed, her head hanging toward the floor, gasping. When he came to her, she kept pointing at her throat. "They are choking me," she whispered hoarsely. After hours of prayer the attack finally let up.

This effectiveness of his prayer suggested to Father Alt that things might still take a turn for the better. He would point at the apple tree in the yard and say, "Just as that tree is now coming into bloom, the same way all will become well with you too." Unfortunately, a week after Anneliese had arrived in Ettleben, Roswitha fell and tore some ligaments in her foot. She had to enter a hospital and stay there for three weeks. Under these circumstances, with no one available to care for Anneliese full time, her parents decided to fetch her home. They came on May 9, together with Peter and Barbara. On seeing them Anneliese briefly regained control. It did not last. She stiffened up and became so heavy that the men had difficulty carrying her to the car. Once inside, they had a hard time restraining her so that she did not cause an accident.

For the remaining weeks of her life Anneliese was buffeted by waves of rage and pain interspersed with entirely lucid and rational periods. Sometimes she would scream for hours. She was continually restless and slept only an hour or two at night. She was usually unable to eat. This alternated with times when she said, "Quickly, quickly, I can eat," and she would tell exactly what she wanted—bananas, fruit juices, milk. And she caused herself a great deal of pain, rubbing her face against the wall, hitting her head against some hard object, knocking her feet against the bedstead, boxing her own face, or biting herself. To prevent excessive injury, she had her family tie her up at night and sometimes also for hours during the day. Even restrained, she was in perpetual motion, throwing her head from side to side, biting herself in the upper arm, or pressing her face into the pillow until she choked.

The day after she returned to Klingenberg, Father Renz came, at her request, to resume reciting the exorcism. About this session he says on the tape,

It is May 10. Once again in Klingenberg. Today *he* said nothing. Anneliese is on the floor, continually turning so her body describes a circle. But she does not react to the exorcism. She hears everything, but *he* says nothing. She defends herself against being held, or against the laying on of hands. I know that she is pleading for help, and I can feel that her head is burning . . . Please, bring me some water . . . Yes . . .

May 12, 1976. Once more *he* said nothing, and there is nothing to report. Will something happen on May 14?

Today it is May 14 . . . Today it is May 17 . . .

During some of the exorcism sessions Anneliese had to be restrained so that she would not injure herself or others with her biting, kicking, and boxing. Usually this was done by her father and by Peter. But she exerted such force that she could not be prevented entirely from moving. Specifically, she would fall on her knees and rapidly get up again, in one session, according to Father Renz, as often as six hundred times in rapid succession, resting only very briefly in between. Or she would hold onto the door frame and rock back and forth. She no longer uttered any of the screams, shrieks, and growls of the demons, or their familiar obscenities and their commentary that had been imbued with such macabre humor. The new demons, whose presence the old ones had spoken about and whose names they did not know, had taken over, and they did not talk.

Dr. Veth had called earlier in the month to remind the family that Anneliese had missed the deadline for handing in the third part of her thesis. An extension could be granted even at this late date, but she would have to hand in a doctor's certificate. On May 17 her father called Dr. Kehler. He had always felt that Anneliese was being treated too protectively by her family, and therefore said that he would only issue the certificate if he could talk to her himself. They agreed that he would make a house call the following day, but Josef Michel called him soon afterwards and canceled it. Anna Michel then telephoned Dr. Wolfert in Würzburg, but he referred them back to their family physician. Father Alt finally procured one from the Ettleben (Werneck) general practitioner, who knew that while there Anneliese had had a temperature. On the basis of this certificate, her deadline was extended. But even that new deadline was drawing closer, and on May 20 Peter and Roswitha told Anneliese that they would not be able to type the thesis for her if she did not do some work on it. Responding almost immediately, she became completely free, and she went down to the living room with Peter. She dictated a four-page outline to him, showing him where the respective excerpts from the literature for each item belonged that she had prepared earlier in Würzburg. They worked for about five hours. Anneliese formulated her ideas so precisely that the following day Peter and the girls were able to type her paper. After the job of dictating was over, Anneliese fell back into her previous condition. When everything was typed, her signature was required before it could be mailed off to Würzburg. But Anneliese was incapable of staying still long enough to write it. The family said the rosary for her, she was then able to sign, and the thesis was mailed off on May 28.

May 30 was a Sunday. On this day Father Alt came with a visitor. This man, Dr. Richard Roth, was a friend of his of several years' standing. He had heard some of Anneliese's exorcism tapes and they had moved him deeply. He told Father Alt that for the first time in a long while he felt prompted to pray again, that they had changed his life. So he eagerly seized on the opportunity of seeing her himself. Father Alt, for his part, also had an ulterior motive in bringing him. He was deeply worried about Anneliese's enormous restlessness, afraid that she would be unable to sustain such a level of arousal very long, that she might "crack up" or break an arm or a leg. He thought that possibly his friend, who was a physician, might calm her down by giving her a shot of some tranquilizer.

The reports of this visit are so contradictory that it will probably never be possible to sort out what really happened. Even the reasons for the visit are unclear. For while Father Alt was looking for some medical help from his friend, Dr. Roth says that he was only scientifically interested and did not go in his capacity as a physician. He was, he said, interested in the problem of defining medically what "life" was, and it was for this reason that he came to see Anneliese. Reading his article on the topic, which he had published years before and had submitted to the Court, we find it hard to see the connection.

Father Alt came out of the Michel house as Dr. Roth drove up. He watched as his friend took some ampules and a syringe out of his black bag and slipped them into his jacket pocket. He and Dr. Roth walked upstairs together to see Anneliese. Peter says that upon looking at her Dr. Roth exclaimed, "My God, she has the stigmata." Later, under interrogation by the Court, he could not remember having made this statement. In fact, he said he saw Anneliese only from the back. To be able to see the stigmata on her feet, he would of course have had to see her from the front. At any rate, he came while an exorcism was in progress. Anneliese was highly agitated, though mute, being held by Roswitha and Barbara while rocking back and forth. She was quite emaciated and her facial injuries must have been obvious. As Father Renz wrote to the bishop on June 2, two days after this visit,

Concerning Anneliese: She has had to suffer outrageously during the past few days, and also her family, who are close to despairing. Anneliese injured herself so seriously that her left cheek is swollen badly, and both her eyes look as if she had been worked over with a fist, with blue, red, and black discoloration.

How come Dr. Roth did not see that? Father Renz is describing the conditions as he observed them at the same exorcism that Dr. Roth witnessed—that much is obvious from the dates. Besides, looking at some photographs that Father Renz took of these last exorcism sessions held upstairs in the hallway where Anneliese's couch had been moved for her, it is difficult to understand how he could have seen her "from the back or sometimes in profile," as he testified at the trial. There is not enough room where he could have squeezed into. If not there, that is, if he had been on the other side, he would not have seen her from the back either, because Anneliese regularly faced that way. Besides, this was not exactly what he told the state attorney when he was questioned as a witness in December 1976.

> We went upstairs in the Michel house. Anneliese Michel stood in the hallway. She was dressed . . . On both sides she was held by two younger women because she kept wanting to hit her head against the door. I do not remember if she gave off any sounds. In the hall it was very dark [*düster*]. I could not see if her face carried any external injuries. I had the impression that her face was slightly flushed and that she looked "fresh."

In other words, he did not see that her face was severely injured, but he did see, in the very dark corridor, that she looked slightly flushed and fresh. Was that from the back, as he said at the trial?

Whatever happened, Dr. Roth testified in December that he had stayed upstairs at the exorcism only five to ten minutes. By the time of the trial it was three to five minutes. He then went downstairs with Father Alt, they had some coffee, and they talked. Father Alt asked him if he would be willing to come if there was a medical emergency, and he promised that he would. According to those present, he intimated that no physician could do anything in this case: "There are no injections against the devil," he was quoted as saying. He later denied having said this. He made some suggestions to the family on treating the contusions on Anneliese's face, which he later said he did not see. Josef Michel made him a present of a booklet entitled, "Victory of the Immaculate One: Reports About Exorcisms." At Josef Michel's request he also wrote out a certificate for Anneliese, something he did not mention to the state attorney in December. It stated that she would be unable to work for another two weeks. This was important for her, because with it she could delay her student teaching, which, of course, she could not do at the moment. But July was not far away, and the resolution would come, and then she could go back to working toward her career.

For June 7 there is a brief sound track of Anneliese's screaming on the tape. These new demons are oddly terrifying. They freeze the heart, for they vocalize entirely without intonation, that is, the sound floats in an eerie, inhuman way: aaaaaah, then a bit higher, aaaaaah, then lower again and somewhat shorter, aaaaah, as if from a broken instrument, unwavering, insentient. Then Father Renz says, "This is how it was on June 7. It has often been this way before. Sometimes she screamed much more loudly all through the night."

Father Alt came to see Anneliese on June 8. It was to be the last time that he saw her alive. She looked very ill. Her face was sunken, her cheekbones protruding, her nose sharp and prominent. Her parents told him that she ate and drank very little. "But that's how it was last summer also. And then suddenly she started eating again." "Is she drinking anything?" "Only some fruit juices and milk. Once she gulped down nearly two liters." If they tried to force her to eat, she spit it out or pressed her lips together very firmly and rapidly moved her head from side to side. "If only July were here," was everyone's comment. She said that July would bring the resolution. It was high time for all this suffering to end.

In a letter to the bishop dated June 24 Father Alt talks about the visit. He summarizes the self-inflicted torture that Anneliese had undergone, how she had bitten a hole into the wall so that some of her front teeth had chipped, how she had gone through the glass door of the hall with her head—although she did not cut herself doing that—how she kept biting her own arm, and how she bit, boxed, and hit everyone around her. He then brings up an idea that was later to be foremost in the minds of the priests, namely, that Anneliese's suffering made sense only if it was viewed as a "penance possession," something she had to suffer to atone for someone else's sins, perhaps someone in her family.

We did not succeed in forcing the demons to speak again. This seems to me to be proof of the fact that we are dealing here with a typical case of a penance possession. In various conversations that I have had with her recently she gave me to understand that things would get very bad again with her. She was tremendously afraid of this and very sad. But she said that she had to pass through that also. In the case of a penance possession, matters are very difficult for the exorcist, because it is difficult to understand the meaning of the penance. This is what Father Rodewyk, S.J., of Frankfurt told me.

The only consolation one has as an outsider is that many souls are going to be saved through this suffering.

Father Renz continued with his exorcistic prayers, faithfully coming two or three times each week and spending at least an hour or more each time. On June 9 Anneliese's sounds—one cannot call it screaming—had changed again. Monotonously and endlessly she kept vocalizing

After a while the call or moan—there is no good word to describe it—changed into a long-drawn-out
               aaaaha, aaaaha, aaaaha, aaaaha
again without any up and down of the intonation of a natural lan-

---

[2] The vowels have the so-called "continental" sound: *a* as in "father," *o* as in "ordinary."

guage, sometimes a little higher, then again a little lower in pitch, like a ghostly bird shrieking over distant waters. Right in the middle of it—while maintaining the same high pitch and total lack of any intonation—Anneliese says, "Absolution." It apparently caught Father Renz by surprise. He says, "That cannot be done just so . . . ," then starts it up anyway, to the counterpoint of the icy, inexorable moan. Anneliese now switches into an abbreviated form of it

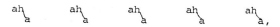

always at the same pitch, then sighs and says in her own voice, with natural intonation, "*I ka ni meh*—I can't go on." Father Renz asks, "How does it feel if I pray? Does it hurt if I pray?"

aa aa aa aa aa
a a a a a ..."I can't ⁺

"Can you still pray?"

aa aa aa aa aa
a a a a a....

Father Renz continues his taped report with, "June 11. Will *he* say or do something today?—June 14, 1976. Last time, on June 14, Monday, *he* has not said anything. Will *he* say something today, June 18?" Josef Michel's voice comes on, saying, "Nice weather. We've had nice weather every day." And while Father Renz says, "Today is June 21," in the background we hear a series of hoarse screams of even length and pitch, mechanical, inarticulate, always the same sound, on and on.

Three days earlier Father Renz had reported to the bishop again. Anneliese's earlier injuries had healed, he wrote, but now she rubbed open her nose, and her knee still had an open sore. During the exorcism she kept going down on her knees, then coming up again, about forty times, then a brief rest, then again about that much, until she was totally exhausted. The previous Friday (July 16) she knelt on the couch, supported herself on her elbows, then jerked up the lower part of her body like a galloping horse. She would stop, rest briefly, then start all over again. On the morning of this letter, that is, June 18, Anna Michel had attempted to do some exorcizing of her own. Josef Michel called Father Renz to tell him about it. "She tried it over and over again, commanding, exorcizing, thinking that she could do something to *him*. Afterwards she slept . . . By evening she had quieted down; she went to mass but had to leave the church and vomit," wrote Father Renz. For Anneliese the day had been frightful, her father told Father Renz. She had raged terribly, had screamed and thrown herself back and forth continually, battering her face and bloodying her nose. Father Renz continues to relate what happened on the last of his tapes.

About a week before her death Anneliese said, "Stop, stop" during the exorcism. At first it wasn't clear to me whether it was she who wanted that or the Evil One, the devil. We were used to such commands from the devil. Therefore I said approximately the following: "Anneliese, we only want to help you. What can we do for you? Do you really want us to stop?" She answered, "Go on." So we continued praying for a while longer.

No matter how terribly she ranted and raged, however, there were always times when she talked with her family and with Peter in an entirely normal manner. One of the subjects they dwelt on longingly was the expectation that all would be over by July. Another topic that came up several times was concerned with getting medical help. Anneliese always rejected the idea. As late as June 30 Roswitha asked her if she wanted her to get a doctor. Anneliese refused. For one thing, she said, she knew that a physician could do nothing for her. For another, she was afraid that she would be sent to the state mental institution at Lohr. "I don't belong there," she would say.

On June 27 Anneliese had a fever. Her family administered cold compresses and it went down again. Josef Michel phoned Father Alt. "It might be a good idea to call a physician," Father Alt suggested. But when Roswitha asked Anneliese she refused. She was worried about the fact that she was still not well enough to go back to Würzburg and do her student teaching. So Josef Michel called Dr. Roth in Frankfurt and had him write out a second certificate, which gave Anneliese another two-week respite. Father Renz continues his taped narration:

> On June 30 she suddenly said, "Please, absolution" during the exorcism. At first I did not understand what she meant, and I asked Peter, "What did she say?" He repeated it for me: "Please, absolution." Of course I immediately gave her the absolution. "Absolution"—that was the last word she spoke to me.

Peter was present at this exorcism, as were Anneliese's parents and her sisters Roswitha and Barbara. Peter measured her temperature before Father Renz started. It was 38.9° centigrade. During the exorcism she insisted on kneeling and getting up again, as she had before. Her father and Peter cushioned her movements as much as they could. Her mother put a pillow where her knees hit the floor. After the exorcism Peter and Father Renz left. Anna stayed for a while. "Mama, stay with me. I am afraid," Anneliese had implored her. Then she also went to bed. Anneliese started throwing herself around again and screamed for a long time. It was past midnight, so her father told her that he had commanded the demons to leave her alone in the name of the Father. It was now the first of July, and the demons were obligated to go out of her. They were supposed to leave her alone henceforth so she could recover her strength. As Josef Michel explained to the police,

> Thereupon Anneliese turned over on her right side and quietly went to sleep. She was quiet all night. Next morning, about seven o'clock, I went to the door of her room. She lay in bed and did not move. I assumed that she was asleep. I went over to the building site. At eight my wife called to tell me that Anneliese had died.

CHAPTER EIGHT

THE TRIAL

One of the first telephone calls Anna Michel made that morning, after telling Josef Michel that Anneliese was dead, was to Father Alt. He was sure that there was a mistake of some sort. Since his friend, Dr. Roth, had promised to be available in an emergency, he got in touch with him in Frankfurt, the location of the latter's practice. Dr. Roth immediately drove to Klingenberg, arriving there early in the afternoon, and found that death had occurred about six hours earlier. He wanted to write out a death certificate but did not have the proper forms with him. So he called Dr. Kehler, who advised him that it might be better if he did not issue the certificate. Instead, Dr. Kehler, as the family physician, went and inspected the corpse. He did write out the necessary document but entered the fact that the death was not due to natural causes. In the meantime Father Alt had also contacted the state attorney's office in Aschaffenburg, and the legal machinery was set into motion. A postmortem examination was carried out. According to the pathologists, Anneliese's death was caused by starvation, possibly aggravated by her tremendous physical exertion during the last weeks of her life. They found her inner organs healthy, including her brain, which showed no damage that could have caused any epileptic seizures, not even on the microscopic level. The fact that her pupils were unusually dilated and that the pathologists thought it curious that her body showed no decubitus ulcers—bedsores, ulcerations of the skin customarily found in patients who had starved to death—was not mentioned later in the Opinion of the Court.

Press releases alerted the news media to the case, which was soon a hotly debated issue. As Father Alt related in a discussion of the trial taped for me in September 1979,

> There were articles by journalists entirely unfamiliar with the case. The anti-Church press seized on it and dubbed the whole matter "medieval." And there were those theologians who, no longer possessing the authentic belief, said, "to hell with the devil." The latter were prominently featured in television, and they wrote lengthy articles for weekly magazines. In the local press any new development always made front-page news.

Yet there was also another commentary, hidden, underground, but persistent. It picked up precisely those arguments that seemed most important to the vociferous detractors of the participants in the *"Fall* Klingenberg—the Klingenberg case," as it was soon referred to, and elaborated on them. There was no devil? Yes, indeed, he existed, and it was obvious from the shape that the world was in that he was more active than ever. Possession was something that nobody really experienced? Not so. A number of persons, both men and women, now reported on being possessed, some by the devil, but most of them by Anneliese. Messages, purportedly from her, spread by word of mouth. It became obvious, it was said, that the demons did not kill her, as was initially assumed. That would have meant that evil had triumphed. Evil can never be victorious. Nor did Anneliese die as a result of the exorcism. She died because she chose to. She offered herself as a sacrificial victim for Germany, for the youth of the country, for the priests. God accepted that. So good triumphed over evil, as it should; it was she who won in the end, and the demons had to return to hell, shamefacedly as always. But before that happened the demons had been forced to work for the cause of good. How appropriate that the Mother of God chose them to give warning to those liberal-minded clerics to mend their ways. Who else was there to tell them to stop tinkering with the time-honored customs of worship, especially the way communion was to be offered? Why, people were not even supposed to kneel anymore. Just think, there was talk of changing the meaning of the Eucharist into nothing more than a shared meal. What good was it if they called it sacred? It was no longer what God wanted it to be, the partaking of the true body and blood of the Lord.

As an expression of this ground swell, people began congregating in Klingenberg to pray the rosary at Anneliese's grave in the cemetery close to the Michel home. Quite unintentionally Father Renz became their hero. He continued giving interviews, published some of his photographs, and even played sections of the tapes for radio and television programs. This added fuel to the controversy while making him the butt of the ridicule and derision of the detractors. Finally, his order advised him to refuse to make any further comment.

As far as the criminal investigation was concerned, the authorities seemed to be dragging their feet. It took the state attorney's office in Aschaffenburg a whole year to gather the evidence, which really did not require any time-consuming detective work since nobody tried to hide anything. There was a rumor that the state attorney's office did not even want to prosecute anybody involved in the matter. But as a result of procedural rules they had to forward their findings to their supervisor, the attorney general in Bamberg. According to Father Alt, nobody had a clear idea of where the matter went on from there, but to the surprise of everyone there was a leak from the Justice Department of the State of Bavaria that there would be an indictment. On July 13, 1977, the Fathers Renz and Alt and Anneliese's parents were notified to this effect. A few days earlier, charges against Bishop Josef Stangl and Father Rodewyk had been dropped.

In the meantime news began spreading over the informal network of those venerating Anneliese that there was a Carmelite nun, a Sister Dorothea, in the Allgäu who had recently been receiving very important new messages for her. She supposedly said that Anneliese wanted to have her body exhumed in time for the trial, which was scheduled to begin in March. The exhuming would bring proof, it was said, that, contrary to what the world and some theologians were proclaiming, there was indeed a hell, demons, a God, a Mother of God, and there existed other spiritual beings. In these messages Anneliese was alleged to have argued that it was true: She had died as a penance to benefit the country, the youth, and the priests. She was chosen to offer proof that there was eternal life. This would become evident during the exhumation, when it would be found that her body had not putrefied, recalling to peoples' minds that there was indeed such a thing as resurrection, because God would resurrect her. The message was to be given to Father Arnold Renz. He should see to it that the exhumation was carried out on February 25.

Anneliese's parents did apply for an exhumation permit, arguing that when their daughter was buried in great haste after the postmortem examination, she was placed to rest in a thin-walled, inexpensive casket. They now wanted to have her remains transferred to a better one made of oak and lined with zinc. The date they requested was February 25. At first the authorities in Miltenberg ruled that it would have to be done with the exclusion of the public, but later they relented and gave permission for a select group of relatives and friends to witness the event. The news spread fast—it was also broadcast over the electronic media—and on February 25, a Saturday, crowds of the devoted and the curious descended on Klingenberg, cameras in hand, to record whatever miracle might occur. A German television network had also sent a crew. Father Alt had come, although he remained in the background. At the appointed time a small procession walked solemnly from the Michel home toward the cemetery. It was composed of Anna and Josef Michel, Thea Hein, Roswitha with her husband, Peter, Barbara, and was headed by Father Renz in priestly robes and stole. Carrying large arrangements of flowers, they walked by the sawmill and entered the cemetery by the main gate. Frau Thora and Dr. Lipinsky, retained by the diocese as the defense lawyers for the priests, were waiting at the grave. In a letter to me dated May 16, 1979, Father Renz relates what happened next.

Anneliese's coffin was dug up. It had a dent on one side, but otherwise it was in good condition. It was carried into the mortuary so her body could be placed into her new coffin . . . Mayor Riermaier came out of the mortuary and said to the Michels (I was standing next to them), "Not surprisingly, after a year and a half, Anneliese is putrefied. She looks terrible. I would suggest that you do not go in. Remembering Anneliese from the past, you have a lovely image of her. Don't spoil it for yourselves . . ." The Michels fell for it and did not go in. Then I was asked whether I wanted to see Anneliese. I immediately answered with an energetic "yes." But at the door of the mortuary I was turned away by the police (there were about thirty policemen present). So I had to leave. Shortly thereafter the new, closed coffin was carried out to the grave and was reinterred.

Those who had stood behind Father Renz during this scene told a slightly different story. According to these witnesses, after saying "yes" Father Renz took a few steps toward the mortuary and then turned back. He simply could not face the possibility that the hoped-for miracle had not taken place, they maintained. But it was Father Renz's version that was picked up by those waiting outside the cemetery. People immediately reacted with anger that Father Renz, "the main man of the exorcism," as one woman said to the television reporter, had not been admitted to the mortuary to see Anneliese. What did they have to hide? Others had supposedly noticed that no cadaverous smell had come from the mortuary. Instead, they said, there was a fragrance of incense or roses. One of the gravediggers, it was maintained, had seen her face and had said that it was white, as if powdered. Another allegedly related that he and his fellow worker had held Anneliese under her arms and by her legs in transferring her to the new coffin. In other words, so people argued in the streets, her bones had held together: She was not putrefied. One person was allegedly overheard saying that he had observed two very well-dressed men talking to each other. One said, "Listen here, this must, under no circumstances, become public, no matter at what cost." What was it that they wanted to keep a secret? Whom were they going to bribe? Who knows, the whispering went, whom they were representing. The state attorney maybe? It was also rumored that the criminal police had photographed the body in the casket, but afterwards nothing was published. "Can't you imagine," people said later, "how eager they would have been to exhibit the pictures if Anneliese had really disintegrated in the coffin?"

The details of the exhumation, considered scandalous by some, heightened the public's anticipation for the trial, which was set to open a month later, on March 30. All the preparatory details were discussed at length in the press, not only in southwest Germany but around the world. According to German law, the selection of the jurors is a complicated process, with lists put together by the city hall in the communities. The city council approves these lists, which should represent a cross-section of the population with respect to age, sex, profession, and religious affiliation. These lists are transmitted to the lower court, where a jury selection committee selects the jurors needed. The president of the county court then decides by lot who is to serve on which days and at which type of court. So the defense lawyers in a case have no voice at all in the selection of the jurors in order to safeguard their clients' rights. Still, it was of interest to know who the jurors were going to be. There were only two: Erich Bäumler, from Alzenau-Albstadt, an engineer, and Josef Becker, a tailor, from Schmachtenberg. Judge Elmar Bohlender would be presiding, and the judges Fritzsche and von Tettau would be assisting him. The prosecution would be handled by State Attorney General Stenger and District Attorney Wagner.

Much publicity in the papers concerned the fact that the Catholic Church gave no moral support to the accused at all. Bishop Josef Stangl was embroiled in a dispute with the officials of his own bishopric over the theological aspects of possession, the existence of the devil, and exorcism. It seemed clear that beyond engaging the defense lawyers for the priests they had decided to throw the accused to the dogs, as it were. This, by the way, was also Frau Thora's impression. For when she attempted to obtain an expert opinion from various theologians on the merits of the case in support of her clients, the reaction was always the same. She could have the opinion, but she would have to accept it unsigned.

Before the opening day of the trial, the press had a field day. Pictures of the accused appeared in all the local papers, together with page-long articles. Given all the notoriety, it was no wonder that early in the day on March 30 there were long lines waiting for the courtroom to open. Most of the curious, and even friends of the accused, had to be turned away because the courtroom had a seating capacity of only one hundred, of which eighty seats had been reserved for the national and international press.

The accused and their friends and lawyers assembled in the St. Agatha parish house, where Father Alt had served as priest before he had become pastor in Ettleben. From there they walked to the courthouse, which was close by. As Father Alt recalled in his tapes,

> The reporter from *Der Spiegel* was there, from *Quick, Der Stern,* and others, some very left in orientation, known to be antagonistic to the Catholic Church. There were reporters from porno sheets and women's magazines. The Norwegian radio system was represented, the Swedish radio, various weekly magazines and, of course, the dailies. There we sat, in the dock, everybody pressing on us, a legion of pointed pencils ready for action, cameras poised. The faces around us seemed gratified to me, as if to say, "There, now we've got you cornered and we can start picking you apart."
>
> Some of the journalists looked as if it really did something for their ego [to know] that they were going to be observers at this particular trial.

At the start of the proceedings, Josef Michel asked to be heard. He said that since this was a case of possession and involved the devil, everyone should first kneel down and pray. The presiding judge, Elmar Bohlender, rejected this suggestion, saying that this was not a church but a court of law. Then some procedural questions had to be taken care of. As KNA (Katholische Nachrichten

Agentur, the Catholic News Agency) reported, the defense made a motion to drop all charges against the defendants, which was rejected. Complaints by the defense against the criminal investigators were termed irrelevant, as was their motion to declare as prejudiced the court-appointed medical expert, Professor Sattes. The confiscation of Father Renz's tapes by the investigator was rescinded. State Attorney General Stenger lodged a protest against that action and demanded that they be reconfiscated because they contained important evidence. According to Father Alt,

> I was the first to testify on the same day. We had agreed among ourselves that this is how we would do it, because I was younger than Father Renz and better able to withstand the stress. Anneliese's parents did not testify in their own behalf. I was completely calm, I had prayed, and I had said, "Lord, this is your affair, not mine. Please guide me."
>
> The questioning went on for four hours that evening. For two hours I spoke without interruption.
>
> In his introductory remarks the judge had said that this was a matter of two civilians facing the Court, not two servants of the Church. What was involved, he said, was that some citizens violated the law; it was a neglect in the sense of the law. It was therefore very important to state clearly that this was not an attack against the faith, against the exorcism. The only point to consider, he maintained, was the fact that the girl had starved to death. But then he wanted to know everything about the exorcism, and I had the feeling I was being exhibited to the public.

We should interject here that during the trial the judge has the right to direct questions at anybody: the defendants, the defense lawyers, or the witnesses. In this trial, apparently, Judge Bohlender more or less assumed the role of the prosecutor. Father Alt continues:

> I also felt I was being ridiculed by questions such as, "I assume, Father, you're not married, are you?" and everybody would laugh.

During the interrogation I said various things that he seemed to find unpalatable. For instance, I said, verbatim, "Your Honor, you may laugh about this, and even fifty million people may laugh about this, if I now tell you that we did cast out six demons. I stand by what I am saying, because I am here representing also the authentic belief of the Catholic Church." He did some swallowing on that, the people in the courtroom sat up, and next morning it said in the newspapers "Even if fifty million laugh . . ."

When he confronted me with the assertion that, to be sure, modern theologians most certainly no longer believed in the devil, I told him that this was not to be considered simply my personal faith, that it was not my responsibility either. I knew what I had experienced, I knew what was written in the Holy Scriptures, which I was thoroughly familiar with, and I referred him to the statements of Pope Paul VI concerning the devil.

This lengthy testimony and exchange between Father Alt and Judge Bohlender is given only a few lines in the KNA report. According to the latter, Father Alt never thought that the girl was dangerously ill. He actually was her spiritual counselor only until 1975. Anneliese conceived of her suffering as penance for the priests, for the German youth, and for a certain unnamed person. She wanted the tapes to become public so that people would believe that there was a devil. Father Renz, according to the same source, stated that if this would have been a physical illness, not possession, he would have been the first to call for medical help. He spoke of the various demons, whom he said he recognized from their different voices. That Anneliese did not want to eat, he said, was due to the influence the demons had on her. Father Alt:

I was later questioned twice more by the state attorney's office. Since I also had to negotiate with them on behalf of the diocesan office, the impression arose that I was the true moving force behind the entire case, and it was I who was responsible that things happened the way they did.

There was some legal maneuvering to get Bishop Stangl to appear as a witness in the case, which was blocked mainly by Father Alt and his defense attorney, Marianne Thora. Calling a bishop to testify was, in and of itself, nothing extraordinary. But both of them felt that it would be unfair to put a frail, gentle old cleric through what was basically a superfluous exercise. What he had to say was fully covered in the files. After a while even Judge Bohlender gave in on that issue, and Bishop Josef was not cited.

On April 5 the physicians who had known and treated Anneliese were called upon to testify. They brought out nothing that they had not already stated to the criminal investigator or mentioned in their letters to the state attorney. The only appearance that generated some excitement was that of Dr. Lüthy, who, as was known from articles on the case, was adamant in denying that he had sent Anneliese to consult a Jesuit. Father Alt:

> Dr. Lüthy came in, very handsome, graying at the temples, six feet tall. But when he started testifying in his clipped "high-German," he oddly deviated from the form set by the other physicians, who had been objective, calm. In response to the question, "Did you say that if Anneliese saw *Fratzen* she should consult a Jesuit?" he answered with obvious agitation, very stridently, "No, I have never said that," so that everybody who heard him had to think to himself, "Well, now, something obviously happened there that was not quite kosher." Anneliese's parents afterwards shook their heads. "We must say, we have never experienced anything like that." "The man did say it," Anna Michel added. "I was there, I heard it myself when he said, 'You'll have to go to a Jesuit.'" And, of course, they would remember, because that was when they finally realized what was going on.

The other physician with whom the defendants were also unhappy was Dr. Roth. He could have done a great deal to take the heat off Father Alt, who had, as he averred, called him in to get medical advice when he started worrying about Anneliese's condition. Father Alt:

Dr. Roth . . . was cited three times. At first he was to appear as a witness for the prosecution. Then the state attorney made some inquiries and he was cited again, and then a third time. He kept vacillating, "Well, I may have been wrong there," or, "It seems that I completely forgot about that" [i.e., that he had written certificates for Anneliese].

The KNA does not mention the Dr. Roth affair. In the Opinion of the Court, which is the final report encompassing the case history, the arguments, and the sentence, Dr. Roth's name is listed under the witnesses who testified under oath only on April 3 and 7 but not on April 17. To gain some idea of the impact Anneliese's case was having, we should try and reconstruct what might have happened to Dr. Roth, a well-known and respected physician. Father Alt maintains that Dr. Roth told him after the trial that he could not testify any differently because people who spoke against Satan, that is, for the defendants, would be punished for it. It almost sounds as if the man had had a conversion experience. The first part of it was obviously what happened when, upon hearing a few of Anneliese's exorcism tapes, he said that it had changed his life, that he started praying again. The second part may have come when he saw Anneliese—very clearly, I think—her emaciated figure, her swollen, battered face. It must have gone through him like a knife, like one of those rare flashes of insight that people sometimes experience. If Satan had that kind of power, how could anyone voluntarily confront it? So he did not. Never at a loss for a witty comment, Father Alt remarked, "Now he is afraid that Anneliese will come out of the grave and take revenge on him. He must have seen too many Dracula films."

After the physicians it was the turn of the young people to testify. Friends still recall with fond amusement how Roswitha would not let herself be cowed. When State Attorney Wagner asked her why no physician was called to attend Anneliese, she exclaimed, "What do you mean, a physician? What for? Possession is not like breaking a leg, you know!" Father Alt:

It was a pleasure to listen to them. Peter and Anneliese's two sisters testified in a manner admired by everyone present.

They were neatly dressed, had a fresh, engaging manner, and
never got tangled in any kind of contradiction on which they
could have been attacked. Anneliese's girl friends also testified in the same style. They told what a nice person she was,
what conversations they had with her, how interaction was
with her. They had seen how she was sometimes sick and
looked ill, and how she spent time in bed, but said that
Roswitha had told them that she had been sick that way before, and it would pass.

On April 5 Judge Bohlender ordered that the letters written by
the Fathers Alt and Renz to the bishop be read in court. The defense had protested against this order, using the argument that
they were confidential and that their confidentiality was guaranteed by the concordat, an agreement between the pope and the
German Government regarding the regulation of ecclesiastical
matters. The state attorney had also agreed to let the matter rest,
but Judge Bohlender insisted. Father Alt:

Bishop Josef had given the letters to the state attorney's
office under the seal of strictest secrecy because he wanted to
be sure that it was understood there that no one had thought
that the girl could die, and so forth. Now they were actually
going to read them in open court. When they started I
jumped up and said, very loudly, very excitedly, "I feel myself exposed by the reading of these letters, as a servant of
the Church and as a priest. I am appealing to our Constitution that these things not be made public. And I am reminding you of the concordat." But they did it anyway.

I should note here that as long as the trial ran we made it
a habit of buying thirteen different newspapers every day to
see how the press was doing the reporting. Beginning with
my first testimony on opening day, I had to bear the brunt of
their attacks. They said I was like an animal trainer, like the
director of a play, the Boss, Rasputin. Now that the letters
had been read, they had more to write about. "Alt Smelled
the Devil," one headline said. Suddenly I was at the bottom
of it all. Increasingly, a condition had developed where we
were systematically run into the ground. It was depressing.

On Friday, at the end of the first week of the trial, the Court heard some exorcism tapes presented by Father Renz in order to demonstrate that the exorcistic prayers produced reactions in Anneliese that, within the terms of the *Rituale Romanum,* indicated that she was possessed. Father Adolf Rodewyk was also called up and testified that of the thousand or so registered cases of exorcism that he had data on, no one ever died. Exorcism, he pointed out, was a prayer, not a magic formula. He was convinced, without a shadow of a doubt, that Anneliese had been possessed. He compared possession states with hypnotic ones, where the subject was without a will of his/her own while the state lasted and entirely normal when the state was not present.

Other witnesses, such as Peter and also Thea Hein, pointed out that Anneliese did not want to consult a physician, that she was deathly afraid of being judged insane and of being committed to the state mental institution at Lohr. Only Ernst Veth, the director of the Ferdinandeum, slanted his testimony against Father Alt, saying that when he came to see him on May 1 to tell him of Anneliese's possession, he didn't mention the need for medical advice. "There was no need to then," argued Father Alt. "She was in good physical condition."

The testimony of Professor Sattes, the expert witness recruited by the Court, was scheduled for the following Monday, April 10. He was a psychiatrist at the Neurological Clinic and Polyclinic of the University of Würzburg, where Anneliese had been a patient. He never knew her personally. The collection of documents submitted by him consists of an essay and a letter in which he answers the question whether Anneliese could have survived had medical help been given earlier.

The Court asked Professor Sattes to comment on the following questions:

1. Did Anneliese Michel suffer from a mental illness and, if so, which one?

2. Could her death have been prevented by consulting a physician, possibly coupled with force-feeding, either in June 1976 or at what time?

3. Could her relatives or other persons who had seen her

shortly before her death have recognized her precarious condition and progressive physical deterioration?

4. Was there any indication on the tapes that she was counseled to reduce her intake of food and drink, or that she was given other instructions that might have caused her death and, if so, when and by whom?

In his essay Professor Sattes summarizes Anneliese's life story and medical history. This is done hastily and quite carelessly. As a result, there are two weighty errors. One is that Anneliese supposedly had two seizures in 1969, when in reality one occurred in 1968 and the other a year later, in the fall of 1969. The other is that Professor Sattes uses the earlier statement of Dr. Lüthy, namely, that he put Anneliese on Dilantin in August 1969, although the files also contained its retraction. Presumably, after checking his records Dr. Lüthy specifically denied this, stating that her Dilantin treatment did not begin until September 5, 1972. The Tegretol medication is mentioned offhandedly, with Professor Sattes overlooking the length of time that Anneliese took this drug. He gives the impression that she took it only until the summer of 1975, when it is obvious from the documents that she continued with it until almost the time of her death. Basing himself on *two false assumptions,* Professor Sattes then states that the Dilantin treatment had "successfully suppressed" the seizures, when, as a matter of fact, she had been free of seizures for two years without the benefit of this medication. This supposedly lengthy suppression of seizures with the aid of Dilantin then resulted in the disease seeking another way out, turning it into a "psychogenic psychosis." As support for this hypothesis, which he states as indisputable fact, Professor Sattes cites Dr. Lüthy as having suspected the start of a paranoid psychosis in September 1973. He did not. He specifically stated on February 9, 1977, "At this point in time it could not be stated with certainty that there was the beginning of a psychotic symptomatology." Dr. Lüthy continued the Dilantin medication and added Aolept drops (periciazine), "which I customarily prescribe in case of neurotic developmental disturbances in children and young people." A neurotic disturbance is not a psychosis.

The summary does admit that there is no indication that anybody encouraged or ordered Anneliese to fast. There is mention of the fact that Anneliese handed in her thesis at the end of May 1976 but not that she dictated the third part of it during that month.

As to the tapes, the report of Professor Sattes speaks of their "great monotony." Anneliese's speech is "unnatural," the sentences being very short. Quite generally, "one gains the impression of a clearly assumed psychogenic posture." It is obvious, he says, that Fräulein Michel "assumes the role of a person dominated by one or the other devil. Some statements make that quite clear." Professor Sattes does not specify that he listened to the tapes himself. He probably did not, for there are many mistakes that he, a well-known and careful researcher, would not have made. It will amuse the reader, for example, to hear that "upon being asked, she admits, in one instance, not only her identification with the devil but also with Hitler or Eichmann" [*sic* for Fleischmann, the ghost of the fallen priest of Ettleben], or that whoever listened to the tapes for Professor Sattes—such tedious tasks are usually delegated to assistants—gained the impression that "snotnose" was a name given to the Virgin Mary. The statement that a comparison between the 1975 and 1976 tapes demonstrated no differences is, of course, patently incorrect, as we have seen, and once more demonstrates the negligence with which the data were handled by Professor Sattes and his staff.

The evaluation of the case repeats the mistakes in the chronology of the medical history. "Epilepsy-like seizures" are called "epileptic, without a doubt," and Dr. Lüthy is given credit for having suspected the start of a paranoid psychosis, or a "mental illness involving delusions." The statement that "repeated electroencephalographic investigations indicated a locus of damage in the left temporal region" gives the mistaken impression that there had been many such tests producing those results, when in reality there had only been two that pointed to any such supposed damage. But Professor Sattes then declares categorically that "the deceased suffered—without any doubt at all—from epileptic seizures." He again repeats the erroneous statement that since she was under anti-epileptic medication since 1969—which she was *not*—there

were no further grand mal seizures. The reason why Professor
Sattes is so anxious to prove, without a shadow of a doubt, that
Anneliese was an epileptic is contained in the following statement:

> The finding that the deceased suffered from epilepsy is of
> great significance because it is a matter of experience that
> particularly persons suffering from this ailment not infre-
> quently exhibit very clear, exaggerated, and in themselves
> pathological religious attitudes, and that within an epilepsy,
> even if there are no more severe seizures, there may be
> depressions as well as delusional episodes.

In other words, Professor Sattes uses the epilepsy theory because it gives him a convenient way, a serviceable model, to account for Anneliese's depressions as well as her attacks and "delusions." The final ten pages of his statement hammer away at these
same ideas. She was suffering from delusional ideas about being
sinful, from hallucinations involving the devil. Such ideas, he says,
can be seen quite often in religious people who suffer from depressions. Her inability to go to church, according to Professor Sattes,
was another psychotic condition. Psychiatrists often have to deal
with persons, he points out, who have the delusion that they are
"possessed," who very graphically tell about how they experienced the control of devils or other evil powers.

> As a rule, these are disease symptoms that may occur
> within the framework of affective psychoses, especially in
> cases of delusions concerning the fear of having sinned, in
> endogenous depressions, also with schizophrenia, or with or-
> ganic brain damage, as in the case of a delusional psychosis
> associated with epilepsy.

Anneliese must have been sick in these terms as early as 1973,
he maintains. She gave reality to affectively strong conceptualiza-
tions. But beginning in April 1976 she lost control, sick concep-
tualizations became delusional ones, so that, according to Professor Sattes, there was now a severe psychotic disease best
characterized as a psychogenic (psychologically induced) psycho-

sis produced by the patient herself, by autosuggestion. The exorcism confirmed her psychotic attitudes and made everything worse. If a priest and a neurologist would have made it clear to her up until April 1976 that she was sick, they could have saved her by talking her into taking nourishment. Beginning in June only forcefeeding could have saved her.

Reduced to its simplest terms, Professor Sattes's proposition boils down to this. Beginning in 1969, Dr. Lüthy's medication successfully suppressed the epilepsy-like seizures that were really epilepsy. Since, we suppose, Anneliese was destined to be sick, the epilepsy now turned into a psychosis, namely, into seeing those *Fratzen,* and, helped by the exorcism, into an even worse mental illness, the possession. The glaring fault of this model is, of course, that things did not happen this way. The seizures were not suppressed by the Dilantin—they stopped on their own—and the *Fratzen* did not arise as a result of the suppression. In fact, they appeared much earlier, as we know from her life history. What is truly astonishing, however, is the authoritative tone with which this reconstruction is offered up as the absolute, unshakable truth. No scientific statement, of course, ever is or can be that. This is a construct, a hypothesis. It could not possibly be anything else.

After Professor Sattes handed in his opinion, the Court asked for such additional clarification as a statement of whether Anneliese would have survived if the exorcism had not been carried out. Professor Sattes was of the opinion that she would still be alive without it. In the conclusion to this supplementary statement he says that from an objective standpoint the accused should have realized that Anneliese needed medical help.

> Subjectively, however, they were of the conviction, on the basis of their religious, nonpathological beliefs, that only divine help was available for the deceased. I do not see how I could designate this belief, probably still held by the accused, as sick.

In his oral statement to the Court, he was considerably less restrained. Father Alt:

Professor Sattes had let it be known that he was not going to talk about religion. But given the facts of the case, he could not avoid the subject. It was his opinion that what the defendants held as belief definitely was beyond normal psychological and religious conceptualization.

Judge Bohlender then requested that Professor Sattes pay close attention to us, because it might be possible that, due to lack of mental competency, he may not be able to sentence us. He mentioned some legal provision—paragraph 20 or 21, I believe. The man, would you believe it, actually made an effort to observe us.

When Frau Thora asked him during cross-examination what he would have done for Anneliese, Professor Sattes answered that he would have tranquilized her, force-fed her, and treated her with electroshock, all presumably against her will.[1]

The defense lawyers thought that it might be useful if they, too, provided a psychiatric opinion formulated by experts of their own choosing. It could be expected to be more favorable than the one supplied to the Court by Professor Sattes. However, Frau Thora encountered nearly the same difficulties as with the theologians: Nobody wanted to have his name connected with the case. She finally located two psychiatrists who were willing to do the job, both of whom were connected with the University of Ulm. "That was far enough away; they did not feel threatened," she quipped. She submitted their names to the Court, and they were subsequently appointed as expert witnesses.

The two men were Dr. Alfred Lungershausen and Dr. Gerd Klaus Köhler, both of the Department of Psychiatry at the aforementioned university. Dr. Lungershausen was the chairman of the department and Dr. Köhler taught there. In addition, Dr. Lungershausen was the director of the University Hospital at Günzburg, while Dr. Köhler was the medical superintendent of a psy-

---

[1] According to a 1979 federal district court decision in Boston, a mental patient has the right to refuse the injection of mind-altering drugs and seclusion at a state hospital. The judge ruled that such measures were an affront to human dignity.

chiatric clinic in Duisburg. Dr. Lungershausen had some minimal interest in possession. His name appears as the second author of an article by Dieckhöfer, published in 1971, entitled "The Problem of Possession: A Casuistic Contribution." Dr. Köhler, on the other hand, had done research on epilepsy. His bibliography lists several articles by him on this topic.

What these two psychiatrists submitted is a complex document consisting of a lengthy joint essay that includes the results of the examination of Fathers Alt and Renz, commented on earlier. There is also a preliminary paper by Dr. Köhler and a summary by Dr. Lungershausen. The long essay is thrown together hastily and without any discernible outline. The bibliography, to start with the last element, is a nightmare. Some of it is in alphabetical order, some of it is not. Various authors referred to in the text cannot be found in the bibliography and, conversely, many items in the bibliography never appear in the text. In other words, the bibliography is padded. It is also instructive for other reasons, for it demonstrates how old, by scientific standards, some of the quoted authorities are. Bräutigam, who is cited for the curious—to say the least—correlation between sleep-epilepsy and humility wrote this article in 1951. Others cited as authorities for the constitution of an "epileptic personality type" or the "psychic structure of epileptics" date back to the 1920s. No wonder: That whole approach has long been discarded. Yet, oddly, it is still trotted out here in great detail in order to cement the shaky arguments for Anneliese being an epileptic. The hypothesis that the perception of odors—what we call "olfactory hallucinations"—was located in the hippocampus of the brain dates back to the late 1800s and is attributed to J. H. Jackson, who is again not referred to in the bibliography.

Their discussion of the tapes covers only a single page out of a total of 103, simply saying that they have nothing to add to Professor Sattes's evaluation. As to the text, it is unedited, tediously repetitious, and the principal point seems to be to give recognition to Professor Sattes. They are completely blind to his obvious inconsistencies. They do note, for instance, that Dr. Lüthy did not start Anneliese on Dilantin until the fall of 1972, yet they agree with Professor Sattes that Dilantin suppressed the seizures. They

repeat his assertion that Dr. Lüthy suspected the start of a paranoid psychosis, which he did not. In 1973, they note, Anneliese
underwent a serious paranoid psychotic episode. In 1975 she developed the delusion of possession. It was not brain damage. It
was a psychogenic psychosis. And on and on in this way for
many pages. When taking off on their own, they get tangled in
contradictions, as they had in their evaluations of the Fathers. The
priests offered content and form for Anneliese's psychotic behavior—in the exorcism, that is (page 81 of the joint essay). Both
priests evidenced a high degree of readiness to accept the content
offered by Anneliese (page 82). In a case of mental illness such as
Anneliese's, biological and psychosocial factors support each
other—or oppose each other (on the same page). Would she have
starved without the exorcism? Probably not; on the other hand,
probably.

To demonstrate their scientific stature, they then offer some
ideas of their own. These are, however, always elaborations upon
what Professor Sattes had said before them. In other words, they
never let go of his shirttails. Anneliese's psychosis had its origin in
her childhood (Sattes): She had a disturbed sexual development involving a conversion-hysterical reaction formation. She
identified with her authoritarian father's superego while suppress-
ing her own feelings of hatred, thus making her aggressive. The
priests acted out of religious conviction (Sattes): True, and this
conviction arose "from naive—not to say primitive—religious
views. Both of them leaned toward magico-mystical ideas that
were, to say the least, unusual for theologians of our time." Psy-
chiatrically, while Father Renz had a calcified brain, Father Alt
was abnormal. Only because Professor Sattes did not have access
to the entire file could he have come to the conclusion that no psychiatric exploration of the priests was necessary. Anneliese's demons were the expression of naive piety. Exorcism made matters
worse (Sattes): Anneliese was the disease center. The radiation
emanating from her attracted mainly uncritical bigots, who then
also got sick, something encountered regularly in cases of so-
called possession. It was all very pathogenic.

As to diagnosis, Drs. Lungershausen and Köhler devoutly em-
braced the model offered by Professor Sattes, adding a few sugges-

tions of their own. Her personality was determined by the epilepsy. On this basis there was the development of a schizophrenia-like epileptic psychosis, or maybe a psychogenic paranoid epileptic psychosis combined with depressive and delusional disturbances, or, then again, possibly also a paranoid-hallucinatory schizophrenia-like psychosis. No wonder that in its Opinion the Court felt the need to state that this terminological logjam was of no import. It all meant the same thing—which is a matter of some doubt.

There is one good idea in all this chaff, a suggestion that indicates that some independent weighing of the evidence did, after all, take place. This is the observation that noxious substances affecting the brain can cause periodic disturbances in persons suffering from convulsions. Anneliese was clearly subject to such intermittent episodes. The idea is simply inserted—perhaps for the sake of completeness—but never developed. In a similar vein—and only in his own preliminary report—Dr. Köhler remarks that although the drugs used for the treatment of epilepsy could themselves produce a psychosis, this is not known to be the case with Tegretol. And he leaves it at that. The observation is absent from the joint report. During the hearing Tegretol came up once more. Father Alt:

> Dr. Köhler spoke of Tegretol, [saying] that it could, with long-term application, produce what he called a "shifting of the field," and that for this reason it was a dangerous drug, but the Court did not pick up on that. Dr. Lungershausen admitted that possibly there were religious matters that psychology had no key to. In every other respect both went along completely with the theories of Professor Sattes.
>
> Frau Thora was very disappointed. She thought these two psychiatrists would speak in our favor. We had talked extensively with them. During a pause I went up to Dr. Lungershausen and said, "Dr. Lungershausen, you are thoroughly familiar with my case. Please tell me: How do you explain the condition in which I found myself during that night, when I was so severely beset by something? How do you explain that all of a sudden there was a fragrance of vio-

lets and everything was over? After all, I had been completely calm; I did not even know Anneliese at the time; I had only heard about her." He answered, "Well, that is something known from statistics," and when I asked him to tell me what he meant, he just smiled, as if to say: How could anything be explained to a simple priest?

Even the parents unwittingly added to the precarious position that the priests increasingly found themselves in. They put out a statement in which they reiterated their consternation at being cited before a court of law for doing something that was in accordance with the teachings of their church. Several times in this statement they repeated the assertion that they had entrusted their daughter "body and soul" to the care of the Church and the priests. This had been precisely the argument the prosecution had used, namely, that the priests had also assumed responsibility for the physical well-being of Anneliese when they undertook their exorcism, and it was through their negligence, in this respect, that she had died.

On April 19 the prosecution presented its case. They demanded that all four defendants be found guilty of negligent homicide due to failure to act. The priests should be sentenced to fines. The parents, the state attorney argued, should not be punished, since losing their daughter was punishment enough.

The defense, especially Marianne Thora, in a very well-written, cogently argued summation, demanded that the defendants should be acquitted. Anneliese had refused medical help on the basis of her previous experience and had placed her life in the hands of God, thinking of her death as one of penance. This was her privilege, her constitutionally guaranteed right.

When, on April 21, Judge Bohlender made public the Opinion of the Court, it became clear that the hypotheses of the experts had been accepted uncritically, in their entirety, as though they were a statement of indisputable fact, not conjecture and nondemonstrative inferences, as, in fact, they had been. The tone of the Opinion waxes patronizing at this point, while in the rest of the document it is coldly juridical. Of course, runs the Opinion, the parties to the affair could not know that the epilepsy had metamorphosed into the psychosis, when this is what had, in fact, taken place.

The Opinion further argued that in May 1976, at the latest, the patient no longer had any ability to decide her own fate freely. The exorcism and the influence of her environment aggravated her illness. By not calling in a physician all four defendants had become guilty of negligent homicide. Had Anneliese been taken to a clinic and treated properly, she would have survived.

The sentence stunned everyone: half a year's prison terms, suspended for three years, and court costs for all four defendants. Even the journalists disagreed with the Court—and said so to the defendants. The defense lawyers made it known that they would appeal the sentence, but to date no one has done so. Father Alt, who had the best chance of having his sentence revised, refused to appeal. This was a matter for God, he said; worldly courts could not pass any judgment on it.

If the legal matter has in this manner been laid to an uneasy rest, the Anneliese legend has not. "Seers" keep spreading messages about her or attributed to her. They are not only from Anneliese's home region. Some are reputed to live in Switzerland and in Alsace-Lorraine. She is "very high in heaven," one such message said. She continues speaking of a judgment day in these messages, and dates are circulated as to when this might come about. The latest one was connected with the falling to earth of Skylab. When this event produced no reaction from heaven, the dates mentioned in subsequent prophecies became somewhat more vague. Other events also added to the legend. Ernst Veth, who had spoken against Father Alt at the trial, died shortly afterwards of heart failure. A priest in Aschaffenburg who had publicly and vituperously attacked the defendants also died suddenly. Two men who had built and exhibited a float spoofing the exorcism during Carnival in Klingenberg had an accident. Anneliese's grave has many visitors every day. They come to it privately or in busloads and say the rosary. She has become the focal point, the center of a religious revival, very conservative, very much embedded in folk tradition, in a way picking up where Barbara Weigand had left off, in accordance with the prophecy Anneliese had written down: "You will fulfill Barbara Weigand's mission."

CHAPTER NINE

THE RELIGIOUS ALTERED STATE OF CONSCIOUSNESS

THE MYTH OF MENTAL ILLNESS

The accused in the Klingenberg case were sentenced because they allegedly had been responsible for the sick girl and had not provided medical help for her. Although legally an adult, she had not been capable of deciding for herself, it was said, and she therefore should have been forced to submit to treatment for her own good. Professor Sattes told the Court what that would have involved: immobilization with tranquilizers; force-feeding, and treatment with electroshock therapy. To her dying day Anneliese refused to submit to that kind of brutal interference. The Court held that if she had refused, she should have been subdued by force in order to save her life. Professor Thomas Szasz, well known for his lifelong struggle against what he calls the "myth of mental illness," likes to point out that in the Western world there are only two kinds of people whose personal integrity may legally be violated. These are the criminals and those who are considered "insane." The question then arises: Was Anneliese insane? That depends, of course, on how insanity is defined.

One way of defining insanity is to say that it evidences itself in abnormal behavior. The problem with this definition is that it is quite impossible to give a general statement about normalcy. What is deviant or aberrant within one kind of context may be entirely normal within another. Put somewhat differently, if a person acts according to the rules prevalent in his own culture, and if his behavior is consistent with the expectations of his society, then his behavior is normal. To view behavior in this manner is termed "cultural relativism," and the attitudes reflected are basic to anthropology. Anthropologists are convinced that behavior must be studied holistically, in the context of the institutions, values, and meanings of the culture to which the person in question belongs. To do otherwise will lead to skewed and invalid conclusions. As Anneliese's case demonstrates, the psychiatrist working in a large, pluralistic society would do well to adopt this kind of anthropological posture. Had the psychiatrists who saw Anneliese as a patient been trained to also look at the culture that had decisively shaped her, namely, a Catholicism deeply rooted in peasant tradition, their diagnosis might have been entirely different. Ideally, they would not have immediately set up the equation—so disastrous in Anneliese's case—of convulsions signaling epilepsy. They might have attempted to discover other possible reasons for their occurrence. The question is: What causation might we propose? One direction worth exploring might be some special characteristic of Anneliese's nervous system.

HOLY PLACES, HOLY TERRORS

Anneliese was, from all accounts, endowed with a nervous system that was more sensitive than that of most people. In persons involved with their religion, going to church on Sundays produces a certain mood, a stimulation that makes the occasion pleasantly different from that of the workaday world. For Anneliese the excitation was often so unbearable when she was a teenager that she became sick to her stomach; as the mass reached its high point she felt like she had to run out of the church or else she would scream. Or remember her reaction to seeing pictures of Hitler in a movie theater. To others her age he was an object of loathing, of morbid curiosity, perhaps. In her he aroused an icy, all-engulfing terror.

An even more telling example is provided by what happened to Anneliese in San Damiano. She was physically incapable of entering certain precincts there. Thea Hein took that as proof positive that the girl was possessed by demons who could not suffer to be close to holy places. But what makes a place holy? Why is it that around the world, in all religious systems that we have knowledge of, there are certain geographically fixed spots that are singled out as special? Is it merely their interesting land formation, their beauty, their significance for survival that sets them apart, as some anthropologists have suggested? All these factors may play a role in one place or another. But the legends about these shrines nearly always relate how they were discovered in the first place. It happens quite accidentally. Someone feels or experiences something strange, something miraculous, not just anywhere in the general area but at a specific spot. This "something" is there objectively, welling up unexpectedly like a new spring, as it were. Scientists hope that someday there will be instruments to tell what this special quality might be. Until such time it is only the overly sensitive nervous system of the "shamans" or "mystics" that registers and reports it.

In San Damiano Mamma Rosa first discovered this special emanation and translated it into her own religious idiom. It healed her. She saw a vision of the Virgin Mary and it affected the pear tree, making it bloom out of season. Some years later both Father Alt and Anneliese perceived the effect independently of each other. Father Alt, obviously also endowed with a supersensitive nervous system, visited San Damiano[1] and recorded his impressions for me in July 1979:

---

[1] The Catholic Church does not recognize San Damiano as a shrine.

I wanted to take pictures of the shrine . . . but when I got to a distance of about ten meters I could no longer walk. It was as if I were paralyzed from the hips down . . . The film tore in my still camera and the motor in my movie camera refused to function. All over my body I had this feeling of having been whipped with nettles, a terrible burning sensation.

When he drank at the well located at the shrine, "instantly the entire 'infestation' was gone. I felt fresh, healthy, happy, as if a burden had been lifted." And as he began walking farther into the shrine, ". . . I had the feeling that the earth started vibrating . . . [and] I was vibrating along with it, as if I had strayed into an electrical force field . . . The current went through me and somehow transformed me, made me shudder with awe . . ."

For Father Alt there was, first of all, the physical effect. Drinking the water of the San Damiano well made him feel relieved, fresh, healthy. It freed him of the paralysis that he conceived of as a demonic infestation. He came away with a conversion experience, making him decide that as a priest he should spend more time in prayer from then on.

That Anneliese's experience was qualitatively similar can be concluded from her files. She noted that after being in San Damiano she always felt well for several weeks. For her it also translated itself into a religious transformation. "I was enlightened in San Damiano," she told Mechthild Scheuering. And in her revelations there is a statement saying that it was in San Damiano that she "shuddered with awe," making her realize that "every priest was a Christ."

"SHAMANS" OR "MYSTICS" IN SOCIETY

Persons with an overly sensitive nervous system may be found in every type of known society. One might imagine such a person as being saddled with a brain in which everything that comes from the outside reverberates, as if it were a telephone network in which something that the speaker says does not go to only one hearer but to ten. Eventually the brain can no longer cope with this constant hyperactivity. Something has to give. Scientists such as Barbara Lex maintain that there will be a discharge caused by all that tension building up in the parasympathetic nervous system. This discharge, which can assume a number of different forms, usually takes place during or close to adolescence.

In one instance, Black Elk, an Oglala Sioux, told his biographer, the Nebraska poet John G. Neihardt, how he had become swollen as a nine-year-old child, had fallen insensate and had stayed that way for twelve days and nights.

To take an example from another part of the world, the Hungarians have a tradition about shaman or *táltos* children. In the 1950s the Hungarian folklorist Vilmos Diószegi collected an impressive amount of material about them. *Táltos* children are said to fall into a prolonged catatoniclike state, or they run away from home and when they come back they are bloody and are clothed in tatters. It may be assumed that this results from seizures they suffer, during which they injure themselves.

Anneliese's seizures probably also fell into this category. She had five of them: one in 1968, one in 1969, two in 1970, and one in 1972, plus a smaller one in November 1972 that she did not mention. They usually occurred at night, so that no one ever observed her when it happened. She described them mainly as a frightening feeling of pressure, paired with the inability to move her arms or to scream. Her physicians called them "epilepsy-like," and since they were unaware that they could be caused by anything else, they then assumed that they were indeed epileptic. After her third seizure—the one that she had when she was in the sanatorium in Mittelberg—an EEG was recorded of her brain activity, but the results were inconclusive. And when Dr. Lüthy later prepared an EEG—he did so several times—it always checked out normal, a physiological alpha pattern.

ANNELIESE OUT OF CONTROL

Only when Dr. Schleip did a test on her while she asked her to sleep in her laboratory—a situation in which Anneliese could not exert any conscious control—was there something that Dr. Schleip described as a pattern of irregular discharges in the temporal lobe of the brain. She interpreted this as meaning that the "epileptic fits" originated there, and that there was probably a "brain-organic damage" at that spot. Persons who do have an injury in that part of the brain, especially if the injury involves the medial or basal cortex of the temporal lobe or parts of its covering, suffer from hallucinations, disturbances of reality, and such sudden subjective sensory fits as smelling unpleasant odors. Anneliese had not told Dr. Schleip about the *Fratzen,* but she did mention the stench and also the brief absences, that is, fits of unconsciousness that she suffered from since October 1972. So it is understandable why Dr. Schleip was so sure that she had pinpointed the right cause for Anneliese's complaints. During the autopsy, however, there was no lesion in the temporal lobes, nothing at all that would have lent support to Dr. Schleip's diagnosis.

A DIFFERENT REALITY

We know from reports of hypersensitives that, aside from the physical aspects, they *experience* something that most often involves seeing. During his period of lying as if dead (in a catatoniclike state), Black Elk had a grandiose, very complex vision of his people, the Sioux nation, passing through many different stages. The *táltos* children see a master *táltos* coming for them, with whom they must do battle. And Anneliese began seeing her *Fratzen,* those demonic, frightening countenances. This matter of seeing something, a different reality, past or beyond or within the ordinary one, turns into a condition for the hypersensitive, a lingering captivity. It is as if the brain, after the tremendous discharge of the seizures, were incapable of returning to "business as usual." As Anneliese said, "This is not a depression, this is a condition." She was talking to Dr. Lenner, so she did not mention the *Fratzen,* whose appearance carried the depression in its wake. The condition may linger for years, as in the following case reported to me by one of my students:

When I was about fourteen years old I suddenly hit a point where I could not deal with school or any large number of people at all. This rapidly grew to where I had a very difficult time being with anyone at all. It made me extremely uneasy—I seemed to have lost all knowledge of how to communicate. I could not talk at all many times, other times I could but did not like to. I spent many days walking five to twenty miles because I could not bear to walk into the school building. Being in the city was also disturbing. While walking in the country, I felt at peace, open to the natural world and personless. Everything was vibrant and filled with power and life. I often sank up to my knees into the earth, which was a homey being radiating light. Plants and stones were larger than life, colorful, and brightly lit. Sometimes I would feel spread out over the earth as far as I could see on the flat land. In the mountains I would suddenly see the entire mountain range and then come shooting back into the insides of a leaf. During this time I was rarely hungry or tired. I slept erratically, anytime, day or night, for short periods. Most foods seemed nauseating. I could not eat at meals at all. There was too much noise, there were too many people, too many things happening. I'd get up late at night or early in the morning when the house was quiet and eat some granola dry. It was the only thing I could stomach. I was never cold during this time, occasionally quite hot, although it seemed to have no relation to my clothes or the weather. I never felt any pain, except once, which was quite a deep gash in my foot. The pain was only momentary and the gash healed fast. I almost always walked barefoot but was not bothered by heat or cold. Only snow made my feet ache after a while. I used to play with fire a lot, putting burning matches to my hands and feet, picking up coals, putting out candles with my fingers. I could feel it dimly, but I never blistered or hurt.

In January 1975 I quit school altogether and nearly totally isolated myself for several months. I sometimes worked with my animals [she owned several horses] but mostly stayed in this intensely alive world. I was also tremendously strong during this time. I remember moving railroad ties around

with very little effort, something that requires a great deal of
effort of me now. I don't particularly remember picking them
up. I lifted one end, then moved them where I wanted them.
I drifted in and out of "reality." The times when I was in
contact with other people and the world became rarer and
rarer.

In addition to hallucinating and, to some extent, suspending
such normal physical functions as eating and sleeping, this student
also underwent another reaction wherein she was more or less immobilized in a catatoniclike condition, which she interpreted as an
irresistible need for sleep:

> I hit a spell when I slept for four days. I got up to eat once a
> day, maybe, and went straight back to bed. The woman I was
> staying with thought that I had mononucleosis and took me to a
> clinic. They could find nothing wrong with me. I was extremely
> disoriented. I had no sense of time.

In this case the initial seizures apparently went unrecognized:
"When I was fourteen I suddenly hit a spot . . ." There is, in the
widest sense, a religious experience ("The earth was a homey
being radiating light") involved with seeing. This student's experience extended over several years.

THE CALL FOR HELP

Hypersensitives perceive of this lingering condition, in which what
they see and experience interferes with ordinary reality, as a kind
of captivity. The *táltos* children "do battle with the older *táltos*"
in an attempt to free themselves. Anneliese spoke of the "hole" in
which she found herself and from which she could not escape.
They therefore turn to the healers of their respective societies for
help. The *táltos* children go to knowledgeable older *táltos* or shamans. Anneliese, as a member of a society with intensive specialization, consulted the representatives of two distinct and competing
groups, the psychiatrists and the priests.

Whatever the professional orientation of the curers might be, they all need to clarify, first of all, whether the case presented to them warrants their interference. To this end, they need to evaluate behavior. The basic question is always the same: Are we dealing with the genuine religious experience of a clinically healthy person or is this possibly some physical illness reflected in deranged behavior? In non-Western societies the specialists have an unbroken tradition to inform them as to precisely what symptoms to look for. This makes it possible for them to distinguish between a hypersensitive and someone who "merely sits at the edge of the ocean and tries to empty it out with a leaky basket," as one curer remarked to an anthropologist.

In Anneliese's case, unfortunately, the psychiatrists had no such tradition to rely on. Dr. Lüthy had some doubts as to whether Anneliese was really an epileptic. Convulsions can have various causes. Twice during his interrogation on February 9, 1977, he spoke of the probability, not the certainty, of such a diagnosis. Only when another attack occurred did he feel reassured enough and went ahead with an anticonvulsant medication. Whether he actually suggested to Anneliese that she should seek advice from a Jesuit is not really that important. What is important is his vehement denial of it. For had he said it, that would imply, in the eyes of his colleagues, that he was willing to admit that a religious experience could be an alternate diagnosis. Instead, within his professional culture he had to insist that her report confirmed his diagnosis: Convulsions and religious "delusions" together spelled epilepsy.

RELIGIOUS EXPERIENCE AND STATE OF CONSCIOUSNESS

A religious experience involves the switching into a different state of consciousness, popularly often referred to as a trance. Generally speaking, the human brain is capable of spontaneously assuming a considerable number of different states of consciousness. With training, several more can be added, as persons engaging in meditative practices know full well. Of these states, as psychiatrist Roger Walsh points out in an article on the subject,[2] Western behavioral sciences used to recognize only three as "normal": the ordinary one, dreaming, and sleeping without dreaming. In addition, the accepted position held by these disciplines (i.e., sociology, psychology, and psychiatry) was that the ordinary state of consciousness was optimal, capable of analyzing and evaluating perceptions in any other state, acting, in a way, as the measure for the validity of their insights or cognition. Actually, Walsh argues, we should view the states of consciousness as a set, within which the various discrete states are nested as subsets. Although they do have certain traits in common, each one has its own specific perception, affect, and cognition. Experiences a person undergoes in one state of consciousness can neither be validated nor rejected on the basis of insights gained in another.

NEW FRONTIERS OF PSYCHOLOGICAL ANTHROPOLOGY

Of the various states of consciousness to which the human brain can be tuned, the one of greatest importance to anthropology is the religious one. Interest in this state was evidenced relatively late among the subjects treated by psychological anthropology, as we learn from a recent (1979) book by anthropologist Erika Bourguignon. Initially psychological anthropology in the United States in the 1920s and 1930s grew out of a concern for the relations between culture and personality. It differs from American psychology by its cross-cultural comparative methods. It was mainly due to the burgeoning utilization and public acceptance of experimentation with states of consciousness during the last twenty years that anthropology added the topic to its range of subjects. Also, the anthropologist knew from fieldwork how ubiquitous, in particular, the religious altered state of consciousness (RASC) was. Ethnographic studies have shown that there is practically no society or religious group that does not use RASC as the central feature of its ceremonial observances. Far from being the symptom of

[2] *Am. J. Psychiatry* 137:663–73.

severe mental illness, as the experts at the Aschaffenburg trial so confidently proclaimed, what Anneliese engaged in was a very normal human activity.

THE PHYSICAL DIMENSION OF RASC

Anthropological works dealing with RASC in many cultures describe the faces of individuals in RASC as being distorted and grim, which was how Anna Michel characterized that of Anneliese, as did Peter and Anna Lippert. "Her face became rigid, a demonic mask," was an oft-heard expression. The subjects exhibit strongly dilated pupils. This we also know to have been true of Anneliese. Father Alt noted it, and so did Anna Michel. "Our Anneliese's eyes became very black," she said.

Not only the faces of the entranced but also their extremities become rigid and stiff. Anneliese's cramped hands were often described as "turning into paws." It was said of Father Pio that while celebrating the mass he had a hard time making the sign of the cross because his hands were so stiff. Anneliese mentioned her stiffness innumerable times. Her legs were like two sticks, she said. The curious manner of walking that results from this condition is often reported. I have seen it quite frequently in the Apostolic churches in Yucatán. It was Satan who made her so stiff, Anneliese claimed, and her guardian angel did gymnastics with her to overcome it.

As a sign of great internal agitation, subjects in RASC may tremble. Some do so very slightly, as in American congregations, where strong manifestations are decried; others may twitch visibly, as Father Pio often did during mass. Or they may perform very rapid movements, such as those reported of Anneliese, who frequently trembled and twitched. According to Father Renz's notes, she might also look as though someone were shaking her. She jerked as if pushed from behind, threw her head from side to side, and fell on her knees at a very great rate of speed.

Once in an RASC, a person will not respond easily to external extraneous stimuli. He is "gone," he cannot be addressed. He simply does not perceive what goes on around him. You can talk to him, even step on his hand by mistake when he is prostrate on the floor; he remains oblivious to it. On one of the tapes there is an example of this phenomenon involving Anneliese and Father Renz. The latter is intoning a Latin prayer and the demon is growling and screaming. The telephone rings very loudly; it must have been in the same room. It is clear from the way Father Renz's voice level changes that he turned in the direction of the phone, but there is not even a trace of any reaction in Anneliese's vocalization.

EVENTS IN THE BRAIN: THE TESTIMONY OF THE TAPES

Such striking behavior patterns, which are very different from the way people behave in the ordinary state of consciousness, must be the result of corresponding changes in the brain. To discover these would be of the greatest scientific interest, but the question remains as to how one can gain access to them. Recording brain waves does not seem to be the answer. In the first place, it is quite possible that these changes take place so deeply in the brain that they would not be recorded by electrodes taped to the skull. Also, many subjects move a great deal in RASC, so that the brain-wave tracings would be contaminated by so-called movement artefacts. In most religious communities, furthermore, the use of the necessary electronic equipment would be entirely inadmissible.

There is a possibility, however, of understanding something of the respective brain events by another, indirect, route, namely, by examining the speech patterns of subjects in RASC. As a trained linguist, I was fascinated to discover in the literature repeated reports that entranced people also spoke, either intelligibly—in this case in a strange, strained manner—or in unintelligible syllables. Within their own religious community, such speech was interpreted as the message of a being from the separate reality, or an unknown language. In Christian churches it was called "speaking in tongues." Subsequently an analysis was carried out[3] of RASC

[3] For further details, see my book entitled *Speaking in Tongues: A Cross-Cultural Study of Glossolalia* (Chicago, 1972).

utterances of speakers representing the following religious communities and dialects or languages: a "Streams of Power" congregation on St. Vincent Island (Black Caribbean English); a tent revival in Columbus, Ohio (Appalachian English); various main line churches in Texas (English prestige dialect); Apostolic congregations in Yucatán (Mayan); Apostolic congregations in Mexico City (Spanish); a spirit mediumship ritual in Accra (Ga, a Kwa language of Ghana, Africa); a Christian Fellowship congregation on Nias Island in Indonesia (Niasian, an Austronesian language); and a healing cult on Borneo (Rungus-Dusun). All these utterances shared some striking characteristics. The vocalizations were very rhythmical, like scanned poetry. The utterance units were of equal length. For example, if a speaker intoned, "ulalala dalala, takan dalala ulala," then the next time he said it the entire unit lasted about the same time. Some speakers needed more time for a unit utterance, others less, but they always obeyed this rule. Occasionally a speaker became tired. After uttering his vocalization, he needed a recovery period during which he might mumble something. Then he would resume his pattern once more. Viewed generally, an utterance—something like a sentence in natural language—started out in the medium range of the speaker, then rose to a peak when he was one third done, and descended until it was hardly audible. Virtually everyone did it this way.

This was a most significant finding because, by contrast, natural languages do not act this way. Or, to be more exact, speakers in the ordinary state of consciousness do not handle their speech pattern in this manner. To be sure, there is what might be called a characteristic speech melody for each language. But, beyond that, the intonation of the sentence can be arbitrarily changed, often overriding the language-specific melody, in order to accommodate meaning. To give an example, take the following sentences: *John is in the garden; John is in the garden; John is in the garden; John is in the garden*—depending upon what the speaker wants to emphasize. There is no case where the same melody is continually repeated, as happens during RASC. In addition, of course, there is hardly an instance in speech in ordinary consciousness where all sentences are of the same length.

To complement the preceding observations, the various sound tracks were also examined with the help of a level recorder. This recorder is an instrument used in the phonetics lab; its needle jumps wherever there is an emphasis. In the previous sentences the needle would trace a peak at the words "John," "is," "in," or "garden," depending on where the stress fell. For utterances during RASC the resulting curves exhibited a peak at the end of the first third of the unit utterance with monotonous regularity.

The striking regularities described above tell us that the brain processes during RASC are entirely regular, obeying very stringent neurophysiological laws that are different from those obtained during the state of ordinary consciousness, when the level-recorder tracing of speech shows a random distribution of curves. They also differ from the pattern obtained from speech during hypnosis. Because of the regular and predictable shape of the RASC speech curve, it can now be used to determine whether, during a certain ritual, the speaker was actually in RASC or not. This was, of course, an important question that needed to be investigated in Anneliese's case. For this purpose an entire half hour of her utterances—the speech of the demons—was transcribed with the level recorder from a tape made on October 22, 1975. And, indeed, Anneliese's vocalization checked out exactly the same way as all the others analyzed previously. This meant that Anneliese had most certainly been in RASC during the exorcism sessions. Almost instantly she came up with a very complex system. In addition to a brief shout, she utilized two basic forms, a scream and a growl. Two variants of each are given in Figure 3. She either screamed or said something with the same intonation, as shown under (a), or she growled or said something with a different intonation, as can be seen under (b). Most of her utterances, moreover, were very loud and had a grating quality about them. Yet when she switched to the ordinary state of consciousness, her voice was not hoarse. The probable reason was that in the altered state she used the ventricular folds, the superior or false vocal cords, not her true vocal cords. The false ones are located a bit higher. This may also be the reason why she was sometimes able to vibrate two registers simultaneously: She was activating both structures at the same time. It is quite a trick, and Tibetan monks train themselves in the art.

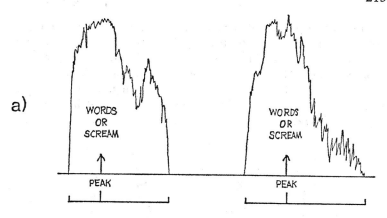

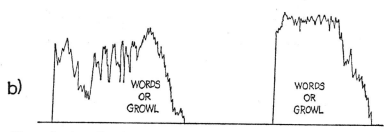

Figure 3. Anneliese's vocalization presented schematically. The curves are simplified from level-recorder tracings. (Brühl and Kjaer, Copenhagen, Model 2305)

Up until the end of October practically all of Anneliese's utterance units were three to four seconds long, often combined into seven-second phrases. This is what prompted the psychiatrists listening to the tapes to remark that her speech was "primitive" or "grotesquely monotonous." This monotony was not merely due to the equal length of the units. It was reinforced by the fact that the intonation pattern was always the same. This comes about because once the altered state is instituted, a person temporarily loses control over his speech and becomes the instrument expressing a kind of "pulsing" brain activity. It is, by the way, close to impossible to imitate this manner of talking when one is in the ordinary state of consciousness. The autocratic rule of the pulsing brain activity accounts for certain peculiarities of the meaningful, i.e., demonic, utterances we hear on the tapes. For instance, that heartrending *"auf alle Ewigkeit verdammt—damned for all eternity"* is not only

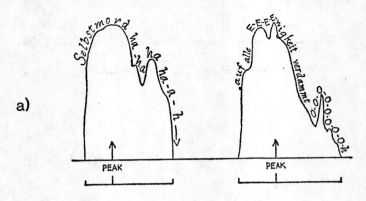

Figure 4. a) Meaningful utterances in the grip of the regular trance intonation.

b) One of the many possible intonations of the same phrase in the ordinary state of consciousness.

accented on the "E" of *Ewigkeit*—the peak of the utterance at the end of its first third—but also concludes with an "o-oh," which makes marvelous sense but is also necessary because of the demands of the descending intonation, which in turn is an expression of what the brain does in this state and from which it will not deviate. Figure 4 renders it graphically, showing how the trance intonation dominates the melody of the natural language (a), which is given for comparison (b). The second phrase in Figure 4 reads "*Selbstmord, ha ha*—suicide, ha ha," referring to Hitler's death. Contrary to the German intonation, which would require the stress to be on the first syllable, it falls instead on the -*mord* part, and the "ha ha" fills out the descending line of the curve. The idling pattern, the growl, is three to four seconds long, and so we get "*Ich hab's gedürft, hihi*—I was allowed to do it," or "*leider, leider, leider* . . .—unfortunately," which is repeated until the three to four seconds are used up. Even the inability of the "demon" to ask an outright question is due to these same constraints. In German the interrogative intonation rises at the end, as it also does most of the time in English. But the intonation of the trance phrase drops much lower than any sentence in a natural language, and it is impossible to ask a question that way.

HORROR OR JOY, HEAVEN OR HELL

Anneliese's religious experience was one of horror and despair. The question arises: Is entering the RASC always terrifying? The answer is no. In fact, most of the time it is highly rewarding, affording intense joy or euphoria. People feel intoxicated; they get "high." Anneliese's experience is much rarer. The arousal of the religious trance is like a train traveling at a high rate of speed. Suddenly it comes to a fork in the rails. Invisible hands throw the switch either toward the high road or toward the low road. If the train travels along the high road, its passengers will arrive at the place of happiness; in the opposite case, they will be carried along the low road and will end up at the fiery pit of horror. As to the brain, this is quite literally true, for buried in its limbic system, the seat of emotion, there is both a pleasure and a punishment center. All humans carry within them both their own heaven and hell.

As to the road that leads there, Sheila Womack, an anthropologist at the University City Science Center in Philadelphia, believes that we are dealing with a path laid out chemically. According to Dr. Womack, under the stimulation of the religious trance the brain synthesizes chemical compounds called endorphins. These do two things: They block certain connections between the left and the right hemispheres of the brain so that the brain as a whole can no longer check on what is going on, and they permit access to the pleasure center in the limbic system. The path to the punishment center must also logically be marked in this manner by a biochemical change, but what that is we do not at present know.

Anneliese's case, however, provides some tentative clues. We know, for instance, that when possessed Anneliese exuded a very characteristic stench. During exorcism, which is designed to cure the demonic possession, this chemical malfunctioning, and with it the stench, disappeared. Father Alt specifically remembers the following incident:

> After the exorcism we were sitting around, relaxing. I sat next to Anneliese. She was "free," and we were talking pleasantly. All of a sudden I had the feeling that "something" was going to happen. Moments later I smelled the stench, and then she screamed.

That we are dealing with actual, measurable biochemical changes in the body during what is experienced as a demonic attack is supported by the following observation by Father Alt:

> During the time I was suffering from demonic infestation, by running some tests on myself I noticed that suddenly I would develop a considerable iron deficiency, as well as a drop in manganese. My kidneys did not function properly; there was a drop in potassium nitrite and other substances. In other words, I was leached out.

Anneliese, as well as others having had a similar experience, always used a lot of obscenities during RASC, which provides a tie-in with a behavioral abnormality called coprolalia. In medical parlance it is known as the Gilles de la Tourette's syndrome. It is an affliction where people utter obscenities in bursts, called verbal tics, apparently with little control over their behavior. Dr. Womack suggests that the Christian "speaking in tongues" and the coprolalia uttered by Anneliese, for instance, have the same underlying brain process, except that one is an expression of a positive experience and the other that of a negative one. Research seems to confirm this, since there is certainly no difference in the intonation of the speaker in tongues and of someone like Anneliese when both are examined with the help of the level recorder.

In medical terms, one might then speculate that Anneliese's experience represents something like a malfunctioning of certain systems. This agrees with the view of the hunter-gatherer societies that have survived and have the longest unbroken tradition involving the religious trance. They take the positive experience to be the normal one, the one to be expected. To them the negative one can be caused by shock; for instance, it can occur if a mistake is made in the execution of a ritual. They consider it a sickness, something that needs to be cured. Catholic tradition proceeds along similar lines. Demonic possession is relatively rare; it could be caused by a curse (i.e., a social shock) and it needs to be treated by exorcism.

THE DIMENSION OF MYSTERY

What are the psychological manifestations of RASC? What do people experience in this particular state of consciousness? Psychiatrist Roger Walsh points out in the same article mentioned earlier that "perceptual sensitivity and clarity, attention, responsivity, sense of identity, and affective, cognitive, and perceptual processes all vary with the state of consciousness in apparently precise and predictable ways" (p. 665). So, if cognition and perception vary with the state of consciousness, it stands to reason that the reality perceived in one state need not be identical with that perceived in another. In fact, it most certainly will be different. Moreover, even the quality of the reality perceived in ordinary consciousness needs to be questioned. Eugene G. d'Aquili, professor of psychiatry at the University of Pennsylvania, warns that although "the question of the validity of the perception of the world during altered states of consciousness . . . remains still unanswered, [we] cannot affirm with certainty the state of external reality even given ordinary consciousness."[4] The reason we need to be skeptical as to our ability to judge what is "real," he says, is because "we must be vividly aware that it is real to us only insofar as it is structured by the analytical mode of thinking." The analytical mode, of course, is a hallmark of the ordinary consciousness and thus, as Walsh also cautions, cannot be used to evaluate the validity of perception in any other state. This is also the conclusion that d'Aquili comes to: "Whatever criteria we use to judge one state of awareness are not applicable to the other state because we are really dealing with two separate worlds" (p. 273).

The psychiatrist reiterates here what anthropologists know from fieldwork. In the world view of peoples around the globe, ordinary reality is accompanied by its twin reality. Carlos Castaneda coined the term "separate reality" for it. Regardless of whether or not we accept the opinion of the psychiatrists about the ephemeral quality of any kind of reality, we must certainly realize that the separate reality has social validity. In the universe of societies uncounted millions of people act in such a way as to demonstrate that in their experience the separate reality unquestionably exists "out there." However, it looks different to different societies. In other words, while the ability to enter into RASC is a physical ability all humans share, the cultural perception of the reality encountered in the state is culturally patterned. To use a simile, the separate reality might be thought of as a vast space. Each kind of religious system can encompass only a small section of it. In the same manner, as various countries are inhabited by people speaking different languages, having different heroes, and living under different systems of government, the separate reality is also very distinct in its many parts. For instance, although Hindus of India, traditional

4 *Zygon* 13: 257–75.

Chinese, the Yoruba of Nigeria, and Roman Catholics all profess
agriculturalist religions characterized by a godhead surrounded
by an aura of specialists, they obviously also differ in many
significant ways.[5] In large, modern, stratified states a further distinction is introduced by the Western, so-called scientific, tradition. For at least two centuries this tradition has emphasized the
preeminence of the ordinary state of consciousness as the source
of knowledge, to the exclusion of all other states, for which training was no longer offered. This produced a situation where, as
Walsh says, "it is very difficult, if not impossible, to recognize the
limitations of the usual state of consciousness if that is all that one
has ever known" (p. 665).

In Anneliese's case these two traditions—on the one side that of
the agriculturalist winegrowers; on the other that of the scientific
establishment—clashed head on. The strategy of the latter was to
declare that while the religious faction might hold any belief it
pleased, to say that it experienced anything the likes of demons
was definitely sick. What this demonstrated was an abnegation of
the validity of experience if this experience had not taken place in
the ordinary state of consciousness. Dr. Lüthy dismissed Anneliese's report about seeing devilish countenances as something
that she never experienced. This is incomprehensible to someone
who has, in his terms, been there. For experiences in RASC carry
a tremendous sense of reality. Its objects are three-dimensional;
you can walk around them and examine them from all sides, as
Carlos Castaneda discovered. According to Lame Deer, a Sioux
holy man,

The real vision has to come out of your own juices. It is not
a dream; it is very real. It hits you sharp and clear like an
electric shock. You are wide awake and, suddenly, there is a
person standing next to you who you know can't be there at
all. Or somebody is sitting close by, and all of a sudden you

[5] I have recently completed the comparative study on which these observations are based. It will be published under the title "In the Dreaming: A
New Look at Religious Behavior."

see him also up on a hill half a mile away. Yet you are not dreaming; your eyes are open (p. 64–65).[6]

THE DEMONS AND THE CHURCH

Anneliese's story is one of experience. She saw the *Fratzen;* the demons possessed her body. During the exorcism ceremony the priests, her parents, her sisters, and others present all saw and heard evidence of the reality of demons: They had acted on the girl's body and had spoken through her mouth. Yet not even their own Church, whose official dogma affirms the reality of Satan and his cohorts, would support their claims. The modern Catholic Church seems to be of the conviction that the Western scientific approach is the mode of the future. Many of its theologians have turned to the view that demons are really only symbols of something that properly belongs to the domain of ordinary reality. As Tübingen theology professor Herbert Haag, much quoted during the trial, says in his book *Abschied vom Teufel* [Farewell to the Devil],

> If we contemplate the concepts of "evil" or "the power of evil," then we are dealing with an undefined term, something only conceptualized. It should be clear that "evil" as such does not exist. "Evil" exists only insofar as it assumes shape in a person through what he wants and does. "Evil" does not exist, only evil people (p. 8).

This is the emancipation proclamation of the Western scientifically oriented Catholic from his agricultural tradition. Theologians like Professor Haag are, of course, in good company. If Weston La Barre, an anthropologist who reduces religious behavior to Freudian terms, says, "Nothing down here but us people," then this is a statement of the same belief. So is the following quotation by Carl G. Jung: "What used to be called demon is now called neurosis."

---

[6] Lame Deer/John Fire, and Erdoes, Richard, 1972. *Lame Deer: Seeker of Visions.* New York: Simon and Schuster.

Dr. Köhler copied it out in his separate Opinion, but he did not know how to go from there, so he deleted it.

THE EXPERIENCE OF POSSESSION

Haag maintains that if you do not believe in the devil you will not believe in possession either. There are two errors in his argument. The first is that the core issue of possession is a belief in it, a holding to the position that it is true. It is not. It is an experience in RASC, one undergone quite regularly by people in many different religious rituals. The second error is the belief that possession occurs only in conjunction with the devil. In the majority of cases it does not. Many Pentecostal sects and, more recently, charismatic Catholics are routinely possessed not by the devil but by the Holy Ghost.

Western psychiatry is better informed here—at least it admits that the phenomenon exists. In fact, it has assembled quite a body of theory about possession, most of it with the idea in mind that it is definitely very sick. From psychoanalysis comes the view that what we see here is a symptom of hysteria caused by sexual conflict, according to Freud. Drs. Lungershausen and Köhler said that Anneliese had a touch of conversion hysteria because her father was an authoritarian and she hated her mother, something that Dr. Lenner thought was very obvious. They maintained that this approach fitted Anneliese's case quite neatly because on occasion she suffered from paralysis. Other psychiatrists argue that possession is a regression to childhood behavior or, as they see it, a retreat into a pathological defense. On the other hand, there is the view that possession may, after all, not be all that sick because it does serve the needs of the ego, providing for a temporary venting of repressed drives.

As might be expected, anthropologists are greatly interested in possession. Erika Bourguignon devotes considerable space to it in her book on psychological anthropology and has written a small monograph about it. Pointing out that women experience possession more frequently than men, she notes that "the possession trancer achieves [power] by abdicating her own self . . . making room for a more powerful self who takes over her body and who performs powerful acts while residing in that body" (p. 262). This is a view that agrees remarkably well with what the Catholic Church considers a test for the presence of demonic possession. She finds that possession trance tends to occur most often in complex societies dependent on agriculture or agriculture and animal husbandry. In such societies women are brought up to be obedient and nurturing rather than independent. In stressful situations they would not turn to spirits for help in making them personally more powerful. Rather, they seek out authoritative beings of the separate reality to act in their place.

As to its role within religious ritual, Bourguignon finds that possession trance involves the impersonation of another, alien, entity. It centers on performance and thus needs an audience. Most often possession trance is followed by amnesia. The audience is important for this reason, too, for it can recall to the trancer what transpired during possession. Although Father Renz also expected to see amnesia in Anneliese, this was not the case. She watched everything like a spectator peering through a hole, as she often insisted.

The imagery of possession trance, Bourguignon continues, is passive and sexual. The possession trancer may consider herself the wife of the spirit, as is the case with the Fon of Dahomey (Africa), or, in Catholicism, in the marriage of nuns to Christ. The possessed is often also called the mount of the spirit, as reported from Umbanda, a mediumistic healing cult of Brazil, or she is considered his vessel or victim, as in Anneliese's case.

EVOLUTION OF RASC

Regardless of what the experience during the religious trance might be, it can last for varying periods of time. During a religious ritual, such as a Pentecostal worship service, it may extend over a period of twenty minutes or so. With some subjects it may take much longer before a return to ordinary consciousness can be achieved. Observations during fieldwork indicate, for instance, that when people are having visions, these tend to dissolve within about forty days, never to return.[7] In the case of a cult "upheaval," an entire congregation in Yucatán was in a more or less continuous religious ecstasy.[8] The episode lasted about forty days. This forty-day period seems to represent something like a biological constant. According to Tibetan belief, the soul remains in limbo for this period after a person dies. It also appears in the Bible: Jesus fasted in the desert for forty days, for instance.

In the case of the hypersensitives, the altered state of consciousness continues—"I live on a different plane of consciousness than other people" Anneliese said—while the forty-day episode arises from it as from a base line. Anneliese, for instance, experienced such an episode in the summer of 1975, which held her in its grips for about this length of time.

The forty-day cycles are a cruel experience, even if they are of the positive variety. Periods of enormous excitement alternate with seeming "death," that is, a catatoniclike state. The subject feels a burning heat, "the fever of the Lord," as one informant said. Due to the tightness of the neck muscles and the pressure on the stomach, the afflicted person can eat or drink only occasionally, when the brain briefly lets up. Sleep is almost impossible. There is constant motion and the urge to inflict pain on oneself. Fasting and pain, in turn, feed back into the trance, fueling it. The pupils are strongly dilated, so that light or colors are painful to the eye. And the agitation of the brain is expressed in the speech pattern of the RASC, reflecting the perpetual pulsing of the brain. In Anneliese's case the episode was made even more violent because she was going through the negative variant and because of her hypersensitivity. No one knew what to do for her, so she suffered all the way through it, as did the congregation in Yucatán. The cycle can, however, be interrupted, as happened in another village in the same area a few years later. Profiting from knowledge gained as a result of the earlier occurrence, the second congregation sought help and was able to terminate the episode after four days.

[7] Felicitas D. Goodman, Glossolalia and Hallucination in Pentecostal Congregations. *Psychiatria Clinica* 6:97–103, 1973.

[8] Ibid., Disturbances in the Apostolic Church: A Trance-Based Upheaval in Yucatán. In: *Trance, Healing, and Hallucination*, New York, 1974.

If nothing is done, the low-level, stubborn excitation of the hypersensitives will persist for a long time, with only brief interruptions. These are intervals where the subject is more or less able to stay within the ordinary state of consciousness. The positive experience may last for three to four years, the negative one even longer, possibly six to seven years. No wonder that persons who experience this think of it as a kind of captivity. Anneliese spoke of it as the hole in which she found herself and from which she could not escape. All societies that we have reports on therefore possess methods for interrupting and terminating the biologically fixed cycle, thereby freeing the afflicted person of his captivity. The cure is not a drug but rather a ritual manipulation of the brain that makes it possible for the subject to gain control over his behavior, to "tame the spirit," as many societies see it. Exorcism is just such a ritual, and since it is the central issue in Anneliese's story, it will be treated in greater detail in the next chapter.

CHAPTER TEN

WHY DID ANNELIESE DIE?

People who suffer from some sort of brain damage or from certain kinds of biochemical imbalance, for instance, have no control over their everyday behavior. Nor can they be cured by teaching them to assume such control. Rather, they need medical help. Anneliese, by contrast, had problems controlling her own behavior because she was caught in RASC. And for that a different kind of cure is possible.

THE CURE

During ordinary consciousness the brain tends to process the stimuli received from the external world in a linear fashion. One is aware of the linear passage of time and can count, name, and speak. During a religious trance the brain is much more inclined to view everything holistically, seeing the total image rather than its details. What humans have apparently known for a very long time, judging from the antiquity of the respective rituals, is that the healthy brain can be taught to switch from one mode of processing to the other. So if a person is held prisoner in the holistic mode of the religious trance, he can be taught to revert to the sequential mode by means of proper manipulation. This is the basic goal of rituals, be they secular or religious.

As an example without religious context, the student of mine mentioned earlier continued to be caught for prolonged periods in the altered state of consciousness. Two years after the initial onset of her experience she decided on her own to move to an environment that was strictly structured, something that her own home was not.

I was almost sixteen when I decided I had to stop because I was unable to do what I wanted to in the normal world. What triggered this was one day when I could not find my horses anywhere on their pasture. I looked for quite a while and never saw them until one whinnied at me, and I suddenly became aware of them. I decided I had to leave home. I had several plans but ended up spending the summer with my aunt and uncle, who lived on a very definite schedule. The routine helped a great deal in structuring the way I dealt with the everyday world, and I managed to keep on a fairly even keel. The next year I spent at a boarding school with its rigid schedule. By the end of that year I began to feel more comfortable with people and had a few friends.

The next summer and school year I spent with the mother of a friend, going to a private high school. I was excited at being able to enjoy being with people and spent a great deal of time with some friends. I had spells of clarity and brightness, but they were not a constant state. Once the floor of the school building where I was waiting for someone began to ripple like a pool of water. A footstep would cause a still place from which concentric rings would form and expand until they bounced off the wall and returned, producing crisscrossing patterns of ripples. I decided to see if the walls would ripple, but instead they began to vibrate, moving with the ripples running up against them. This went on for some time and then stopped. In April that year I had a continuous dream that I was traveling down a long, winding road, where I encountered many beings and made my peace with them. The dream ended with my climbing a hill that overlooked where I had traveled. I then awoke, feeling quite joyous and feeling that now I was whole. I then had a series of very vivid, continuous dreams, and my altered state appeared as isolated incidents. The dreams became spaced weeks apart, with the last one toward the end of December 1978. Since January 1, 1979, there have been no involuntary incidents of an altered state of consciousness.

While secular rituals, such as establishing a routine, are of the hit-or-miss variety, religious curing rituals are of admirable effectiveness because they have been honed to perfection by thousands of years of use. For this reason it is very regrettable that because of the events surrounding Anneliese's death there are now demands in Germany that the exorcism be changed or forbidden altogether.[1] Efforts in this direction are based on the mistaken notion that Anneliese's death was caused by it. It will be demonstrated that it was not.

"ATTACKED BY DEMONS"

The exorcism, as well as other curing rituals of the same class in many different non-Christian religious systems, aims at switching the brain activity from the holistic to the linear processing mode, bringing the trance under control by enforcing a linear structure. The way exorcism does this is, first of all, by imposing time limits:

---

[1] During her fieldwork in Bolivia, Dr. Libbet Crankshaw, an anthropologist with the University of Connecticut, came across a case of two sisters suffering from demonic possession. Due to special circumstances, one sister was treated both in an American psychiatric hospital and also with prayers from a Methodist minister—quite unsuccessfully. The other sister came under the care of a Catholic priest, whose exorcism succeeded in curing her. This incident was related to me in a personal communication.

There is a beginning of the ritual at a certain agreed-upon time; there is a middle; and then there is an end. At the start of the ritual the afflicted person is encouraged to institute the altered state, mainly by means of cultural suggestion, the expectation that this will happen. To induce a religious trance is relatively easy. The reason is that humans are so thoroughly patterned genetically to be able to do this that we are very susceptible to any kind of strategy that would induce the state. When, during that hectic summer episode of 1975, Anneliese began seeing dark little animals scurrying around and clouds of what seemed like insects, those around her also saw it. Later her mother was "attacked by demons," as Josef Michel told Father Renz. Father Alt entered into the altered state simply as a result of hearing what was happening to Anneliese. The examples that Father Rodewyk cites also give evidence of this learning aspect. The two girls, Germana and Monica, whose demonic possession he discusses in detail were of the same age, were friends, and worked at the same mission station in South Africa. It was an observation that Dr. Schleip puzzled over, as we know from her letter to the state attorney. "I am entirely unaware of the fact," she wrote, "that an induction could take place in the environment of a person suffering from a psychosis, such as an epileptic psychosis, caused by brain-organic damage. This kind of psychosis lacks the empathetic quality of a true paranoia." Even with true paranoia, she remarked, an induction (of the same behavior, that is) is extremely rare. She was absolutely right. The reason for the induction phenomena was that Anneliese suffered from neither an epileptic psychosis nor a true paranoia.

With the expectation that the religious trance would set in and the demons would start speaking, Anneliese learned the switch-over very quickly. In the notes Father Renz kept of the first few sessions, when he was not making any tape recordings, we read, for September 24, 1975 (the date the first exorcism took place), that "Anneliese or, rather, the demons were very quiet in the beginning." By September 29, he writes, "Anneliese began trembling as soon as I arrived."

MAINTAINING THE TRANCE

Once induced, the trance needs to be kept going because a great deal of work has to be accomplished during this phase of the episode in order to rid the sufferer of his affliction—in Anneliese's case, of her demonic possession. There are a number of strategies to maintain the trance. One is the continuous recital of the Latin formulas. It is reminiscent of the drum signal used in so many societies to accomplish the same purpose. Another tool is the introduction of features that are designed to "irritate the demon," thereby keeping the arousal high, a precondition for the altered state of consciousness to continue. Father Renz followed up all the suggestions listed by Father Rodewyk in his works on exorcism and added some of his own. Astutely he noted if something was useful and then exploited it to the fullest extent. Making the sign of the cross, sprinkling holy water, placing the stole on Anneliese's shoulder, exhibiting pictures of the crucifix or of sacred personages, bringing a reliquary to the exorcism, reading relevant Bible passages or sections from Barbara Weigand's work, saying the rosary, singing songs to the Virgin—all served the same purpose. How important the continued maintenance of the altered state was for the overall curing purpose can be seen by the fact that in one astounding instance the demon himself suggested what might be most unpleasant for him: the recitation of the Litany of the Five Sacred Wounds. If something did not work, Father Renz dropped it. The description of the demon as an animal with ten horns decorated with diadems and having claws like a bear did not ring a bell with the demon, who was, after all, a twentieth-century creature, not one belonging to the first century. So Father Renz did not repeat the reading of that part of the Book of Revelation.

The work of switching the brain from holistic to sequential processing is carried out by using a number of tools. It is this kind of processing, for instance, that was operative when the demons were ordered over and over again to say the specific prayer formula, "Hail Mary, full of grace." The most important and most obvious tool, however, is the asking of questions: What was the demon's name? Why was he smitten by eternal damnation? Why was he present in the possessed person? What was the hour and the day of his projected exit? By whose permission was he present? These were some of the questions posed by Father Renz to Anneliese's demons, as prescribed by the *Rituale Romanum.* Other queries referred to such problems of the day as the conflict in the German Catholic Church between traditionally held concepts and those newly introduced by the Second Vatican Council. What we see here is the important community-building function of the rite. The possessed person needs the community as audience before which he plays out his experience. Conversely, the community needs the possessed person through whom its religious experience is confirmed and amplified. The answers of the demons—as messages they were forced to enunciate directly from the Mother of God—still serve as guidelines of conduct today for those who attended the exorcistic sessions.

To judge by Anneliese's testimony, the work of the exorcistic ceremony was accomplished in gradual steps. Thus, for example, the Mother of God at first appears only indirectly at the rite. We know of her presence because the demons say that they must obey her. Two weeks into the exorcism the benevolent personages from the separate reality of Catholicism start speaking to Anneliese in person. And there is even hope that the most persistent of the possession conditions, the *Fratzen,* will disappear, for the Mother of God promises her that they will be replaced by visions. In neurophysiological terms, the exorcism is increasingly switching the behavior away from the pain center and toward the pleasure or reward center. Simultaneously, the characteristic stench begins to fade during the exorcism—something noted by all the participants —and a pleasant fragrance appears instead. The report on pleasant fragrances is so persistent that it may be a translation of the neurochemical changes of the religious altered state of consciousness leading to the pleasure center into olfactory terms.

PREDICTIONS OF JUDGMENT DAY

How difficult it was for Anneliese to block the pathway to the pain center can be understood from the constant refusal of the demons to leave, and from their grudging and occasional vacillation in granting some compromise to the Mother of God. It can also be illustrated by the predictions of a judgment of fire—something like a Third World War—that the demons dwelled on so persistently. Anneliese startled some of her girl friends in the Ferdinandeum with that prediction. "Anneliese was very pessimistic about the future," they said. "One should close the doors and the windows and pray in order to be saved." It is obvious what is going on here in neurological terms: The judgment represents confinement to the pain center; blocking the pathway to it is the closing of doors and windows; and prayer affords access to the pleasure center.

Predictions of what amounts to the end of the world are not peculiar to those who suffer from demonic possession. Christian and non-Christian groups have produced similar prophecies. But with an access to the pleasure center, and thus to the positive aspect of the experience, these prophecies usually involve *la terre sans mal,* the land without evil, for instance, for Indian societies in South America, or a kingdom of a thousand years with Christ as its ruler for the Christians, where the lame can walk, the blind can see, and death loses its sting. What seems to happen in both these latter instances is the hope that the altered state of consciousness, and with it an access to the pleasure center, can be instituted permanently. At that point, of course, the world perceived during the ordinary state, the reality of everyday living, sinks out of view, the "world" comes to an end—a very desirable event. Unhappily for those cherishing such hopes, the altered state of consciousness is unstable. Eventually it literally evaporates, dissolves, and with it access to the pleasure center also is blocked. The chemistry of the brain rights itself and the prospect of eternal bliss is lost.

In Yucatán such an episode took place in a millenarian congregation, one predicting the end of the world and the arrival of Christ. When, after about forty days, the congregation as a whole returned to ordinary consciousness, it was a very sad experience. It was so hard for the congregation to cope with the fact that the end of the world did not come about in August 1970 that the prediction lingered with new dates for months and years. This is one way in which to understand the mass suicide that took place in the Jonestown colony in Guyana. Rather than allowing ordinary reality to take over again, they made a pact to die, which would cause the ordinary world to go away forever, and would afford the members of the sect an entry to the separate reality permanently. "Today we will all die," one of the guards told a man of the entourage of Congressman Ryan, and he smiled.

THE END OF THE EPISODE

The afflicted person needs to be trained to terminate the religious trance on command, upon being given a signal. This is a most important lesson to learn because it represents the assurance for the afflicted that they can function without difficulty in the world of ordinary consciousness. In neurophysiological as well as psychological terms it represents the repairing of the barrier between the two types of consciousness, the ordinary and the altered one. It is the erecting of the dam that Anneliese spoke about in that tragic note begging for help that Father Alt found in her room. Accordingly, it is much harder to learn than to initiate the episode. We know how often the demons refused to accede to Father Renz's request for a break in a lengthy session. Many times the sessions went on and on because the demons would not stop screaming or growling at the signal of the final benediction.

In ritual terms, an exorcism is successful if the demons have answered all the questions, made their obeisance before the Holy Ones, and have left. Relapses are occasionally reported, but they are usually brief and easily dealt with. No further afflictions have ever been reported. This is entirely clear from the case histories compiled by Father Rodewyk. It is also traditional knowledge in non-Western societies, and it agrees with what anthropologists know based on their fieldwork. There is usually a social or psychological reason for the relapse.

AN OCCASION OF HIGH DRAMA

The person possessed is the center of a great deal of attention. The exorcism itself is an occasion of high drama, enjoyed both by the patient and by those surrounding him. The drama itself may be heightened by the return of the entity that is supposed to be expelled. The Russian ethnographer A. F. Anisimov describes in great detail a marvelously exciting exorcism carried out by a Tungus (Evenk) shaman. In this case the context is not Christian, of course, and the spirit to be evicted is a disease spirit. After a long and dramatic contest between the shaman and the disease spirit—involving negotiation, debate, much invective, the sacrifice of a reindeer, commands on the part of the shaman, and defiance by the spirit—the latter is cast out, only to be discovered hiding in some unexplored part of the patient's body. It is finally swallowed by one of the spirit helpers of the shaman, a spirit loon, who flies over the abyss of the lower world and expels it through the anus so it cannot return. In this case the patient is permanently cured.

THE EMERGENCE OF THE RELIGIOUS SPECIALIST

The ordinary person comes out of the religious experience with greater mental health. Unmanageable stresses become dulled, life is faced with renewed courage. In other words, the experience aids in adapting to harsh and painful changes—this is one reason why, in the modern age, we see a worldwide proliferation of sects and cults that have ritualized the religious trance. For the hypersensitive the rewards are proportionally more significant. Black Elk, for instance, became a holy man, a visionary leader of his people. The Hungarian *táltos* children grew up to become diviners, healers, individuals able to control the weather. Mainly, they exhibited the ability to see the dead. This ability has survived into the present. In the summer of 1978 stories of a woman from the village of Putnok who could see the dead, a *halottlátó,* made headlines in Hungary. As long as there has been a written record of Hungarian history, this was one of the standard titles of a *táltos*. They are also called "men and women of knowledge," which will ring a bell with those familiar with Castaneda's work. Jolán of Putnok, now in her late forties, can see the recently dead, and she can hear them: They talk to her. In her case, the gift arose after an unspecified illness during her teens. At first she thought that "everybody saw the dead." There are many eyewitness cases of her ability that are the talk of the country. Crowds of people seek information from her concerning missing kin or unexplained deaths.

In the brief time allotted to her, Anneliese began to evidence a number of these same gifts. She became telepathic, knowing, for instance, who was praying for her in some other town and at what time. She began divining, telling those around her that May and June 1976 would be very bad for her, and July would bring deliverance. She was mercifully not aware that this meant her death. The dead visited her, as we know from her diary. There was Siegfried, the recently dead nephew of Father Roth. Had she lived, she could have chosen any role from the models available to her. There was Therese Neumann of Konnersreuth, the lover of suffering, whom she might have followed into penance to save souls. "Reserl," as she was often called, was from the same general area of Germany as Anneliese. And she venerated Barbara Weigand, wrote revelations in imitation of the latter, and might have followed in the footsteps of this visionary, whose home was only a short distance from Klingenberg. It was not to be. The task still remains to try and discover why Anneliese died.

ANNELIESE OUT OF CONTROL

There is sufficient evidence to support the contention that Anneliese was indeed not sick, that she was not an epileptic, that what looked to the uninformed like symptoms of a disease were actually manifestations of a religious experience. We may even assume that after a great deal of suffering she would have recovered on her own. Or she might possibly have discovered some way to bring about her own cure without the aid of others, as happened in the following well-known case involving an Indian civil servant by the name of Gopi Krishna. In an autobiographical account entitled *Kundalini: The Evolutionary Energy in Man* Gopi Krishna relates how after seventeen years of meditation something extraordinary and very frightening happened to him. Quite suddenly his body became stiff and heavy and was awash with coursing currents of energy that burned him and did not let him rest day or night. He could not eat properly, was unable to feel any affection for his wife and children, and walked the streets at all hours. None of the religious specialists, Yoga teachers, and others that he consulted had ever experienced anything like it and were unable to advise him. He did not turn to any psychiatrist, for he was quite familiar with Western literature and was sure that they would not recognize his affliction as anything that they could remedy. Gripped by unbearable terror, he was driven to the edge of death by a lack of food and sleep, continually wracked by the pain of the fiery currents engulfing him, his skin feeling as if it were pierced by hot needles. It was in such dire extremity that he remembered an interpretation that made sense with respect to all the various counsels that he had been given, namely, that in activating the creative energy of his body he had made a mistake, as sometimes happens. Instead of the energy flowing up the left side of the spine, it was inadvertently circulating through the *pingala,* or solar nerve, on the right side. Perhaps he could correct this mistake. Gathering up his waning strength in one final effort, Gopi Krishna concentrated on the base of his spine and attempted to divert the flow to the left, to the *ida,* or lunar nerve. He heard a sound like a nerve thread snapping, and all of a sudden the flow of energy became cool and brilliant, comforting and invigorating. The experience left him with a number of extraordinary abilities, attested to by Professor Weizsäcker, whom he visited in the offices of the Research Association of Eastern Wisdom and Western Science in Germany. He and Professor Weizsäcker collaborated on a book dealing with the biological basis of religious experience.

Anneliese did not even have to affect the cure herself. She was treated with the exorcism, the "treatment of choice" in cases such as hers. So what went wrong?

THE FALSE PARADIGM

For a very long time—surely since the Age of Reason appeared on the scene—the West has assumed a particular posture toward religion. This involved the idea that it was all right, and even virtuous, to believe in religious concepts such as God, Christ, heaven, possibly even Satan and hell. As Professor Sattes wrote in his Opinion, that was definitely not to be considered pathological. But anything that smacked of experience—say, if somebody maintained that last night Jesus came to see him, or that he was possessed by demons who spoke through his mouth and tormented him—that was sick, a delusional psychosis in modern parlance. Earlier such persons were shunned, ridiculed, ostracized, or, in severe cases, locked up in asylums. Of course, not all modern psychiatrists work with this paradigm in mind. This is why it was regrettable that the Court consulted clinical rather than cross-cultural psychiatrists. Even more regrettable is the fact that Anneliese had the misfortune of encountering only clinical psychiatrists.

How differently representatives of these two specialties may treat the same kind of patient is illustrated by an incident—related by the American psychiatrist E. Mansell Pattison, a consultant to the Public Health Service Clinic on the Yakima Indian Reservation—involving a young Yakima Indian girl whose case is strikingly similar to Anneliese's experience.

Dr. Pattison arrived on the Indian reservation one morning in December and was told by the public health doctor that he had just treated an adolescent Indian girl. He had been called by the family and encountered the girl running around in the house in a state of panic: incoherent, babbling, agitated, muttering about ghosts and afraid of dying. He had given her a chlorpromazine injection (i.e., an antischizophrenia drug) that put her to sleep. His diagnosis was acute schizophrenic psychosis. Dr. Pattison asked that the mother and daughter come and see him in the clinic. He found the thirteen-year-old Mary to be well developed and healthy, but she was hunched over, kept her eyes downcast, and hardly spoke. The mother told him that Mary had played with

some other girls in the moonlight at a summer camp. They looked
up into the trees and saw ghostlike human figures whom they recognized as their tribal ancestors. A conversation ensued between
the girls and the ghosts. No one suffered any ill effects from this
excursion into the separate reality except Mary. A ghost followed
her, jumped on her, and tried to choke her. Mary struggled against
the ghost. She gasped for breath and then screamed for help. The
counselors finally had to take her to the local hospital, where she
was given a chlorpromazine injection. From then until Dr. Pattison saw her—a period of about four months—she could not rid
herself of the ghosts. During the day she went to school and performed well, but at home she would see ghosts at the window and
was terrified. She saw blood on the field when she went walking,
and was afraid the ghosts would kill her brothers and sisters. She
was frightened and would cry and scream. Sometimes her parents
would take her to the hospital for another chlorpromazine shot.
When her mother asked the psychiatrist whether he thought her
daughter was crazy, he answered that he did not know because although the girl seemed withdrawn, she was logical and in touch
with reality in her conversation. The mother then explored the
question of whether the psychiatrist "believed in religion." Reassured on that point by his answers to a number of shrewd questions, she told him about her father, who had been a witch doctor
and had cared for the entire tribe. Before he died he said that his
power would pass on to one of his grandchildren. Apparently this
was her daughter, although she had never mentioned the matter to
her. She did not think that it would be realistic, in this day and
age, for the girl to accept the gift of her grandfather. Dr. Pattison
encouraged the mother to go through with her idea of asking the
grandmother and some of the old Yakima women to rid the girl of
the ghosts, telling them that Mary did not want to fight with them.
The old women carried out the exorcism the same night, without
Dr. Pattison being present. When he came back a month later, the
mother and daughter were radiant. They thought he was a great
doctor, for Mary had been healed. She had no relapse during the
many months that Dr. Pattison followed the case. In other words,
Dr. Pattison rejected the paradigm proffered by his younger colleague, who thought that Mary showed an acute schizophrenic
psychosis, to the benefit of his patient.

ENTER THE DRUGS

A further development of the false paradigm leads to the conclusion that all seizurelike activity is, of necessity, the symptom of an illness, which, with the advent of powerful new drugs, should be treated with the latter. What distinguishes Anneliese's case from all the others previously mentioned is the fact that *she is the only one who, almost from the start of what anthropologists call her shamanistic illness, was given anticonvulsant drugs.* These seriously interfered with what her brain was designed to accomplish. Table 1 provides an overview of what happened in this respect.

TABLE 1

Fall 1968		1st seizure
August 25, 1969		2nd seizure
June 1970		3rd seizure
	A. Unknown anti-convulsant drug; first probable appearance of *Fratzen*	
Fall 1970		4th seizure
		Fratzen continue
June 5, 1972		5th seizure
		Fratzen continue
September 5, 1972	B. Dilantin	*Fratzen* continue
		depression
		stench
		absences
November 8, 1972		last, usually unreported, small seizure
September 3, 1973		*Fratzen* continue
		depression
		stench
		absences

September 7, 1973   C. Aolept
                         (periciazine)
                         added
November 28, 1973   D. Tegretol   *Fratzen* continue
                                           absences probably stop
                                           depression ⎱ (stop, then
                                           stench   ⎰ resume)
March 9, 1976   Tegretol,
                         last known
                         prescription

Drug A: Unknown anticonvulsant. Anneliese told Father Alt that she had her first religious experience in Mittelberg. She was also given her first anticonvulsant medication there. We know that as a child she was sick a lot. Quite possibly this may have predisposed her toward opening up the pathway to the pain center. "We were in her from the beginning," the demons said. On the other hand, this pathway may simply have been opened up by the composition of the drug itself. That the development took this direction during this time is attested to by circumstantial evidence, namely, by the change in her that everyone noted when she returned from Mittelberg: her deepening depression; her inability to feel affection; her shunning of sexual expression. While the latter was determined, to a considerable extent, by her culture, which places great value on premarital chastity, it was still a warning that something was wrong.

Drug B: Dilantin (phenytoin sodium). In September 1972 Dr. Lüthy put Anneliese on Dilantin. According to the *Physicians' Desk Reference* (PDR), Dilantin is designed to control grand mal epilepsy, presumably by affecting the motor cortex. It can have very unpleasant side effects in the central nervous system, causing, among other things, insomnia and headaches, both of which Anneliese complained about. It also affects the chemistry of the brain cells, causing them to lose sodium at the synaptic junctures.

Dilantin is a pretty unpleasant drug, the administration of which can really only be justified because grand mal seizures are even worse. For Anneliese it was a disaster. As she told Dr. Schleip, "almost daily since October 1972" she began having deepening depressions and absences—a mere four weeks after the start

of the Dilantin medication. What she did not tell her was that at
the same time the *Fratzen* also became terrifyingly frequent
callers, appearing much more often than before. What Dilantin
apparently did was to cause, or at least aggravate, a disruption in
message transmission in the brain—thus the absences. It most
likely also intensified the chemical changes that opened a pathway
to the pain center—thus the greater prominence of the *Fratzen,* the
stench, and the frightening depression.

ANNELIESE TURNS TO THE CHURCH

By the summer of 1973 Anneliese had understood that Dr.
Lüthy's medication did nothing to blot out or dissolve the terrifying ghostly countenances. They kept appearing out of nowhere,
frightening her during the most innocuous activities, harassing her
and bringing with them that indescribable icy dread, the threat of
annihilation. Nor did it free her of the stenches that welled up occasionally. This is what she was talking about when she insisted
that she didn't want to consult a physician. It was this particular
ailment that she knew they could not heal.

If the physicians proved ineffective, at least her faith offered an
interpretation for what the *Fratzen* were: devils, demons. That
made sense, since everything fit: their appearance, so terrifying
that she always refused to describe it; the horror of hell attached
to them; the mood of damnation. As a Catholic she was aware of
the fact that the Church also had a number of remedies, powerful
weapons to chase demons away: prayer, blessings, and, if all else
failed, exorcism. With admirable consistency she therefore began
demanding religious support. Not that she was immediately received with open arms. It took an intervention from the Savior to
get her to forgive the fact that some priests continued doubting
that she had demons pursuing her, as we know from the following
diary entry:

29.10.75
I must confess that when I thought of Father Herrmann and
Father Habiger I often felt resentment against them, because

in 1973 they would not believe me that Satan was molesting and tormenting me. Last night the Savior let me feel that these priests had done the right thing, because at that time they had no visible proof. Only Frau Hein and Father Alt had those. (The "Black One" always sneaked off.)

It is questionable whether the priests deserved forgiveness. For it was their timidity, their shilly-shallying that, in the fall of that year, drove her back to Dr. Lüthy, mainly because her parents were also doubtful about the religious origin of her affliction. When Dr. Lüthy then said, as they averred, that they should see a Jesuit, they must have been left thunderstruck.

Drug C: Periciazine. Instead of discontinuing all medication when Anneliese told him about her religious experience—the *Fratzen,* the fear of damnation, the judgment of fire that she foresaw— Dr. Lüthy added another anticonvulsant. Periciazine affects the central nervous system. It is used to reduce its "hyperexcitability." At the very least this drug set up an action that was in conflict with the need for discharges in Anneliese's brain.

Drug D: Tegretol (carbamazepine). Since Anneliese could feel no improvement, she turned to the health services of the University of Würzburg when she started attending the PH there. On November 28, 1973, Dr. Schleip switched her over to Tegretol. That the chemical changes produced by earlier medications were still reversible at that point, is proven by the fact that for a few weeks Anneliese felt greatly improved, since she was out from under the burden of Dilantin plus periciazine. The relief did not last. But Anneliese continued taking the drug conscientiously anyway. In her written statement to the Court Dr. Schleip gave the impression that she informed Anneliese that she would have to take the Tegretol indefinitely. This is not, however, what Anneliese reported. She said that she was told that while she was on this medication she could not get married. With youthful exuberance she kept repeating to Peter and to the priests that at the clinic they said that within half a year the Tegretol would take care of whatever was wrong in her brain, the exorcism would free her of the demons, and then they could get married. This expectation was so important to her that it even became part of her revelations.

If Dilantin and periciazine were bad for Anneliese, Tegretol was worse. In fact, Tegretol brand carbamazepine is infinitely more dangerous. Anneliese was changed over to it because both Dr. Lenner and Dr. Schleip guessed that her continuing depressions, the brief absences, and the stenches that she suffered from were really epileptic petit mal seizures, and Dilantin was not indicated to alleviate those symptoms. However, the PDR alludes to the suspicion that Tegretol may lead to birth defects when given to women of childbearing potential. So it is very difficult to understand why they chose it at all. In addition, it has extremely dangerous side effects, possibly causing serious-to-fatal modifications of the blood cells. For this reason, according to the manufacturer, before being put on Tegretol patients must be checked for any blood abnormalities and afterward, on a weekly basis for changes in their blood during the first three months of taking this drug and every month thereafter for two to three years. There is no indication in Dr. Schleip's letter to the State Attorney's Office that this was done. Peter stated emphatically that during the entire time that Anneliese was under the care of Dr. Schleip she never once had a blood test.

According to the PDR, the action of Tegretol, a brand of carbamazepine, is obscure. It is metabolized in the liver, and its serum half-life is between fourteen and twenty-nine hours. This does not mean, of course, that modifications it might have wrought in the brain chemistry or elsewhere while it was in the body could not persist beyond that time. What it produced in Anneliese, apparently, was a kind of seesaw effect, making her feel well sometimes and poorly at other times. This is the "periodicity caused by noxious substances" noted by Dr. Köhler. But so committed was he to the model he had taken over from Professor Sattes that he did not think further along these lines. After all, we can read in his Opinion that Tegretol is not known to cause a psychosis, and he viewed Anneliese as psychotic. Consequently Tegretol had nothing to do with the matter.

TEGRETOL AND EXORCISM

Initially the rite of exorcism did indeed seem to effect a cure. Tegretol apparently did not, in the beginning, interfere with those neurochemical processes. More and more, the ritual was starting to block access to the pain center and rebuilding the path to the pleasure center. The exorcism was "freeing her," as she kept saying. Even as late as Christmas 1975 she told Peter that she felt better than ever. With a sort of body intuition she even foresaw a complete cure, something like the snapping of a nerve fiber that Gopi Krishna had experienced. This is what the persistent prediction of the demons may have meant, who talked about leaving *"wenn's kracht*—when it cracks or crashes."

At the very same time, though, just when she was improving subjectively something sinister was going on that she was not aware of on the conscious level. For Father Renz was entirely right: The exorcism should have accomplished its job much faster than it actually did. Her brain may have been prepared to carry out the appointed task on October 6. But then the Tegretol prescription was renewed, and in contrast to the moderate arousal experienced on October 6, Anneliese's screams on October 7 blew the roof off. The Mother of God then told Anneliese that the demons would finally be cast out on October 31. That makes marvelous sense, because on that day the forty-day cycle that had started with the exorcism came to an end. But on that same day Dr. Kehler gave the family another prescription for Tegretol. So the grand casting out of demons turned into a terrifying struggle between the youthful power of Anneliese's brain and the action of the drug. It is quite possible that the difficulty Anneliese experienced in attempting to institute RASC at the outset of that session was already a danger signal that something was going wrong. In the end the drug won out and the demons announced that they were back. Even after the grand casting out, there was an instance of this irritating effect of Tegretol. On December 17 the prescription was renewed. It was followed by an agitated exorcism session on December 19. Roswitha remembers that Anneliese often took less than the three tablets per day when her prescription was beginning to run out, and then made up for it as soon as it was renewed by taking more than the prescribed dosage.

THE EVIDENCE OF THE SOUND TRACKS

The tapes also reveal other subtle changes. In November we can hear how Anneliese's throat seems to be constricting occasionally. The invective *"Drecksau—dirty sow,"* that she used so often turns into *"Drecksack—dirty sack."* Speaking in linguistic terms, the end of the syllable is no longer open, ending in a vowel, but unreleased due to that strong double "k" (equivalent to "ck" in German spelling). This begins to interfere with the trance-induced melody of the utterances: It often no longer attenuates into a barely audible conclusion. By the end of November the screams, only three to four seconds long earlier, begin to stretch into howls of eight, ten, eleven, or even fourteen seconds. *"In alle Ewigkeit verdammt, o-oh"* turns into *"verdammt in alle Ewigkeit"* (see Figure 5), with a rather flat peak at the wrong spot from the point of view of a true trance utterance.

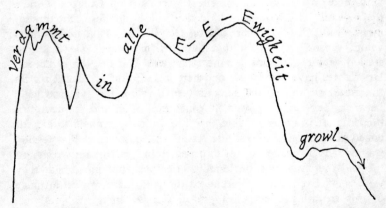

Figure 5. The phrase *"auf alle Ewigkeit verdammt"* modified into *"verdammt in alle Ewigkeit,"* November 9 (simplified curve).

ANNELIESE MOBILIZES HER DEFENSES

Eventually, of course, Anneliese understood what was happening on the bodily level. She did not pinpoint the drug as the source of the inhibition, but she did intuit that what she needed was to overcome some sort of breaking action. So she tried to shock the systems back into their proper functioning by means of strategies she had explored in the summer of 1975. They are known the world over for inducing the religious altered state of consciousness and keeping it going and are thus most likely physiologically informed. She inflicted pain on herself, fasted, and choked herself—all powerful tools for altering body chemistry. And she exposed herself to cold, which induces a shivering reaction designed to mobilize the body's defenses. No wonder that, to her amazement, it was a friendly voice that kept urging her on to do that, as she told Father Renz in their conversation on February 1. But it was to no avail. The religious altered state of consciousness could not be called up anymore. As a consequence, the *Fratzen* dissolved, the demons fell silent on February 29, and, as is fitting at Easter, so did Jesus, their positive counterpart.

DID TEGRETOL KILL ANNELIESE?

Immediately after these events, that is, on the Monday after Easter, Anneliese's girl friends described how they heard Anneliese laughing "in an unnatural way." She would laugh, then stop, laugh again, and on and on in that way. This is clearly a pattern that leads into the ones recorded in May and June by Father Renz (see Chapter Seven), qualitatively totally alien to the pattern heard during a religious altered state of consciousness. Anneliese, trained to give voice to brain events, now provided a vocal representation of something that cannot be described in any other way except as a drug intoxication. This may be the reason why her pupils were so strongly dilated at the moment of death. I possess a tape, prepared in London, of a patient who, about ten years ago, was put on a very high LSD 25 dose during psychiatric consultation. The man tried to speak but was unable to do so while under the effect of the drug. Instead, he went into a vocalization that in its own way is as frightening and chaotic as Anneliese's. It is much faster than hers, but it also varies erratically in pattern, as hers did at the end.

By the beginning of May, at the very latest, the destruction accomplished by the Tegretol medication had become irreversible. Roswitha says that during the first week of May, when Anneliese and she were in Ettleben, Anneliese took only a few of the tablets. Both she and her mother were sure that after her return to Klingenberg she no longer took any medication at all. Yet her condition did not improve. In fact, things got progressively worse. Due to the effect of Tegretol on the various formed elements of the blood, especially the platelets, patients taking Tegretol bruise easily. We are reminded of Father Renz's description of Anneliese looking "black, red, and blue" after she had hit herself in the face. Ulceration of the gums is another symptom that these patients suffer from. Two days before her death Anneliese asked Roswitha to brush her teeth, something that she had earlier always refused to allow. This time she not only requested it but also wanted it to be done with alcohol. She may have felt the soreness coming on. Even her involuntary fasting was most assuredly due to some hitherto unrecognized effect of this terrible drug. Her death by starvation, which the pathologists attested to, was atypical, for she had no decubital ulcers on her, the telltale sign of death by starvation.

If a patient is taken off Tegretol, this can, according to the PDR, precipitate a *status epilepticus,* with fever and hypoxia. Anneliese could no longer swallow the drug, and towards the end she showed all three symptoms. The *status epilepticus* is a rapid succession of epileptic spasms. The uncontrolled, enormously rapid movements during the last two months of her life were most likely an expression of this condition. During the final few days of her life she had a fever. And she died by lying down and not moving again. Yet death occurred about eight hours later: She gradually choked to death as her red blood cells ran out of life-giving oxygen.

EPILOGUE:

EXIT THE DEMONS

All of this is, of course, a hypothesis, a construct, as the opinions of the experts had been, based on what we know about Anneliese. But there are some corroborating witnesses they paid no attention to, witnesses that the Court did not think to call and the defense did not cite either. These witnesses are the demons: Judas, the betrayer; Lucifer, the fallen angel; Cain, the slayer of his brother; Nero, the mass murderer; Fleischmann, the fornicating priest; and Hitler, whose name sticks in the German throat like the dead rat of the Russian proverb ("You cannot swallow it and you cannot spit it out"). Turning him into a demon and exorcizing him was a masterful stroke. A ghastly lot. But they are nevertheless of the separate reality, and they know more than humans.

The demons knew the secret of Anneliese's death. They were in her from the beginning, their spokesman testified. They wanted to stay in her—it was much better than hell—but the priests made things so miserable for them that on October 31 they felt they could take no more and they left. Tricky as the demons were, however, they left one of their number behind. That way they could make sport of the priests in case they changed their minds, for their unnamed confederate kept the door open for them. And, indeed, once cast out, they thought better of it and returned, although they knew that henceforth the priests would definitely have the upper hand; no matter how obdurately they would resist, the days of their stay would be numbered. These were the age-old rules of the game. They knew them, and so did the priests. Only this time things were different. They had hardly begun setting up shop again in their old abode when they began to sense something ominously amiss. There were now in their human shelter other demons whose names, they said, they did not know.

Listening to the tapes, one hears how, at first unnoticed even by the demons themselves, these unnamed, strange demons sickened them, like miasmas rising from a swamp. Their strident screams, the very beating of the demonic heart, began to falter, stretching into strange, unwieldy howls startling even to them. They weakened to the point where they needed more and more rest, saving their strength for occasional outbursts. Their unnamed foes were so cunning, doing their lethal work completely in hiding, that they even had the demons fooled into thinking that it was their enemy of old, the Savior, who was causing their discomfort. Finally they woke up to what was happening. They were in mortal danger. Only if they fled would they survive. Except that by now those other, sinister, nameless ones had been at work in the night. They were trapped in a net of steel that was being pulled ever tighter around them until they began to choke. In a state of great alarm, the demons gathered up the last ounce of strength. "We want out, out, out, out," they screamed, over and over, pitiably, hopelessly. Their screams became so heartrending that they even touched the exorcist. But it was too late. Some more twitching, screaming, and a few last growls. Like a candle flickering into darkness when deprived of air, so the demons collapsed. Very shortly thereafter, on Good Friday, the Savior also died, as he had the first time. In a cataclysmic *Götterdämmerung,* a twilight of the gods, their entire world was obliterated, was wiped away, and vanished. Despite all his exorcistic ploys, Father Renz could not bring it back to life. "It was no longer possible to tell whether what Anneliese said was hers or a demon's," he remarked. "She screams, and I don't know why."

The new and unnamed demons now had the field to themselves. They got hold of Anneliese's voice, but they had nothing to say, nothing at all. Erratically they toyed with it, giving off inhuman, mindless, neutral sounds. For a while they tarried, jerking the girl's body as if she were a rag doll. But soon they tired of the game and left, while she sank into death.

What the demons bear witness to is the fact that with all its cruelty the old system was still human and had human rewards and remedies. There was sin and there were devils, but there was absolution for one and exorcism for the other. The new demons now arising from the nightmares of this terrible century are outside the human cosmos. "You can pray all you want, you can scream for help, it's no use, the heavens are deaf," Anneliese said. She knew. For while she was still clamoring to the gods of her world for succor, she fell victim to the new demons of her age. And for them there is no exorcism.

BIBLIOGRAPHY

Anisimov, A. F. 1963. The Shaman's Tent of the Evenks and the Origin of the Shamanistic Rite. In: *Studies in Siberian Shamanism*, ed. Henry N. Michael, pp. 84–123. Toronto: University of Toronto Press.

d'Aquili, Eugene G. 1978. The Neurobiological Bases of Myth and Concepts of Deity. *Zygon* 13:257–75.

Bourguignon, Erika, ed. 1973. *Religion, Altered States of Consciousness, and Social Change*. Columbus, Ohio: Ohio State University Press.

———. 1976. *Possession*. San Francisco: Chandler and Sharp.

———. 1979. *Psychological Anthropology: An Introduction to Human Nature and Cultural Differences*. New York: Holt, Rinehart and Winston.

Büttner, Wilhelm. 1974. Schippach und Barbara Weigand. In: *Fränkischer Hauskalender und Caritaskalender*, pp. 3–21. Würzburg: n.p.

Cohen, Denise, and Marks, Frances M. 1975. Gilles de la
    Tourette's Syndrome Treated by Operant Conditioning. *Brit-
    ish J. Psychiatry* 126:315.

Diószegi, Vilmos. 1958. *A sámánhit emlékei a magyar népi
    müveltségben*. Budapest: Akadémiai Kiadó.

Goodman, Felicitas D. 1972. *Speaking in Tongues: A Cross-Cul-
    tural Study of Glossolalia*. Chicago: University of Chicago
    Press.

——. 1973. Glossolalia and Hallucination in Pentecostal Congre-
    gations. *Psychiatria Clinica* 6:97–103.

——. 1974. Disturbances in the Apostolic Church: A Trance-
    Based Upheaval in Yucatán. In: *Trance, Healing, and Hallu-
    cination: Three Field Studies in Religious Experience*,
    pp. 227–364. New York: John Wiley.

——. 1980. Triggering of Altered States of Consciousness as
    Group Events: A New Case from Yucatán. *Confinia Psychi-
    atrica* 23:26–34.

Gopi, Krishna. 1971. *Kundalini: The Evolutionary Energy in Man*.
    Boulder, Colo., and London: Shambhala.

Haag, Herbert. 1978. *Abschied vom Teufel*. Einsiedeln: Benziger.

——. Elliger, Katharina, Bernhard Lang, and Meinrad Limbeck.
    1974. *Teufelsglaube*. Tübingen: Katzmann.

Jungnitz, I., H.-M. Fink, A. Jans, and J. Lunkenheimer, 1978.
    Materialien zur Exorzismusfrage (Fall Klingenberg). Mainz:
    Bischöfliches Ordinariat, Abteilung Öffentlichkeitsarbeit.

Kiesler, Berta Maria. 1965. *Padre Pio*. Salzburg: Erzbischöfliches
    Ordinariat.

La Barre, Weston. 1970. *The Ghost Dance: The Origins of Reli-
    gion*. Garden City, New York: Doubleday & Co.

Lame Deer/John Fire, and Richard Erdoes, 1972. *Lame Deer:
    Seeker of Visions*. New York: Simon and Schuster.

Lex, Barbara. 1975. Physiological Aspects of Ritual Trance. *J. Altered States of Consciousness* 2:109–22.

——. 1978. Neurological Bases of Revitalization Movements. *Zygon* 113:276–312.

Di Maria, S. n.d. *Die Muttergottes in San Damiano?* Hauteville/Bulle, Switzerland: Parvis.

Neihardt, John G. 1961. *Black Elk Speaks.* Lincoln, Nebr.: University of Nebraska Press.

Ornstein, Robert. 1972. *The Psychology of Consciousness.* San Francisco: W. H. Freeman.

Pattison, E. Mansell. 1973. Chapter 21: Exorcism and Psychotherapy. In: *Religious Systems and Psychotherapy,* pp. 284–95. Springfield, Ill.: C. C. Thomas.

Pfeiffer, Wolfgang M. 1971. *Transkulturelle Psychiatrie.* Stuttgart: Thieme.

1976. *Rites of the Catholic Church as Revised by the Second Vatican Ecumenical Council* (orig. published as *Rituale Romanum,* 1614). New York: Pueblo.

Rodewyk, Adolf. 1975. *Possessed by Satan,* trans. Martin Ebon. New York: Doubleday & Co. (orig. published in German as *Dämonische Besessenheit.* 1963. Aschaffenburg: Pattloch).

Walsh, Roger. 1980. The Consciousness Disciplines and the Behavioral Sciences: Questions of Comparison and Assessment. *Am. J. Psychiatry* 137:663–73.

Womack, Sheila. 1979. An Analysis of the Therapeutic Effects of a Pentecostal Church on Alcohol and Drug Addiction. Unpublished manuscript.

——. 1979. From Coprolalia to Glossolalia: A Possible Link Between Gilles de la Tourette Syndrome and Speaking in Tongues. Unpublished manuscript.

ABOUT THE AUTHOR

Felicitas D. Goodman was born in Hungary and attended school in Transylvania. It was not until she immigrated to the United States after the Second World War that she was made aware of the infestation by vampires of her home province. She was trained as a translator and interpreter at the University of Heidelberg and worked for several decades as a multilingual scientific translator and abstractor. This was neither profitable nor very stimulating. So at an age when others begin thinking about a retirement cottage at the seashore, she returned to graduate school at Ohio State University to learn something new. Her first choice was linguistics, in which she earned a master's degree in 1968. Programmed, early on, to believe that science, to be valid, had to be dull—something that linguistics had not exactly disproven—she was thrilled to discover anthropology. Here, apparently, this axiom had not yet been accepted. It was love at first sight, especially since she was allowed to pursue a long-cherished interest in religious behavior. After completing fieldwork in Mexico City and in Yucatán, she wrote a book about speaking in tongues. She then did her dissertation on yet another aspect of religious behavior, namely, crisis cults, and received her doctorate in 1971. From 1968 to 1979 she taught linguistics and anthropology at Denison University. Since that time she has turned to full-time writing and research, while teaching anthropology and comparative religion during the summer at Cuyamungue Institute in Santa Fe County, New Mexico.

As a sideline she also "accumulated" four children who, in turn, have presented her with five grandchildren to date.